Second Wife, Second Life!

A LOVE STORY

Marjorie Holmes

DOUBLEDAY
NEW YORK LONDON TORONTO SYDNEY AUCKLAND

PUBLISHED BY DOUBLEDAY
a division of Bantam Doubleday Dell
Publishing Group, Inc.
666 Fifth Avenue, New York, New York 10103

DOUBLEDAY and the portrayal of an anchor with a
dolphin are trademarks of Doubleday, a division of
Bantam Doubleday Dell Publishing Group, Inc.

Book design by Tasha Hall

Library of Congress Cataloging-in-Publication Data

Holmes, Marjorie, 1910–
    Second wife, second life! : a love story / by Marjorie
Holmes. — 1st ed.
        p.   cm.
    1. Holmes, Marjorie, 1910–   —Biography—Marriage.
2. Schmieler, George P.—Marriage.   3. Authors, American
—20th century—Biography.   4. Physicians—United States
—Biography.   5. Wives—United States—Biography.
I. Title.
PS3515.04457Z473   1993
818'.5409—dc20
[B]   92-33890
                                                 CIP

ISBN 0-385-41293-2

CONTENTS

INTRODUCTION

"What Will You Talk About, Dad?"

This book is about the most exciting adventure of my life: my second marriage, to an incredible man, after our children were grown. An experience filled with the surprises, pains, and problems that must be common to any second marriage. But above all, the sheer delight in sharing for the first time almost everything I thought and felt with another human being.

Shortly after we met, George and I went to Ocean City, Maryland, to spend a few days at his son's vacation home. A drive of about a hundred miles from my home on Lake Jackson, near Manassas, Virginia. "But, Dad, you hardly know this gal," his son Jeff worried. "What will you talk about?"

Talk? We talked all the way, nonstop. Though George had driven there so many times he claimed he could find it blindfolded, we were talking so hard we missed the turn to the ocean, found ourselves in Delaware at midnight, and had to drive fifty miles back.

We were married a few months later, and have been talking ever since. George is a very loquacious but eloquent man. Oh, the joy and wonder of conversations with George: his descriptions, his jokes, his lengthy dissertations; his love of beauty so vividly expressed; his colorful stories of patients, other doctors, and people he has known.

"He may drive you crazy," Jeff's wife Tanya warned me, "but you'll never be bored."

George gets long-winded sometimes; I have to flash our hand signal meaning *"Zip it up, George,"* if only to get my work done—or some sleep. He listens to other people, however, as avidly as he talks. His response to my own ideas and discourses is always pertinent, understanding, calling for more from both of us. We sing a kind of eager duet of words . . . there's so much to observe, so much to think and feel and say!

A lot of it about ourselves. We will never cease to marvel over the miraculous way we found each other.

Reliving it through words.

One's own life story has a fascination for most of us. George and I often talk about our life together as if we were just discovering it. In this book, much of it taken from my journals, you will find the story of my life with George, often revealed in conversations that are, to us at least, the blood and heartbeat of a truly happy marriage.

Second Wife, Second Life!

CHAPTER ONE

Choices

It began in Manassas, Virginia, as I sat at my desk overlooking frozen Lake Jackson, wondering what to do with the rest of my life . . . or the year ahead. Or for that matter tonight, which was New Year's Eve 1981.

Outside, I could hear the water groaning under its heavy burden of ice and snow. A solid-white floor. But just across the way, a swarm of boys had cleared an expanse for skating. I could see their lithe young bodies bending forward, shooting gracefully across the ice, hear their shouts and sometimes the whack of their sticks, playing hockey. So brisk and blithe in their youth, I wanted to be out there too. I'd been restless all day, my spirit like the frozen water, wanting to break free.

I suddenly had an impulse to grab my own skates and rush down to join them . . . I laughed at the very idea. Okay, I'd been a good skater as a girl growing up in Storm Lake, Iowa; most of the kids were. The older boys taught us, and often skated with us. I still skated.

But right now, *at my age?* And a *widow*. Absurd.

One thing sure, however. I did not *feel* old . . . or look it. (At least not *that* old. Impossible!) I was in excellent health. I did ballet exercises every morning, jumped on my trampoline, swam three times a day all summer, danced and ran and water-skied. In fact, my latest book was on health, energy, and staying young. As for being a widow—after thirteen months the word still seemed strange. Desolate, yet vaguely intriguing.

Actually, to be almost *starting over* . . . Doing things I hadn't had to do before. Making decisions—about money and cars and where to live. Choices, decisions. Without a husband, there are so many to be made. Even deciding what to do about New Year's Eve. My best friend, Hope, was having a party— but I dreaded the fifty-mile drive on a cold windy night, to Washington, D.C. . . . Or I could see the old year out with a bowl of chili and a kindly couple up the road. Or tag along to the club where my daughter Melanie and her Greek musician husband, Haris, were performing.

They had flown home from Athens, to be with me when her father died last year. My own house was small—a remod- eled cabin that had begun as our summer place. Luckily, later we had bought the larger house next door, mainly for family gatherings after my husband retired. The only two houses on the point, with a lovely view of the lake. But Haris had commit- ments in Greece; they would be leaving in a few months. And my other children were scattered.

For the first time, I'd be alone. My family was already concerned.

"Please come with us tonight, Mother," Melanie implored when I told her I'd finally decided to stay home. "I don't feel right about leaving you by yourself on New Year's Eve."

"Don't worry, I'll be fine," I claimed. "I'll work on my New Year's resolutions."

"But you need to get out. You've really got to get out more, Mother. See your friends in Washington, meet new peo- ple, have fun." Her tone was teasing, but her eyes sweet with caring. "Gee, you might even meet Somebody Special."

I told her not to worry, I'd be out a lot on speaking dates this spring, and in the summer teaching at the Georgetown Writers Conference. "I'll meet a lot of people. And—who knows?"

"I hope so, Mother." She kissed me and ran off to put on

her stage makeup, which only enhanced her natural beauty—so fair but vaguely Oriental, with her almond eyes and high cheekbones. Returning, she crouched by my side—my last late child —born, at first to my dismay, when I was forty. But what a blessing! A dancing angel—gentle, merry, sweet, and wise. And very close to God. The most spiritual of my four children.

"Mother, listen. Much as we all loved Daddy, we know things were very hard for you. He was sick so long, and . . ." She hesitated. "You deserve to be *happy!*"

"Honey, I'm not sure I'd even want to marry again."

"I'll bet you do want to, and I'll bet you will!" she claimed. "Mother, I really feel something wonderful is going to happen to you in this new year. In fact, I predict that you're going to meet somebody who will change your life. And when you're ready, I want you to try a prayer that worked for me after my divorce from Rick." Holding my hand, she closed her eyes, and said softly, *"Please, God, send me somebody special. A wonderful man I can love, and who will love me."* Her face was shining. "I prayed this faithfully three times a day, for just a few months, and suddenly there was Haris!"

I smiled, and promised to try it. "But if I ever do marry anybody, he'll have to be *very* special. He'll have to meet my specifications."

Later that night, listening to the celebration in New York, watching the couples dancing to Guy Lombardo, I felt as I had that afternoon seeing the skaters . . . Left out, missing things. *Before the Parade Passes By* a voice was singing there—and in my heart. Beautiful but disturbing. Life is short, I didn't want the parade to go by without me. I wanted to be there with them, in the arms of a man who danced divinely, and . . . and . . . I fantasized.

In my longing I got up and danced with myself. But it didn't help. I turned the music lower, and tried to concentrate on my future. Mainly where to live. Melanie was right. It was lonely here on the lake, especially in the winter, and would be worse when she and Haris left. Also, the roads were bad. And I dreaded moving, I knew I'd be homesick for the sky, the woods, the water, a place where I could swim . . . My mind wandered to Melanie's prediction. It was comforting, enticing. Who knows what the future will bring? Gee, I might even meet a wonderful guy who had a place on the shore!

I laughed. But I also decided to try her prayer. And while I was at it, to write down the things I would really desire most in a man, should the miracle ever occur. It was midnight. And just as the clock in Times Square struck the magic hour, and bells rang and people shouted, I opened the journal on my desk, and began to list them:

1. He must be a man of faith, devout.
2. In good health.
3. Professional, successful.
4. Intelligent, well read.
5. A good talker and listener.
6. Romantic, sexy, and ardent.
7. A good dancer. (Not absolutely necessary, but why not ask for what you want?)

Boy, if I got all that—never mind a place on the shore!

On a bright February morning (exactly a month from the day I started taking Melanie's advice) the telephone rang. "Marjorie Holmes?" a rich male voice announced. "You saved my life, I love you!"

I gasped, astonished but curious. Some nut, I thought—but didn't hang up. As a writer you learn to listen. The voice, as it went on at some length, was refined. He was a doctor from Pittsburgh, he explained, who had lost his wife eight months before. He'd been devastated. Lonely, wild with grief, on the verge of suicide. When, only a month ago, on New Year's Eve, he found my book *I've Got to Talk to Somebody, God.*

"It was at the bottom of a pile of her things. I'd been cursing God and wanting to die, when something impelled me to drop to my knees and reach into the closet beside our bed. And there it was—the only book there. I read it that night, and it made me realize how precious life is. I read it over and over. But I never write to authors, let alone try to contact one. It's hard to believe I'm actually talking to you now. The book was published years ago—I had no idea where you lived, or if you were even alive, until a few days ago," he informed me. "On my way to Florida."

Friends there had been begging him to come—even offered to send his plane ticket. And his family was emphatic about his getting away. "You've *got* to, Dad." If he insisted on driving, he could stop over, as usual, with his son Jeff, a lawyer in Silver Spring, Maryland. And there, for the first time, he learned that the author of that book lived somewhere in the Washington, D.C., area.

"I knew I had to call you. But I've had a terrible time tracking down your number. The paper you write for wouldn't give it to me, but I found out your married name, and began to dial." Finally, he reached a pleasant man who said, "Why, yes, her husband was my cousin, who died about a year ago. Her number's right here."

"Somehow I already knew," George said. "Please listen, if you are still free, may I come to see you?"

I was pleased and touched. Yes, I was free, I assured him. "And I'd really love to see you. But unfortunately, I'm leaving on a two-week speaking trip."

"I'll wait!"

"Oh no, you can't do that."

"I'll wait," he declared. "Just promise me you'll call as soon as you can when you get back." His voice was cheery but urgent. *"We haven't got that much time."*

To my amazement, he waited. When I returned, my mailbox was stuffed with envelopes postmarked Silver Spring. Opening them, I began to laugh—so hard I almost cried. They were stuffed not only with romantic notes but with jokes, poems, valentines, items marked simply "interesting," and comic strips. Still wiping my eyes, I held up a fistful for Melanie. She laughed too as she read. "At least this guy sounds *'interesting,'* Mom. I've never heard of anybody else being courted with cartoons!"

I called him, as promised, and suggested we could meet somewhere for dinner, in Georgetown perhaps. "No, no," he protested. "I'll come get you."

But I was so far away, I explained. "And I live on a winding country road, you might get lost."

"Don't worry, I'll find you."

He not only found me, he arrived an hour early. I had just gotten home from the hairdresser. *My first date,* I realized as I drove. Expectant, bemused, and curious. What would he be like? Was it possible I *was* about to meet a man who might change my life?

It was only five o'clock. I was still trying to decide what to wear when Haris called me on the intercom. "Somebody just drove up. That man is here!"

"Oh, dear. Entertain him until I'm ready."

Trying not to panic, I replenished my mascara. But my hands were trembling so I gave myself two black eyes, and had to redo my makeup. Thank goodness for Melanie and Haris. At least this would give them a chance to look him over. They felt responsible for me. Finally, wearing my best little black suit with rhinestone buttons, I took a deep breath and joined them.

He leapt to his feet, and there he stood, this tall handsome prince with his arms full of roses. He had curly gray hair, a little mustache, and the bluest eyes I ever saw. Never had I seen a more handsome man at *any* age, let alone ours. He was beaming like a schoolboy as he handed me the flowers. I held them to my breast, not knowing what else to do with them, and we both just gazed for a minute, discovering each other.

"You're so *little!*" George exclaimed, but he sounded delighted. "I could put you in my pocket."

"And you're so tall!"

"Never mind, we'll match."

He held out his arms, and suddenly we were hugging, in spite of the flowers. While a voice announced—I could hear the words clearly in my head: *"You will marry this man before Christmas."* . . .

Absurd. I didn't believe them. I don't pay attention to voices.

We took off in his white Cadillac. Just down the road he reached out with an air of authority and pulled me closer to him. We ate at a charming old church restaurant right there in Manassas. He was gallant and poised and charming, seating me and ordering my dinner. He was also very funny. Never had I felt more comfortable with anyone, or so well entertained. And, holding hands as we walked back to the car, he began to sing— old songs we both remembered, in the sweetest male voice I ever heard.

George was almost too perfect, but he was for real. He'd brought his worn black doctor's bag along to prove it. Later, while I made coffee, he opened the bag and we sat at the long pine table looking at pictures of his family: His wife, Carolyn— slim, fair, and serene. Two attractive sons: George Jr., a doctor like his dad; Jeff the lawyer. And a daughter, Diane (now chief microbiologist at the hospital), gently beautiful like her mother . . . But the ones that most fascinated me, of course, were of George and his wife together: On beaches in Florida, where they spent two months every winter. Or Cuba, where they owned a condominium until Castro took over. On cruises to Bermuda. "We always put our marriage first," George explained. His mother was happy to keep the children. "We spent plenty of time with them at our cottage on Lake Erie every summer. And we always took them along to Skyline Drive every fall."

"My goodness, when did you practice?"

"Between vacations," he laughed. "And I worked hard. Although it's been years since I made house calls, or kept the office open till midnight to put the kids through college . . . Work and play, love and pray. Those are the words I've always tried to live by. They're like a framework, a support—the four points of the cross."

He got out his prescription pad and drew a cross to illustrate:

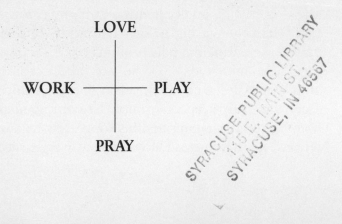

"Love at the top," he said. "Prayer at the bottom, the foundation. And work and play to give it balance. Balance, that's the whole secret. Work too much and you have no time for yourself or your family. Play too much and you haven't fulfilled your responsibilities. You need both. Play refreshes you, takes your mind off your worries, you really work better.

"But love and prayer," he declared, "they give you inner strength. Love is the most important. To love your wife and children next to God. But also to love people, your friends and neighbors, and with me, my patients.

"But if I didn't love God first," he stressed, "I couldn't love other people so much." George paused, his voice unsteady. "The way I loved Carolyn . . . Or the way I love *you* now." To my surprise, he lifted my face and kissed me.

I was thrilled but bewildered. Unsure of myself. I couldn't think what to say except "That's beautiful. And your wife must have shared the same philosophy."

"Oh, she was wonderful." He went on to describe their marriage. She was not only his sweetheart and companion, but housekeeper, secretary, nurse. "Carol handled everything—payments, investments, bills—I didn't even answer the telephone." Keeping their social life at a minimum, they spent nearly fifty ardent years living only for each other. "Neither of us was ever untrue to the other. We didn't even flirt," he claimed proudly.

Thus, when his wife died suddenly, almost in his arms at their Lake Erie cottage, he went into shock. "My whole world collapsed. I was like a child lost in a strange city in the dark. I just stood there and screamed. Then I grabbed a bottle of sleeping pills."

George told me how the sounds of his agony so frightened one dog, their poodle, it dived straight through a screen and ran. The other, a big golden Labrador, hurled himself at his master, knocking the pills from his hand. "I owe my life to that dog." From that day on, he was like a zombie, literally ill, almost autistic with grief. Silent, broken, and nobody could reach him. To keep his sanity, he continued to practice, but gone were his laughter and his songs. He wouldn't accept invitations, go anywhere. He was losing weight, dying himself.

This was the state George was in that New Year's Eve he had briefly described to me. Now he added more details. As he was cursing God and wanting to die, a picture—his own picture—on a dresser clear across the room, suddenly pitched forward and crashed to the floor. "No logical reason—no wind, no bolt of lightning, just that sudden crash. Curiously, the picture didn't even break, although a little china dog sitting in front of it was shattered."

It was at that point he fell to his knees, and groped into the closet, to find my book. "A book that told me you too had suffered, a lot of people suffer, but with the help of God we can and must go on."

He also told me more about his trip. Halfway to Silver Spring, another incredible thing happened. George found that his car had somehow crossed a high, impossible embankment, and was heading down the superhighway in the wrong direction, with two trucks bearing down on him. He managed to swerve out of their path and smash into a tree. "Nobody was hurt, although they had to call a wrecker to free the car."

The experience was so unnerving, however, he yielded to his son's advice not to drive on to Florida for a few days. Reluctantly, he agreed to unpack at least one bag. Where again he found the book. "I don't even remember putting it in—but there it was, right on top. I knew then that something strange was going on. If you were alive and still in the area, I had to find you." . . .

It was very late when he glanced at his watch. Suddenly he rose and walked to a cabinet, where he leaned, studying me with pleading eyes. Gone was his eager aplomb. "Would you . . . consider marrying me?" he asked.

I shook my head, disappointed for him and for myself. "No, George. You're still in love with your wife. And from what you've told me, I know I could never be the kind of wife she was to you."

"But I love *you* now," he cried. "The past is gone, it's all over. Something happened the minute I heard your voice, it was like waking up from a long nightmare. And when I actually *saw* you tonight! It's not your book, it's you, the wonderful time we've had just in these past few hours. We need each other," he pleaded. "God himself must have brought us together. Please say you'll at least make an effort to know me."

I explained how difficult that would be. He was still practicing in Pittsburgh. I was busy on a new book, and winding up promotion for the one just published.

"When will I see you again?"

"Not for a while. I'm leaving tomorrow for a booksellers convention. And not long after that I'll be flying to Israel for about a month."

"I can take time off, let me go with you!"

"Oh, no," I protested. "It's for research, I'll have to concentrate."

He begged to stay, but I steered him firmly but kindly toward the door. "I'm sorry, George," I repeated, "but you're still in love with your wife."

"No, no, I told you that's all over. It's you I want—*I love you*. I want to marry you. I'll give up my practice for you! I'll come to live here at Lake Jackson."

"Heavens, no, that's the last thing I want."

He looked so forlorn, trudging to the car with his little black bag, I couldn't stand it. "Wait!" I called. I could at least give him a copy of my latest book, *God and Vitamins*. "Thanks for a beautiful evening," I inscribed it, and ran outside to present it to him. Standing on tiptoe, I kissed him good night once more, which seemed to comfort him.

Watching his taillight disappear down the bumpy road, I didn't know whether to laugh or cry. What a remarkable man. I began to wish I hadn't given him the book. Too late now. Kicking myself, I went back into the house. As a medical doctor he would probably disagree with its major premise—that even the highly touted "balanced diet" is woefully deficient in vitamins; and most people would be healthier and happier if we took a lot more. I knew of few doctors who did agree—many scoffed at the very idea.

What had I thrown away? "Well, so be it," I thought. "I'll probably never see him again."

. . .

The next morning the telephone rang. To my amazement and delight it was George, announcing in a voice charged with excitement, "This is fantastic, I just can't believe it. Your book about vitamins—I stayed up and am about halfway through it, and I agree with everything you say. I've been using supplements with my patients for years! In fact, at Pitt I worked with Dr. King, one of the early pioneers in vitamin C." Could he come down immediately?

No, I regretted to tell him, I was packing for my trip. Maybe when I got back . . .

But as I put down the phone I was awed, almost as excited as he was. I remembered hearing somewhere: "There are no coincidences—only Godincidences." Adding them up, I could not but marvel: The falling of the picture. The finding of the book. The accident that could have been fatal, but only kept him from going on to Florida. His finally dialing a number that proved to be that of my husband's cousin. And now this.

"You will marry this man," the voice spoke again. *"You will marry him before Christmas."*

CHAPTER TWO

The Roses

My own marriage was a different story. The Great Depression was less kind to engineers and aspiring writers than it was to doctors. We moved a lot during our early struggles to succeed. (Seven states in seven years.) There were no grandparents eager to keep our children, and no time for vacations. It was almost ten years before Lynn, my husband, felt he could squeeze just a week away from his job. And even after being sent to Washington as chief executive of his firm there, it was a long time before he managed even *one* month's vacation—let alone *four,* like George.

He was a wonderful man, kind, friendly, generous, and outgoing. His staff adored him. "The best boss we ever had," they told me over and over. His clients, mostly prominent builders with whom he had large contracts, respected and admired him enormously. They were always singing his praises as I danced with them at the huge parties they gave at the luxury hotels—usually the Sheraton Park or the Shoreham. "You sure got yourself a great husband," they said. "He's honest, he's tough, but he's a pleasure. Never dealt with a better man." Often they paid him their fondest tribute. "He's *'Mister C'* himself!" (An acronym for his firm.)

But he was a man driven. Perhaps to compensate for the time he had to spend in hospitals. He'd been seriously burned by X rays as a boy.

Unlike George and Carolyn, who kept to themselves, we had many friends. Beginning with our church—Trinity Episcopal, which was right next door to our old Victorian house when we lived in Takoma Park. (Later, St. John's in McLean.) In Takoma only a hedge separated us from the rectory. Ruth and Ray Ryland, the young rector and his wife, became very close in many ways. We cut a hole in the hedge so our children could play together without risking the perils of the street. They came to many a party in that huge Victorian house that we had remodeled; along with doctors and their wives in the neighborhood, people from the office, architects and engineers, and sometimes other writers. We also belonged to half a dozen clubs.

We were a decent, caring couple, mingling with other couples. And, to all appearances, a very happy one.

In addition, we each had friends of our own. Mine were mostly writers. Every few weeks a little group of us, all pros, would meet in somebody's house to have lunch, talk shop, and sometimes read from a work in progress: Dorothy McCardle, who wrote for the Washington *Post*; Cecily Crowe, fiction for *Good Housekeeping*; Pat McGerr, murder mysteries; Carly Dawson, children's books; Jane McIlvaine (later McCleary), novels for teens. Jane had also written *It Happens Every Thursday*—a book about her adventures publishing a weekly newspaper—which was turned into a film starring Loretta Young.

The most famous among us was Catherine Marshall. Dear Catherine! We saw her through two books after Peter Marshall died—and her second marriage to Leonard LeSourd. Not that she needed our advice about her writing. None of us paid much attention to that, anyway. But oh, how we listened when we got into personal stuff like husbands and children. We saw Jane through a divorce and remarriage; and Dorothy through the loss of her husband, Carl. It wasn't our profession that kept us together, it was an escape from our problems. And strong friendships developed.

Lynn's escape was to go deep-sea fishing with his buddies: usually at nearby Ocean City, but when they could all get away,

Atlantic City, or distant ports like Acapulco, Mexico, or the
Bahamas. When the fishing trips were near, he insisted on including his sons. (Mark, the older, was only thirteen when he
caught a huge marlin.) The men also flew to football games—
Michigan, Iowa, or Notre Dame. On rare occasions (three, I
think) they took their wives along.

I encouraged these jaunts. Anything to keep him from killing himself. He worked insane hours and often dragged himself
home too late for dinner, too tired to eat. He was chain-smok-
ing and drinking too much. And working too hard, even with
projects at our cabin. But there was little joy in it . . . Anything to give him respite, cheer him up, keep him from looking
so sad and troubled. Oh, if only we could make him laugh and
be happy with us, the way he always seemed to be with strangers.

Few even suspected our secret agonies. Like a lot of other
people too proud to show it, we lived "lives of quiet desperation," behind the façade of supposed success.

Ironically, in addition to books and articles and stories, I
was writing a biweekly column for the Washington *Evening
Star*. "Love and Laughter," I called it; sketches about the simple
pleasures of everyday life. With categories such as: "Beauty in
Your Own Backyard," "It's Fun to Be a Woman When," "Moments That Make Marriage Worthwhile." Never specifying my
own family—I had a horror of embarrassing them; and avoided
it by using the impersonal "you" instead of "I," which made it
hypothetical, almost everybody's experience, and not exclu-
sively ours. Actually, I was just sifting the gold and the jewels
from the grim realities of married life. Those moments that *are*
precious and sparkling, if you really want to find them. I could
and *must* "write beautiful things for people who crave beautiful
things," as an inspiring English teacher once urged. "There is a
duty!"

But the picture that emerged from this column was false.
Once an unmarried woman, prominent in the press corps,
strode up to declare, "I love your column, but sometimes I can't
read it—I *envy* you too much." She kissed me and gave me a
playful kick. "How can you be so *lucky*? To have a happy
marriage, all those kids, and also a career!"

I laughed and nodded. Yes, I was very lucky, I agreed. But Lynn and I did not have a happy marriage. Love each other? Of course. The very *"of course"* was the problem—to assume, take love for granted.

I hadn't expected this. I had different role models. My parents adored each other and showed it. Dad didn't make much money, but oh how rich Mother was in love. I remember how Dad would hold her on his lap in the big rocking chair, and cuddle. (When the chair finally broke down with age and their weight, they just bought a bigger, more comfortable chair.) Another sweet memory is of Dad watching Mother as she laughed with a little group of friends by the Ferris wheel. "Ain't she pretty?" he said fervently. "By golly, your mother is still the best-looking woman in Storm Lake!"

As children we thought nothing of their displays of affection, although it often made the neighbor kids giggle. Their folks didn't act that way. And, as I came to learn later, Lynn's parents didn't either . . . But that was my dream of marriage. I could hardly wait to marry somebody who was crazy about me, and become the queen of his heart.

When things didn't turn out that way, I was bitterly disillusioned. Outraged at the tricks of nature that confuse and entrap the young. Mad at myself, and Lynn and God. I cried and stormed, begging for something it was hard for my new husband to give me, after all—attention. (The worst possible way to get it.) When we tried to talk about it, we trod on dangerous ground. There were only quarrels, which diminished and ravished us both. I finally realized I had to grow up and accept some ancient truths: There are different *kinds* of love. Romance, and devotion. (An ideal marriage would have both—balance, as George would say.)

But romance, we are warned, is fleeting. Once you are married, the courting is over, the honeymoon can't last. So settle down, take care of each other and be content. This we have come to believe. But for most women (and a lot of men too, I think), one without the other can be misery. And if forced to choose between romance and sheer dogged devotion, I'll bet the women, at least, would take romance.

Lynn and I were loyal, we really cared about our marriage,

and each other. We had four children. Whatever we thought we were marrying for was long gone. Yet we could not separate. We hung on because of habit, duty, and a kind of stubborn devotion to each other's needs.

Ours too began as a whirlwind courtship at the University of Iowa, where I was working after graduating from nearby Cornell College the year before. Lynn was about to graduate as an engineer in June. We met one spring night at a popular inn where, like many students, he waited tables. It was instant infatuation. I noticed his pixie-like ears and his engaging grin as he balanced a heavy tray on one palm over his shoulder, heading for the kitchen. He winked, we flirted; he walked me home and kissed me.

We were off to a rollicking start. Parties at his fraternity house (I was dazzled, I'd never been in one before), dancing to the big bands like Paul Whiteman, at the Student Union . . . Hours gazing into each other's eyes, exchanging information. "In case we want to get married," Lynn teased, and a thrill went through me. But the first month was mostly caprice and make-believe. I learned that he'd been born in Holstein, Iowa, only thirty miles from where I was, but raised in the Rio Grande Valley of Texas, where a doctor who didn't know much about X ray, used it to cure a bad case of acne on his back. "Not on my face, thank God. They used it like a sunlamp. I'd lie under it for hours. And boy, was I cooked!" It cured the acne, he said, but now his back was a worse mess, of ulcers. He seemed embarrassed. "I hope you don't mind?"

"Oh, you poor thing!" I cried. "Why should I?"

"Because we *are* in love—everybody knows that, at least I do. And if *you* do, let's get married."

I gasped, again that piercing thrill. "When, where?"

"As soon as possible." Why wait till June? He whipped out a pad and pencil—he had it all figured out. A married couple he knew were leaving their tiny attic apartment. "It's very cute, and the rent is cheap. It'll go fast, we ought to grab it." We could cross the Iowa state line into Illinois, where you didn't have to wait two weeks. His roommate Les would drive and bring Lillian; they'd been engaged two years; they would stand up with us—and who knows, we might get them to make it a double wedding.

My imagination took wings. Love at last! He adored me. He was romantic and daring. I was flattered. It would be an adventure, like something in a movie starring Janet Gaynor. I remembered two lines from a flippant poem I'd written at sixteen, in the style of my idol, Sara Teasdale:

> Oh, to dance down Dinsmore Street,
> And wed the first man that I meet,
> Just for the adventure!

Well, here was my chance.

Lynn wasn't the first man, but we still were almost strangers. Enthralled, excited, we went to see the apartment, which was darling with its quaint old furniture and cozy slanted ceilings. "Let's take it!" I whispered. Lynn blanched when the landlady told us the rent had gone up two dollars, but grandly forked over a five for deposit. Oh dear, it wouldn't be ready for a couple of weeks. We could hardly wait. I was twenty-one, Lynn was twenty-three. But our eager dreaming was now like two children planning to play house.

Never have two people had sillier reasons for making the most crucial commitment of their lives . . . Foolishly, we shared our secret with several other people.

But gradually I came to my senses. Two days before we were to leave, I got scared and tried to back out—at least until after he graduated in June. Lynn was aghast, almost as desperate as George was on that night I had made him leave. He would be ruined, he'd made the deposit, how could he face the guys at the house? He'd have to resign, quit college, not even bother to graduate! He was actually crying when he left.

I cried too. I felt terrible—the poor guy, I'd ruined his life. I lay awake half the night, blaming myself, confused, wondering how to make amends. Then the next day, the roses arrived. Nobody had *ever* sent me flowers, let alone *roses!* . . . That did it. I packed my new pink nightie, and called him . . .

The wedding was beautiful. A gentle minister unlocked his

empty church and even brought his wife along to play a wedding march. Lillian volunteered to sing a weak but sweet "I Love You Truly." And the joyful party returned to Davenport, Iowa, where the hotel dinner cost $1.25—more than we expected—the soup was extra. Lynn was a dollar short, so Les slipped him one as a present. They drove back that night; we would take a bus.

We had not been intimate before our wedding night. There hadn't been much time, for one thing; and in those days *nice* girls *didn't*. Eagerly I got ready for bed, puzzled that my new husband still sat on the couch, as if reluctant to undress. He looked up and smiled, but his eyes were anxious. Slowly he began to unbutton his shirt, then reached over his shoulder for the undershirt. "Lord, I hate to have you see this, I've dreaded it all day."

"Honey, it doesn't *matter*," I told him, helping him struggle out of the undershirt. "It's not your fault." But I was not prepared, in spite of his warning. His back was covered with bandages, clumsily placed. And most of them were stained. When he pulled one off, it bled.

"Oh, *Lynn*, you poor dear! Does it hurt?"

"No, but it looks awful. I'm so ashamed—I'm scared you'll be sorry you ever married me. I shouldn't have rushed you into it, but I wanted you so bad."

"Me too!" I cried. "I wanted you too, don't say such things. You can't get rid of me so easy. I'm your wife now and I want to help you. So pipe down and tell me where to find your gauze and stuff—whatever you use."

Together we pulled off the dressings. The wounds would have to be cleansed. He said Les was good at this, but wasn't always there; usually Lynn just did the best he could. "Oh my God, I hope you don't think it's another reason I asked you?"

"If I thought that, I wouldn't be here. But now that I am, I'm kind of glad. It makes me feel important to you."

Awkwardly myself, I accomplished my first duty as a bride. One I was to perform almost every night for over forty years—the rest of his life. But I honestly *didn't mind*. Then—or ever. It made me feel close to him, tender and needed. And Lynn was always grateful. But I know it hurt his pride. He wanted to be a strong independent husband, not a burden to his wife.

At first, however, we had no idea how heavy that burden would become for both of us.

With no jobs in sight, and still enjoying our fantasy of the madcap honeymooners, we bought an old car for $35 and set off for Texas as soon as he got his degree. We didn't even wait for graduation ceremonies; his parents couldn't come anyway—they were in Arizona with Lynn's younger sister, who had TB. Our destination was San Juan, where they had offered us their now vacant house on a small truck farm.

The old car barely made it over the Ozark Mountains. It would only go uphill *backwards,* so that's exactly what Lynn did—just turned it around and backed over them, while other cars honked and got out of our way. Another adventure! "And wait'll you see the size of a Texas moon and the orange trees."

It's a long way from Iowa City to the Mexican border, no matter what you're driving, but in a car practically breathing its last, it takes forever. By the time we got there I was pregnant; and the job Lynn had been promised in a garage had vanished. But the house was a charming bungalow surrounded by clashing palms and citrus trees, with all the amenities (except electricity, which was dependent on an ailing Delco plant). And with six acres of land we could sure raise cabbage, Lynn said. One good crop could sometimes make a fortune.

He set about it feverishly, while I tried to write, harvesting only rejection slips except for a few poems; trying to blot out my terrible disappointment. It was *not* fun playing house with only a couple of chairs, a bed, and a card table bought at an auction, or cooking on a kerosene stove when you're nauseated. And no matter how huge the moon or sweetly sang the Mexicans, it was *not* romantic. Because our orange blossoms were shriveling fast.

I couldn't understand it. Linda and Casey, a couple even poorer than we were, had moved in with us; they'd been married two years and still could hardly keep their hands off each other. *My* husband didn't even want to hold hands in the movies . . . A lot of my writing wound up in my journals, most of it raging at myself. "Fool, fool, you got yourself into this, you *wanted* to come! Shut up, don't cry—don't make things any harder for him, he's doing the best he can . . . and those darn *ulcers!*"

His doctor had felt very bad when he saw them—the ulcers hadn't appeared until after Lynn left. His advice was to lie in the sun as much as possible. "To dry them up."

More radiation to cure radiation? The doctor just didn't *know* any better. And how could we? We wouldn't dream of suing him, even as the back got worse. The doctor was a very sweet man, who delivered our baby and brought me a gardenia from his garden. (And after marrying George I was glad we didn't; no doctor ever deliberately harms a patient, and if there's a tragic mistake, it haunts him all his life. George knew, he'd once made a serious mistake himself.)

Three days before our little girl was born, I sold my first story. And two weeks later a second one. We were ecstatic. Manna from heaven—now we could pay for the baby! We worshipped her—she was so tiny and beautiful, and she had brought us luck. The luck, however, didn't last. Before the year was over a flood nearly swept us away, a hurricane took the roof off the house, and aphids ate the cabbage. (Just as the market shot up!) . . . After the last disaster, Lynn's father offered to lend him enough money for graduate school. The Depression couldn't last forever. Get more education while you can, until jobs open up.

Incredibly, the old car got us back. Lynn had fixed whatever was wrong with the transmission; it rattled proudly over the mountains; but by the last forty miles the battery was giving out. He kept turning the lights on and off, and we coasted down the last hill into Iowa City, where it gasped its last at our final stop. Rest in peace. (Later we sold it for junk.)

There, between study and classes, Lynn furiously applied for work. His major was metallurgy, but his dream job was in air conditioning: "The coming thing," he declared. Meanwhile, he'd take *anything*, no matter what, to get out of debt and take care of us. One day the heavens opened: He was summoned to Rock Island, Illinois, where a munitions plant was very impressed by his credentials. Starting salary would be sixty a month! All he had to do was come down for an interview, sign up, and look for a place to live.

Again we were ecstatic, our friends (most in grad school for the same reason) were thrilled for us. They bought him a new hat, had a party, and escorted him to the train.

Two mornings later I was shocked when a haggard ghost of a man walked in the door—face ashen, eyes stricken, mouth grim. He was trying to hide its trembling.

"Lynn!" I jumped up so fast I spilled the baby's cereal. "Honey, what's *wrong?* What *happened?"*

"My back. I couldn't pass the physical."

Plunging into a chair, he covered his face and sobbed.

His new hat fell to the floor. I picked it up and held it a minute, remembering how proudly he had waved it from the train. Never before or since have I felt so sorry for anyone. To set off with such high hopes, only to be rejected before he had a chance! I put my arms around him and tried to comfort him. "Don't worry, honey, you'll get something better." He would, I knew he would—he had so much to offer, but right now my heart broke for him. He didn't deserve to be hurt like this. I cringed to think of my own selfish hurts and demands. I promised myself I would never blame him for anything again. He needed me, and I would never, never leave him . . .

President Roosevelt's Work Projects program supported us the next two years: Lynn built a dam and handled welfare clients in Northwood, Iowa; then a two-year stint with Caterpillar Tractors in Peoria, Illinois. They were grooming him for advancement when the miracle happened: He was accepted by the firm of his dreams in New Jersey for their six months' training class. No money, not even expenses, but those best qualified would be guaranteed good jobs. At that point the ulcers were almost dried up, we were encouraged. Selling almost every object we owned, we took off in a slightly newer car, and survived in the thrilling shadow of Manhattan until Lynn graduated, second in his class.

The ladder was there to be climbed. They sent him to Chicago; then Zanesville, Ohio; Texarkana, Arkansas; Philadelphia; and finally, in 1950, after fifteen years, Washington, D.C.

Lynn would have sacrificed his life for that company—they were wonderful to us. The ulcers would recede for a while, then break through more vicious than ever; they had to be cut out and skin grafted from his thighs. Eventually they became malignant and began to devour his body. He also developed diabetes, and had three heart attacks. Yet the firm never failed us. Their insurance paid the medical bills, and subordinates took over until he could recover. They really cared. And he brought in the biggest contracts they ever had in Washington: the White House, the Pentagon, Dulles Airport . . . He was too valuable to lose.

Finally, the battle was too destructive. At sixty Lynn took an early retirement, and we moved to Lake Jackson. But he could not rest, he must keep working—building, fixing, repairing. And as before, although he never drank on the job, at home alcohol became his solace.

There is no loneliness like living with an alcoholic. And there are crises . . . Finally, in desperation, I called Mark. The boy who had caught the big marlin with his father drove all night to talk to him. I will never forget the sight of the two men, arm in arm the next morning as they walked to the car. Beaming, they looked up and flashed me the V for Victory sign, which I eagerly signaled back. I was fighting not to cry until they left.

They were heading for AA.

That blessed organization saved what was left of our marriage, and probably his life. He was more cheerful from then on. He had something to live for now, and rejoiced in the 12 Step Program, where he quickly became a sponsor, spent hours counseling, and rushed to the rescue of everyone he could. He was generous and giving until the end.

That was the state of my life not quite two years later when the telephone rang one bright morning, and a rich male voice announced, "You saved my life, I love you!"

The date was February 2, 1981. His name was George.

By another odd coincidence, it was also on that exact date, February 2, fifty years before, that I had first met Lynn.

The past. The future. It was as if two men stood at the crossroads, beckoning, and I must choose which one to follow.

I was tempted but confused. This too I poured into my journal:

> My study is always chilly before the sun floods in. The little heater Lynn installed for me is purring, and I'm wearing an old flannel shirt of his. Outside, the lake is sparkling, and the cottage-shaped bird feeders dance atop their poles. Birds are swarming, gorging themselves on their breakfast of suet and seeds. Little birds mostly —yellow warblers, black-capped chickadees—and oh, yes, a jaunty woodpecker, his scarlet head shining like satin in the sun . . . What a joy it is to see this as I write. You have to make an effort for this kind of beauty; they won't come unless you put out the seeds.
>
> But sweetest of all are the bluebirds, darting in and out of the houses Lynn built to attract them. We'd heard about how scarce bluebirds were getting. And sure enough, a few days after he'd put them up, a pair appeared to inspect them. We watched them excitedly from the window, fluttering and twittering as if talking it over. Off they flew, but soon were back with a few twigs, and moved in.
>
> "Hooray!" I rejoiced. "Bluebirds mean happiness."
>
> My husband patted my shoulder. "I wish I could have made you happier, Marj. I'm not a word person like you, I feel a lot of things it's hard for me to express."
>
> It's a comfort to remember that I told him, "You do a wonderful job in other ways, honey.". . .

Bluebirds are shy. I remember how he built the big round patio table just far enough away from them, its base an old barrel. I remember our trips to the lumberyard, and the sound of his saw cutting wood. I remember our trips to the quarry for flagstones and rocks. All these things to make us happy: The wall, the steps—some of them cracked and broken after the years of wear and weather; the yard, the garden. The patio—he let us help with the grouting, while he labored somewhere else. But always, always, whenever humanly possible, he was there for us.

My eyes film as I see our boat bobbing at the dock. I can see Lynn standing there, teaching his children how to bait and cast and bring the fish in. He also fished with them, another form of his devotion . . . I remember how proudly he cared for that boat, and pulled the water-skiers—so fast it scared me, but it was thrilling to hear the cry "Hit it!" and the roar of the motor as we sped off. But he always brought everyone safely back.

I don't know just why I'm crying. I thought I had used up all my tears during those years of hurting for him, for all of us. Strangely, I didn't cry after he died. I was so glad for his escape from all the pain. Pain, suffering, sickness had become a way of life. And yet he trudged on; even in his final weeks he kept trying to do things for me. It hurts, it hurts to remember. Yet there is a tender sweetness too . . . I think of that young couple who ran off so blithely to chase a rainbow that wasn't even there! At least for long. I grieve for all that we missed in our marriage. And I grieve most of all for Lynn—who will never find it. For him it's too late to try again.

Yet for me . . . I am happy with a kind of indescribable "color" of joy. Something is singing and dancing within me. I feel almost giddy with this new delight. Like a girl writing in her diary after a thrilling date. Because that's just what I've been having—dates with George. Actually, only two so far in person, but he calls me from Pittsburgh at ten o'clock every morning, and at ten again every night. He told me that he and Carolyn had a special time they'd always think about each other. "Ours was nine-fifteen. Now you choose one for us." I wished he hadn't put it like that, but said, "Okay, let's make it ten o'clock—easy to remember."

He also sends flowers twice a week, usually roses. And writes those flattering but incredibly funny love notes with jokes and clippings. Adding always: *P.S. Don't forget to marry me. As soon as possible, please.*"

I've never laughed so much or felt so at peace with anyone. George seems to be everything I ever dreamed of in a man. That list I wrote on New Year's Eve—the very night George says he found my book. Amazing. I almost forgot the list until yesterday, and haven't told George, but *he fits everything on it* . . .

and more. I didn't even ask that my Wonderful Man also be handsome and could sing!

Why, then, am I so uncertain, not of him but of *myself?* For days his dreams for us have been on my mind, no matter what else I'm doing—packing for Israel, half wishing I didn't have to go. I feel a kind of trembling ache I don't want to stop. His beautiful roses stand on my desk, tall, scarlet, a merry reminder of him. *Roses* . . . The coincidences are almost too much to believe. It was the arrival of roses at the last minute that made me decide to marry Lynn. And this makes me wary, afraid of getting swept away again.

Yet I can't stop thinking about what fun it would be to live with George. The sharing of a thousand delights. We could talk about so many things, not just problems. I wouldn't have to be careful with him, curb my own enthusiasms, or be afraid of hurting his feelings. At least I don't think so. He is so full of love, and so am I. My love, my expressions of love were held back so long.

"You will never be hungry or thirsty for love again," George has promised . . . Can this be true? That's what bothers me. He loved *her* so desperately so many years, will he ever forget? Could he ever love me that much? I want to be sure, I don't want to make a mistake.

Dear God, is this man the answer? I've worked so hard all my life—ever since childhood really, working my way through college, then home and family and writing—the absolute need to write; in my own way I've been as work-obsessed as Lynn. Indestructible though I seem, I know I won't live forever.

"We shouldn't wait," George pleads, and reminds again, *"We haven't got that much time."*

He's right, we're not young anymore, no matter how vigorous we are and young we feel. The prime of our lives is past. "But the years we have left can be the best years of all," he insists.

Lord, let him be right about that too. I want to rest, I want to enjoy. I've used up so much time already . . . Isn't it time I started life over, and gave love another chance?

CHAPTER THREE

Just Get Us Through July

It was May. I was still in a trance, but unable to give George an answer before leaving for Israel in a few days. He kept pleading until the last minute; and at Kennedy Airport in New York, I was thrilled to be paged for a telephone call from Pittsburgh. "Just one more time before you take off: W-Y-M-M? Translation: Will you—"

I broke in, laughing. Who but George? "I get it, I get it, darling, but they're calling our plane. Tell you when I get back!"

"But you will go to Ocean City with me?"

"I promised, didn't I?"

And I did . . . As soon as I got over my jet lag, George arrived at Lake Jackson with his dogs—Ben the golden Lab who saved his life, and a frisky white poodle, Tanjy, who was instantly jealous of me. This time George was driving a spacious Cherokee Jeep; we piled into it and were off for the ocean, except for one stop where I'd left some things to be altered. It was a test of sorts, although I didn't mean it to be. "I know it's late," I apologized, "but I really need them. This shouldn't take long."

"Don't worry," George said. "Take all the time you want."
He went for a little walk—he had spied some wildflowers along
the roadside, and picked them for my first bouquet. Blue corn-
flowers, yellow mustard, and white daisies. "Welcome back!"
he proclaimed, presenting them to me. Then he hung up my
garments and we were off again, with Tanjy nipping and
scratching, doing his best to reclaim his seat beside George instead of me most of the way.

It was a glorious carefree week. Running the dogs on the
beach, swimming, dancing, side trips to Chincoteague to see the
ponies, Assateague for raw oysters that melt on the tongue,
dining at romantic places like Phillips by the Sea. George was a
magnificent swimmer and diver, I discovered, a former lifeguard and captain of the championship Pitt swimming team. As
for dancing, he was the answer to every woman's dream. With
him it was like flying, it was Paradise. He led me blithely
through almost every step ever invented, plus delightful variations of his own. He was such a strong and graceful leader it
was impossible not to follow. (Unlike today, when the most
popular style seems to be wiggling and waving and shaking
yourselves at each other.)

Breathless after that first dance with George, I realized I'd
be a fool not to marry him. I had already fallen in love with his
personality. Now I was in love with his dancing! . . . Before
the week was over I was deeply in love with something even
more important—his wisdom, his imagination, his eloquence,
his *mind*. I'd had only a taste of this before, now we had endless
hours to talk. George was fascinated by so many things, and
expressed himself with such profundity and wit, saying things I
wish *I* had written. I had not brought my journal, but I asked
for paper so I could at least put some of them down.

Easter Sunday, our holiday was ending. We got to church
early to get a seat, and held hands as we waited. George didn't
let go even when the choir marched in, but lustily joined the
singing. He freed it when we knelt to pray, but I noticed he was
fooling with one of his rings; he wiggled it off during the re-
sponses, reached for my left hand, and slid his own wedding
ring on my finger. He was beaming as he whispered, "I, George,
take thee, Marjorie—" Startled, I shook my head and tried to

"*Shhh!*" him, but it made me giggle. George proceeded, although silently this time, mouthing the words carefully: "For better . . . for worse . . . will . . . you . . . marry me?" It was so like him, I couldn't stop laughing. His ring was so big I was afraid I'd drop it, I had no choice but to nod.

Thus while other people prayed, and a few heads turned, I whispered, "Yes, oh yes!" And meant it.

Thrilled, we rushed back from church and called his family in Maryland. "When?" they asked. "June," I heard George reply (four months from the day we *met*). "No, no!" I rushed onto the scene. I had too many commitments this summer. "We can't possibly be married before Christmas."

"*Christmas?*" George gasped. How could we endure being separated so long? We had to, I insisted, we weren't a couple of kids. "That's exactly it," he said soberly. "We're *not* kids, and we *don't* have that much time." I was so adamant, however, he had to yield . . .

Three weeks later, George arrived in Manassas and drove me to the airport for a flight to Allentown, Pennsylvania. I'd promised my son Mark and his wife a brief visit, mainly to see my granddaughter Kathy's dance performance. George would drive on to Maryland for the weekend with Jeff and Tanya and his own granddaughters.

We were in tears at parting, but also cheerful, mature. There was so much to be done before I could get married, even by Christmas. But time was flying, and we had so much to look forward to.

This was the mood I was in when I reached Mark's house and collapsed from sheer joyous exhaustion. The week before had been spent in New York doing interviews and talk shows about *God and Vitamins*. On each one I worked in the fact that I was about to become the bride of a vigorous doctor still in practice, who was himself a pioneer in the use of vitamins. How good God was . . . Then I heard the small voice again, now urging, "*Don't wait.*"

I smiled, overtired, dismissing it, but it wouldn't be still. It went on and on, all night, it seemed: "*Don't wait. Don't wait!*"

I still heard it the next morning dancing in the shower. I know it's foolish to dance in a shower, but I often did when I was happy. I thought of Kathy dancing tonight in the ballet, I thought of George. In sheer exuberance I kicked as high as I could, and suddenly was grabbing space. *"Don't wait!"* the voice commanded, as I skidded across the tub and crashed against its rim.

For an instant I was too nauseated and pain-assaulted to think. Clutching my chest, I crept downstairs; an ambulance was called, the four fractured ribs taped. I was given painkillers, and somehow sat through the beautiful performance. But pain and those incessant words gave me no peace for the next three days. To my dismay, there was no call from George. I was hurt, bewildered, and for the first time afraid. What if his love was cooling? What if his family were advising *him* to think it over, urging *him* to wait? For the first time I realized how great was my need and desire for him.

Finally, on the third night, the call I had been praying for came. Mark explained about the accident and handed me the phone. I was crying so hard I could scarcely speak. "Darling, I'm so sorry!" George said. "I didn't want to bother you, I wanted you to enjoy your family."

"Let's not wait," was all I could think to say. "You were right, something tells me we shouldn't wait."

"Thank God. I was in misery."

He would have come at once—he thought I meant now, or next week. Consulting the calendar a few days later, we chose the Fourth of July. Our honeymoon would start in Canada, where I still had engagements to fill. Meanwhile, we had six weeks to get ready for the wedding.

Becoming a Bride Again

Melanie's predictions were coming true. I *had* met a wonderful man who would change my life in this new year. But even she was astonished. "Mother, I didn't dream it would happen so fast! Why, we're not even *halfway through* the year."

Excited, if now a bit apprehensive, she helped me shop for The Dress. We found it right there in Manassas, after combing all those expensive boutiques in the city. I wanted pink chiffon, which had to be ordered—the Bridal Shop had only white at first. It was beautiful, fitted at the waist, with long flowing sleeves and little sparkling rhinestone cuffs at wrists and throat. "Perfect, Mother, perfect," both my daughters cried. My oldest, Mickie, who had arrived from California, shortened it and took it in at the waist. They also helped me choose the cake and flowers.

We decided to use the patio, scene of two former weddings in the family (Mallory and Judy, Melanie and Haris). Sons Mark and Mallory would take care of patio chairs and parking. Haris called on his Greek friends to cater and provide the music. Everybody wanting to help Mother get married. Even my sister Gwen burst merrily in from Chicago, announcing, "Now, I won't interfere, I just want to *boss*."

The last week they even shooed me off, insisting that I fly to Iowa for my 50th Cornell College class reunion. "Don't worry, we'll take care of everything." So I went, thrilled by the dazzling new diamond ring on my finger, amused to recall a little chant advertising Jergens lotion: "She's young, she's beautiful, she's engaged." . . . I *felt* young and beautiful—more, I believe, than ever before in my life. Certainly a lot more than I'd ever felt as a co-ed on that campus.

At the same time there was this strange feeling that this couldn't be happening. I'd wake up any minute. George was just the handsome prince in a romantic dream. Or he was a movie star in disguise, already on his way back to Hollywood, laughing at my naïveté. Or at the last minute somebody *had* talked him out of it, he'd changed his mind.

This silly anxiety persisted, even though he called me the night before the wedding, and again the next morning when it was raining buckets, to promise me a beautiful day. "I've put in my order to God, sweetheart. Do it for Marjorie, I told him, she's worked so hard. Please do it for her, not me . . ." I was actually relieved when my daughters rushed into the room where I was dressing, to announce, "He's here! George is outside." They had shared the joke of my absurd apprehensions. "You ain't stood up, after all, Ma."

All I could say was, "Hooray! What's he wearing?"

The blinding rain was still falling when George and his entourage set forth from Silver Spring at four o'clock. Yet he kept confidently praying, "Lord, as you parted the Red Sea for those Israelites, I know you will part these clouds for Marjorie." And lo, as they turned down the bumpy country road, the sun broke through.

People were mopping up the chairs, bringing out the flowers. The minister arrived, the music began to play. And there on the patio before our families and a few close friends, George and I joined hands to repeat our vows just as a beautiful rainbow began to arch across the sky.

The whole world seemed to be rejoicing.

The wedding was over. The first major event of July.

Two days later we were off to Canada, to begin a month of engagements scheduled before we met. What an initiation this would be for George—and a test for both of us. "Just get us through July," I kept praying. "If we can make it through July . . ."

First stop Toronto, to do a popular TV show, *600 Huntley Street,* and some interviews. Then back to Ocean Grove, New Jersey, for a speech at the famous historic Auditorium. And finally back to Washington, D.C., to teach a week at Georgetown's Writers Conference, as I'd done every summer for twenty-five years.

George was a trouper all the way. For one thing, he had never flown; although he and his wife traveled widely, it was always by boat or car. "Surely she's not getting you on a *plane,* Dad?" his children gasped. "Where she goes I go," he told them. But he was obviously nervous, under his camouflage of kidding. "Flying's impossible," he whispered as we boarded. "This thing'll never get off the ground."

I urged him to take the window seat, where he sat with his nose pressed against the glass, as excited as a child in a candy store, marveling at the fabulous cloud formations overhead, and the enchanting panorama unwinding below. He was so moved he wiped his eyes; then turned to me, beaming. "Now I know why I married you. To find out what I've been missing!"

Honeymoon

George was so gallant and charming and funny he made a hit wherever we went: the Canadian TV stations, the crowded auditorium at Ocean Grove, New Jersey, and finally the Georgetown Writers Conference in Washington, where he sat enthusiastically through every speech and class. I was so proud of him, and we were so happy. The fact that we were honeymooners seemed almost as thrilling to the people we met as it was to us.

In Canada, however, I suffered my first blow as a second wife. We were dining at a luxurious revolving restaurant overlooking Niagara Falls; violins were playing, the falls a torrent of diamonds under the stars. Sheer paradise until George looked up from our menus to ask courteously, "Carolyn?"

I gasped. However unintentional, it was like a stab. Fighting tears, I stared blindly out the window while he repeated my order for the waiter. The falls still exploded in brilliance, the music played on, but I thought my heart would break.

George himself was stricken at his mistake. "Oh, you poor little thing," he tried to comfort me. "I'm so sorry, I love you so much I wouldn't hurt you for the world!" There were tears in his own eyes as he reached out to grip my hand; but a little smile played across his face. "And yet—please forgive me— somehow, seeing that you *are* so hurt only makes me love you more."

At Ocean Grove the audience was wonderful, and George so handsome and delightful people were asking for *his* autograph. The next morning I gazed at his profile as he lay beside me, still asleep. His brow barely wrinkled, his small straight nose so neatly carved; and that strong jaw and curly hair— gray, of course, and thin on top, but a thick curly tangle behind. It was hard to believe I was his wife. Becoming aware of me, he roused, grinned, and held out his arms . . .

We had decided to stay on a couple of days to swim and enjoy the gulls, the ships, and the fancy white Victorian houses and hotels. But unfortunately that first morning, the telephone rang. It was a dear lady from the Salvation Army asking if I could possibly say a few words this afternoon for the officers at their retirement home. I told her yes, of course; I've loved those people ever since working with them as a member of the auxiliary in Washington.

But my heart sank at George's shocked expression as I hung up. "Why did you accept?" he protested. "You've done enough. Why do you give so much of yourself away? We were going to swim."

"Darling, they're my *friends*. And they give their whole lives away!" We could swim right now before breakfast, I told him, and again when I got back. "You needn't go with me this time, you're tired, you should stay here and rest."

George agreed, but I knew he was upset; there was a strange sense of loss between us and I was miserable, blaming myself. Why had I been so impetuous? This was our *honeymoon*, I should have at least consulted him.

The gathering took longer than I expected. And later when I rushed in, the room was empty. I was disappointed and curiously frightened. George must have gone swimming without me! And he hadn't even left a note.

Heartsick, I took the back stairs and ran down to the crowded beach. The waters were teeming with people; shielding my eyes, I scanned them, screaming, "George! *George!*" in the direction of any man who looked remotely like him. I couldn't find him. I felt like an abandoned child. What had I done to our honeymoon, our marriage before it even began? What if I'd driven him away?

In near panic I finally ran back to the hotel—where George was standing in the lobby visiting merrily with the manager. "Hi, honey, how'd it go?" he asked, introducing me as his bride, and launching into the story of how we met.

I interrupted, I was so glad to see him. "I couldn't find you!" I wailed. "I thought I'd lost you, I thought maybe you'd drowned or run away."

"Why, honey, how could you?" George scolded fondly, hugging me. "You should have known I'd never go swimming or anyplace else without you. You are my life!"

Then finally the last class was taught, the farewell banquet over. Exhausted but exhilarated, we were driving back to Manassas where it all began. We had triumphed. August was upon us, we had made it through July. Now to get ready for the most important journey of all, moving to McMurray, the Pittsburgh suburb where George lived.

I was packing my books and papers when I came across that half-forgotten list. "George, listen, you won't believe this," I said and began to read it to him.

"Who is this guy?" he laughed. "I'll kill him."

"No, wait." I handed him the list. "Look—you fit everything on it and more—you've even got a place on the shore."

"Two, counting Jeff's," George informed me. "Ours is on Lake Erie." He read the list, amused but impressed. "When did you say you wrote this?"

"At midnight New Year's Eve, just as the clock on Times Square began the countdown in New York."

George stared at me, awed at this latest confirmation of the miracle that had brought us together. "Six months ago today! We were listening to the same program—Guy Lombardo. I remember hearing that clock bonging the hour, as I was there on my knees. That's exactly the time when I reached into that closet and found your book!"

CHAPTER FOUR

Lady of the House

We left in high spirits one morning, pulling a U-Haul trailer loaded with my things. Mostly my clothes and office equipment: typewriter, copy machine, worktable, books, and supplies. "Don't bring anything for the house," George advised. "Everything we need is there, and anything else you want we'll buy."

We both felt young and full of joy. And so secure, I thought; how wonderful to be able to start over, with all the romance but spared the financial worries. George sang most of the way and we talked our heads off, reminiscing about our wedding. Grateful that we'd gone to the trouble—neither of us had had a festive wedding before. Matching stories. I told George about the empty church, the empty purse at dinner; and now—sailing through the Alleghenies in an expensive car—about my first long trip as a bride crossing the Ozarks "in an old Model T that would only go uphill backwards."

George was delighted, but his eyes were tender as he patted my knee. "Oh, you poor kids, I admire you."

His own first wedding was less impetuous—they had known each other longer—but very simple, in a relative's home

the year he graduated from medical school. "No trimmings—
like you, we couldn't afford it, but at least as a doctor our
future was pretty well assured."

I dug into my bag for our own wedding pictures, and
looked at them eagerly as we drove. They had just arrived, all
of them wonderful, flattering to all of us. But to my surprise, I
told George, "In some of them you and I are the only ones
smiling. In the ceremony at least, we're beaming at each other,
but our children actually look *sad.*" Melanie was holding my
bouquet with eyes downcast, or gazing at us almost as if she
wanted to cry. (Was she thinking of her father? I wondered.)
And young George, so straight and tall beside his father—lips
tight, very grave.

The later scenes with our families were better, everybody
dancing or laughing and teasing, hanging JUST MARRIED signs on
the car, having fun. But as we studied the pictures together at
lunch, George and I agreed that in spite of their encouragement,
this beautiful event must have been secretly hard on them. "It's
never easy for kids when their parents remarry," George said.
"No matter what anybody's age. Memories hurt, their loyalties
are jolted. And I don't care how old they are, offspring can't
help being wary of the stranger who seems to be taking a
mother or dad away from them."

"I hope they learn to like me," I said meekly.

"They *love* you," he exclaimed. "How could they help it?
But listen, let's make a pact—it's you and me, baby, from now
on. Of course we'll still love and appreciate our children—
they're wonderful, we need them. And they need us. But it's *our*
love that's important, *our marriage* above all else, it's got to
come first."

I slept most of the last hundred miles—I hadn't realized how
tired I was. Toward dusk I was aware of George humming to a
Mendelssohn concerto on the radio, and the patter of rain.
Contented sounds. I'd never felt more peaceful and happy, or so
much a bride. I could sense George's animation mounting the
nearer we got to our destination. Finally, he pulled me closer.
"Wake up, honey, we're almost home."

Across a bridge, around corners, along pleasant shady streets, and we were turning into the driveway, headlights shining on the huge brick Tudor house, half hidden by trees and shrubbery, set far back from the street . . . I'd seen it once before, when my sons insisted on bringing me here to meet more of George's family, and make sure I would be properly taken care of. I was too much in love to care, but I appreciated their concern. After all, widows do sometimes make tragic mistakes. Everybody seemed delighted with each other; and Mother's future home was not only substantial, but bountifully furnished, to say the least.

This time George asked me to wait in the car until he was ready. It was still raining gently, the windshield wiper sweeping the drops away, the music soothing. He took so long I knew he must be up to something. Then lighted candles began to blossom in every window, one by one, and George finally galloped out to open the door for me.

"Strange wonderful George," I thought, my pet phrase for him from the beginning, he was so unique. I wouldn't have been surprised if he carried me over the threshold, he was big enough and nutty enough to try it. But he led me inside, where more candles flickered like fireflies throughout the house. In the kitchen he pointed to the long hand-lettered sign stretched like a garland above the shining cupboards:

WELCOME, DEAREST MARJORIE, TO YOUR NEW
HOME

"I made it myself," George said proudly, "and put it up before I left."

I stood marveling, and deeply touched. "And you even fixed all those candles?"

"Of course. I wanted to have everything ready for you when we got here. Sorry they took so long to light."

"It's *beautiful*," I told him. "I've never had such a welcome. It's like fairyland!"

Lady of the House

We waited until morning to unload the trailer. George called
Charley and Jincy, the faithful black couple who had worked
for the family for over forty years. A friend of Charley's came
too. Jincy looked me over for a minute, and then put her motherly arms around me, although she was about my age. "Now
doan' you worry," she puffed, sensing my doubts. "You be
happy here, we fix this place up *real good.*" The men carried
my heavy equipment upstairs to the bedroom I had chosen earlier for my study.

George Jr. had occupied it while waiting for his divorce to
be final so he could marry Liz. (They were newlyweds too, as of
last November.) The place was in chaos, with a lot of his books
and even some clothes still here, and mine piled everywhere.
They moved some of the furniture and might have to move
more . . . My George said that in time, if I wanted to, we
could build on a wing for my writing.

That would be nice, I thought, but I wasn't sure. The
house, so lovely by candlelight, looked different in the cold
light of morning. Different even from my first brief visit before.
Dark and depressing—maybe because it was still raining. Or
because I was getting uneasy about even staying here.

It was *theirs* so long, I realized that first day, and for a long
time afterward—so full of their memories. George had no idea
how often he called me Carolyn. Of course he didn't mean to, it
just slipped out, and he felt terrible when I reminded him. He
wasn't even thinking about her, he said; but for me each time
was like a fresh wound. "Which I *must control,*" I scolded
myself in my journal. "After all, in Manassas a couple of times I
called him Lynn. But when I asked if it bothered him, he only
laughed. He actually said no, 'it just makes me want to tell him
how lucky he was to have you.' George has an answer for
everything."

But the house was also so full of their *things.* Never, in a
single house had I seen so many *things!* The kitchen was so full

of gadgets it was hard to find a place to cook. There were so many chairs and sofas and love seats in that wonderful step-down living room I never knew where to sit. I felt lost in a dark jungle of furniture and possessions chosen by somebody else, and I must cope with it somehow. But I already knew I couldn't go on living like this—at least for very long.

You Married a Man Who Loves You

It was raining again this morning, it had been raining all week. I woke up with a sense of fear and depression. George was going back to his office; he'd been away for over a month. I would be alone for the first time in this strange, enormous, overstuffed house, and I was afraid.

I followed him upstairs after breakfast, watching as he shined his shoes and straightened his deep blue tie. He has an instinct for coordination—dark trousers, light blue shirt, and a good sports coat of silver-blue, all intensifying the incredible blue of his eyes. I knew he even wore crisp blue lab coats instead of the usual white. For the first time I saw him not as my always well-groomed sweetheart, but dressed for his profession —a doctor who would examine and counsel and treat patients all day. And I was so proud of him I wanted to tag along, if only to make sure I was really his wife.

But my childish fears were evident. George sensed them and turned to ask, "Why, darling, what's the trouble?" He came to sit beside me on the bed, where I was crouching stupidly. "Tell me."

"It's . . . everything's so dark and depressing. I'll be all by myself here," I whimpered.

"You'll be all right, honey. Keep the doors locked, and you've got the dogs to protect you. Besides, the sun's going to shine, it's going to be a beautiful day."

"It's not that . . ." I made a helpless gesture. The dark-brown-and-white wallpaper; the religious statues, the excess of *things.* How could I explain that I felt trapped, choked and buried in an opulent, overstuffed tomb?

This was his *home*.

But following my gaze, George understood. Lifting my chin, he looked straight into my eyes and kissed me. *"I love you,"* he said, with a new intensity, pulling me to my feet. "Just remember this: *You married a man who loves you.* You are the lady of the house now—do whatever you please. Whatever you want *I* want, as long as we live."

I was so relieved I followed him to the car, waving excitedly as he drove away. Lady of the house . . . Lady of the house! *You married a man who loves you* . . . I will never forget those words.

I thought they had freed me. But I wandered witlessly around all day, feeling timid and almost guilty, peeping into rooms, trying to decide where to begin . . . If I even *dared* to begin. I felt like an intruder, I kept apologizing to Carolyn in my head. Knowing how *I'd* feel if some other woman was prowling my house, looking in drawers and cupboards, judging my possessions and my taste, making decisions about what to change.

It doesn't seem fair, I thought. She's gone and I'm alive; I have her husband, I have her home that she must have been so proud of—and George was too. I'm trying to hang on to what George said—I *am* the lady of the house now. Yet I don't want to hurt anybody, it still seems almost an affront to both of them.

I finally decided—the kitchen would have to come first. I went to the basement and brought up boxes and sacks to put things in. Climbing on a little stepladder, I took down items dangling from the ceilings, or crowding top shelves. Then extra pans and dishes and bigger appliances I doubted we'd ever need. By the time George got home the back porch was crowded. He looked a little surprised, but only asked cheerfully where to put them. I suggested a toolshed near the garden. "At least for now. I'm not throwing anything away," I assured him hastily. "Just making room."

Every few days I work up my courage to approach another room. Always with that same sense of anxiety and intrusion, half afraid somebody might come in and catch me. "What are you doing here?" they demand in my head . . . "It's okay," I plead. "I belong here, I'm the new wife, *I'm the lady of the house.*"

Such idiotic dialogues—I actually wished I had a witness. I was relieved the day Jincy came stomping in.

"Good!" she said without preamble. "About time, yes, *ma'am,* I been hopin' for years—every time I dust." Jincy has a gesture more eloquent than words; one broad downward sweep of her arm dismisses everything. From the things she says, I know she really loved Carolyn, but Jincy has her own opinions. And now she was eager to help me. It was a comfort to have her working with me, there in the dining room with its priceless silver and china and glass. Together we took everything down from the glass shelves in the windows that flank the room— both bric-a-brac and treasures; washed everything, and began trying arrangements of what to put back. The green-and-gold goblets, the cut glass, pieces of crystal and ruby and amber—a lot of it stored away in cupboards, now flashing and sparkling like a Tiffany's window in the sunlight.

When we had boxed the rest, I took a deep breath and removed a lace tablecloth, to discover a magnificent teakwood table, matching the lovely Oriental chairs. We polished it until it shone like a mirror to reflect all the dancing sparkling colors. I was so happy I hugged Jincy, and could hardly wait to show George. He seemed delighted, thank goodness, and I hope and pray his family will be pleased. The last thing I want is for them to think I'm acting superior to their mother. But I have to fol- low my own taste, and somehow define my role . . .

The next day I felt better. Hope called and I poured all this out to her. "Marj, stop tormenting yourself," she ordered fondly. "She would do the same thing! *No* woman ever walked into another woman's house without imagining how she'd change it. And if you have to *live* in another woman's house, it's *imperative*—so go ahead and enjoy it." (Hope should know; she was married thirty years to a decorator.)

She was right. I've got to stop fighting with myself, and thank God for having a husband like George, who was so gen- erous and willing to please his wife, and is treating me the same way . . .

Carolyn was an incessant reader—read a book a day,

George told me. There are books all over the house. To my pleasant surprise, I found three more I had written. George was also delighted—they never discussed what they read. When he discovered my book of prayers that night, he had never heard of me. "Why, she knew you before *I* did," he marveled. "I think you and Carol would enjoy each other, Marjorie. You're not a bit *alike,* but I'll bet you could have been friends."

The thought was intriguing—who knows? At least I wasn't as *scared* of her anymore, or quite as hurt when he talked about her or showed me more pictures and slides of them with their family, everyone so beautiful and carefree. I try to be happy for them but oh how I envied her. Not for a single possession. But for those radiant years of being young together, and so in love as long as she lived. There's no denying it, I desperately envy that.

Ghosts and Dreams

We have been home in McMurray about a month now, and there is still so much to be done. I'm still enjoying the challenge of being a new wife after all these years. A *second* wife, like the heroine in Daphne du Maurier's wonderful novel *Rebecca.* An adventure, blissful but often bewildering.

Sometimes, going to the store, or even just running out to the mailbox, I wonder what people think. (If they bother to think of us at all.) Are they curious about me? Do they approve of the woman they see, who is taking the other wife's place? Do they resent me, or want to be friends? It's strange, after being somebody else so long, sure of my own identity. There is also a new person to be dealt with—not just George, but *myself*. I have not only changed my name, there are changes inside me— emotions I didn't know I *had*. Some of them shocking.

One night I had a terrible nightmare. There's a big fireplace in our bedroom, and one night Carol came down the chimney, of all places, and began to upbraid me, ordering me to get out of her house. And George just stood there, grinning; then they walked away hand in hand, laughing at me over their shoulders.

"Honey, it's all right, it's all right!" I woke up in a cold sweat, moaning and whimpering. George was holding me close to comfort me. "I'm right here, don't be afraid." I could feel him taking my pulse. "Can you tell me about it?"

"Don't ever leave me," I babbled, still trembling. "Don't ever die and go away with her!" Then I started, and came to my senses. "I'm not blaming *you*," I insisted as I told him. "Nobody is ever to blame for somebody else's dreams."

George sat up and turned on one of the bed lamps. He was looking at me strangely. "I've had a dream too," he said, "the same dream several times—I wondered if I should tell you, but maybe . . . promise this won't upset you?"

"I hope not, but you can't stop now."

"Carolyn loves you, Marjorie. She has come to me in dreams three times. And she's so beautiful, all in white, and she hands me a rose. Then I notice she's also carrying a book—*your* book, the one I found New Year's Eve." George hesitated. "This too she hands me, she's smiling as she tells me she put it there where she knew I would find it. 'I wanted you to have someone who would love you the way I did,' she says, 'someone who will take care of you when you get sick.'" Again George hesitated, gripping my hand. "Dear, she told me my cancer would return—that she couldn't bear it the first time, it's partly what killed her. 'I know Marjorie is strong,' she says. 'I love her for it, that's why I chose her. I love you, George, and I love Marjorie.' . . . And then she drifts away."

I was stunned. Too astonished and hurt for a moment to respond. Then angry. I didn't want to be somebody else's choice, I wanted to be *his* . . . And *cancer*? I was aghast.

When we first met, George had told me about losing a kidney to cancer the year before. "Everybody thought I was the one who was going to die, not Carolyn." Despite his urgent pleas to marry me, he had taken the precaution of having a CAT scan to make sure he was free before we set the date. "Otherwise I wouldn't put you through it." Yet now it flashed through my mind: as a physician he still had doubts—no wonder he kept reminding, "We don't have that much time!"

Oh, God, no—please—he had completely recovered. The thought of losing him was intolerable: *I* couldn't bear it either, I was not *that* strong—not after having even this brief sweet taste of life with George . . . Then once more I came to my senses —the irony and the absurdity of my panic. It was only a dream —dreams were crazy, they didn't mean a thing—ours even contradicted each other.

I was shaken but suddenly freed. All that mattered was that we were here *now,* brought together by whatever forces direct our destiny, to love each other as I, at least, had never loved before. The wild hurt was gone, swept away by a flood of relief and thanksgiving. I cuddled closer to George to make sure; I was safe in the arms of the most wonderful man I've ever known—wise and kind and romantic, even if he was inclined to dramatize. He was also funny—and somehow his ludicrous attributes helped make it all right. I was the luckiest woman in the world!

And no matter who or what chose me to be his wife, I should fall on my knees. Just let me be *with* him. And no matter what happened, I would always take care of him, as I knew he would take care of me.

Nonetheless, the experience was disturbing.

We went house hunting. George seemed taken aback when I broached the subject of buying, but said, "Of course, if that's what you want." I knew he dreaded the thought; men are like houseplants, they hate to be uprooted; and it would be hard for him to move after half a lifetime here. But I felt haunted—it might be easier for both of us to find something else.

When I first came here, we had talked about building, and explored his land for possible sites—a vast expanse of beautiful sloping hills rich with woods and streams. Years ago George began buying up nearby farms and letting them go back to nature—part of the "clean and green" movement, which helped on income taxes. He had given several acres to Diane and her husband, where they had built a fine country house with plenty of barns, and pastures for their horses. He gave even more land to George and Liz, who were already in the process of building what seems to be a magnificent house with a glorious view.

"If only we were *younger,*" George kept saying the day we went to see it. He pointed across the road to the crest of another hill. "Those five acres have the best view of all. That's where we were always going to build our dream house."

"Why didn't you?"

"Well, the war came along, and the kids were about ready for junior high. We bought the house where we live instead— everything's so convenient, the school so close, not far from the office . . ."

I was too excited to listen; my heart raced, visualizing *our* dream house there now. Why not?

"Oh, honey"—George gripped my hand fiercely—"if only we knew we had ten more *years!*"

"It wouldn't take long," I pleaded. "We've got lots of time left."

"We can't be sure. I should have warned you. In my profession I see people our age dying every day—or often in terrible condition."

I was so disappointed I almost cried. But he was right, much as I hated to admit it. What if we undertook such a project, and something *did* happen to him? Or for that matter to me, strong as I am?

I still got wistful as we watched George and Liz's house going up . . . I knew my own George would do the same for me if I insisted. "I'd build you a Taj *Mahal!*" he declared. But after those dreams, we compromised. He told me to look for another house, and went with me when he could, whistling softly and pretending to like whatever I did. Twice he even whipped out his checkbook. I had to stop him from making a deal—at least before I was sure I'd found what I really wanted . . . And I hadn't, until the other night, driving home by a different route, I suddenly pointed and cried out, "Now *there's* a beautiful home!"

"Like it? Okay, let's take a look." To my astonishment, George swung the wheel into the long driveway, and stopped. "It's where we live."

I gasped. We both were laughing. Incredible as it seems, I

hadn't recognized it for a minute. The other day George had Charley cut down a few more of the trees that hid the house . . . It *was* a beautiful home, I realized. Almost as big as the one young George was building—we'd be fools to throw it away. All it needed was a lot more clearing out, getting rid of the excess and those dark blue walls—sunnier colors inside. I'd start by calling the painter and go on from there. I would make it truly my home now, and we would be happy right there.

Meanwhile, George was eager to show me Lake Erie—just weekends, he assured me—and join the family for a few days in the Blue Ridge Mountains, at Skyline Drive. He already had our tickets for the cruise he and Carolyn took every October. It sounded fabulous, we couldn't miss it—but with so much to be done, I was getting anxious. (I've got a book under contract, I should be writing!) And after Christmas, those "two blissful months" they always spent in Florida. (Maybe I could persuade George one month of Florida bliss would be enough for us.) Then I remember George's cross-shaped symbol for happiness: balance. Love and Pray, Work and Play in equal measure. And once more I hear the firm voice, saying:

"It's what you prayed for, isn't it? It's his life too. Enjoy it with him while you can. You've waited for this too long."

CHAPTER FIVE

Early Adventures
with George

First Walks by School and Stream

Why was I so sad about moving? Giant trees surround us, every window frames their beauty, and we have plenty of space to roam.

We walk the dogs when George gets home, around 5:30, while the sun is still bright but slanting across the hills. The dogs are frantic with joy when they hear him drive in, barking furiously and nearly knocking him down at the door. "They love you better than me," I've accused him.

"They've known me longer," he laughed. "Also, I'm the one that feeds them, they associate me with supper and their walks."

"Our walks," I reminded.

"You bet they are," he said. "I'm so glad you like to come along. Carol took terrific care of our dogs, especially the poodles, she even groomed them—but I always walked them by myself. Now I'd miss you too much, I wouldn't even want to go without you."

The dogs gobble their food, and we're off, out the back

door, past the lilac bushes and a neighbor's garden, to crest the hill where two paths meet for our choosing. Ben leads the way, Tanjy bouncing along behind him. As we go, George begins his daily report of the patients he's seen, describing them vividly and telling me their life stories. And every time we take this journey he adds some bit of poesy or knowledge that I find life-enhancing.

One evening, as we circled the big brick schoolhouse at the bottom of the hill, we noticed the power lines looping up to the supporting pole. The pole was silhouetted against the pink sky, its beam forming a perfect black cross. And just below its outspread arms was a rectangular box I don't remember ever really seeing before.

"What is that thing?" I asked.

"A transformer," George told me. "A very important device for altering the ratio of current to voltage. In other words, a transformer gets the electricity from the large line and reduces it to usable current," he explained, marveling. "Electricity can work miracles for us. It can heat houses, run our machinery, light up the world. But without that *transformer* to reduce and direct it, the electricity would be too powerful for us to use. There would be just a big explosion."

I was amazed. "Gee, to think I could live this long without even realizing—"

George pondered a minute, pointing upward. "See that cross? And the transformer? Christ is like that transformer," he declared, to my surprise, "making it possible for God to show himself to the world. Without Christ and the cross, the power would be too great. The majesty, the wonder of the universe, life and death. People couldn't comprehend it, it would literally blow their minds. But by sending Jesus to live among us and show us the way, God focused and localized his power. His *son* became the light of the world!"

I gazed at George astonished. I had no idea he was so religious. Then a thrill of understanding went through me. He does not preach or try to sound erudite; such concepts just pour out of him, opening my eyes to so many things. I don't believe I will ever see power lines again without thinking of that analogy —the tremendous energy of God, and Jesus the transformer bringing it into our lives to work miracles for us. . . .

Another evening Ben dashed along the path to the right that leads through the woods and to the stream. There the grasses lie long and tawny, a bleached golden color that matches Ben's coat. The whole evening had a tan-gold glow against the vivid dark green backdrop of the fir trees around us. The air smelled sweet and verdant, earthy.

We walked to a pasture where two horses grazed, and leaned on the white board fence. At sight of George they came bounding for him to stroke their noses. Then we turned down to the creek that runs along the gully, bubbling and dancing over rocks at the base of the twin slopes. On the opposite side are houses and lovely green lawns. A man was mowing grass, another burning some brush, the scent of grass and bonfire fragrant. The dogs forded the stream and ran joyfully on the other side. Tiny lavender flowers are scattered along the grassy slopes, like strewn beads or patterns woven into carpeting. George picked one for us to examine closely—an orchid in perfect miniature. While here by the stream other wildflowers grow—wild roses and daisies and black-eyed Susans. George gathered some as we went, and by the time we circled back to the schoolhouse hill I was clutching a bouquet.

The long winged school building lay below, still roofed in brilliance by the falling sun. The grounds were alive with children. Little boys and their dads at a game of soccer. The dogs raced down, barking and yipping along the edge of the excitement. Beyond, two girls were throwing a Frisbee. Ben caught it and brought it triumphantly to us. The girls, about twelve years old, came running and noticed my flowers. "Who gave you those?" they asked. Smiling, I told them, and to their delight George bowed and kissed their hands. "Oh!" they both exclaimed. "We wish *we* had somebody who loved us enough to pick us flowers."

That was the night we encountered the square dancers. Sounds of country music and shouting were coming from the gym. "Square dancers?" I was excited. George said yes, a bunch of them practiced here about once a week.

"Let's go watch! We used to square dance in Dr. Little's basement back in Washington. It's the most fun in the world." I scurried ahead, George followed slowly, but by the time we got there the music had stopped, couples were beginning to pour out. "Dr. Schmieler!" The cry went up from several people who flocked around us, embracing George and welcoming his bride. The caller was beaming. "Come join us. Your little lady wants to, I can tell by the way she's bouncing." He turned to me. "We've been trying to get this guy for years—you persuade him."

"Oh yes, George, please, it's easy, you'd love it."

I caught myself at the expression on his face. Gently shocked and protesting, even as he thanked them warmly and said we'd certainly think about it, but we were very busy and away a lot—we'd have to talk it over.

The glow had gone from the evening, spoiled by the brief encounter. We walked up the hill in silence, exchanging stricken glances, blaming each other and ourselves. It was like that time on our honeymoon when I promised to run off and make another speech. I shouldn't have been so impetuous, I should have asked my husband first. But darn it, I didn't think he'd let me down. Now I was very disappointed, and it stung to realize that George was disappointed in *me*.

He finally spoke as he unlocked the door and we went in. "Listen, if it means *that* much to you, we will do it."

"Not if you don't want to."

He shook his head. "Honey, I'm sorry, but our time together is too precious to waste. Join a club like that and you have other couples after you, inviting you to parties, expecting you to ask them back. Who needs all that?"

"But people need friends," I protested, starting dinner. "Gee, friends were our lifeline wherever we lived. I don't know what we'd have done without them."

"A lot of people feel that way. And Carol and I had one or two couples who became very dear to us. But if you've got something wonderful by yourselves, why scatter it to the crowds? If two people are as happy as we are—at least I hope *you* are—why go chasing outside for excitement with people who don't mean a thing? Guard what you have, enjoy each other, spend every possible moment with the one you love."

"But you said it's important to play too."

"Yes, of course, but play together or with your family. Let the rest of the world entertain itself."

"Isn't that kind of selfish?"

"*No,*" he said emphatically. "Not if you're a good doctor or a good writer or anybody who works hard for the benefit of other people. But remember, you're the boss, we'll go wherever you say, do whatever you want if it makes you happy."

"Happiness is a two-way street," I said meekly. "I want you to be happy too."

"*That's* my girl," George said tenderly, and opened his arms to cuddle me. "My little girl—*mein kleines Kindchen,* as my father used to call my mother in German—his little girl. And, honey, we've got so many *places* to play. Lake Erie—we can still get in a few weekends there—and Skyline Drive coming up in October, and after that the cruise. It's like the Love Boat, I can hardly wait to show you. My dearest sweetheart wife, let's make the most of what we *have,* we are so richly blessed!"

I caught his exuberance. He was right. Never, since meeting George, would I have preferred the company of anyone else, if only because we shared such a feast of words.

For this I had starved. Any woman would be a fool to try to change the lifestyle of such a man. How can you improve Paradise?

Later that evening, George himself proposed a compromise. We could go to the doctors' events, which usually included dancing—Carol didn't care for them, but he'd be happy to take me. And when I had to travel on speaking trips or anywhere else, he would go along. "I just want to be *with* you from now on. I can't bear the thought of you being out in the world alone anymore.

"And you and I don't have to do the same things *we* did every year," he assured me. "Skip Florida next year, if we have to; skip the cruises—we'll always have Lake Erie. That itself is a lot more than most people ever have."

George cupped my face, and gazed into my eyes. His voice was serious. "Oh, Marjorie, it doesn't matter where we are, just so we're together as long as God will let us. Time runs out, you know. Nothing lasts forever."

First Visit to Lake Erie

At last we were off to Lake Erie: the poodle cuddling George like a furry cushion as he drove, Ben sprawled asleep on the back seat. I was thrilled, but I knew from George's whistling that he was a little anxious. "I sure hope you like it."

"Like it? Darling, I was born on a lake, lived on a lake, and jumped into almost every lake I ever saw. But never once a Great Lake—you may never get me out."

Smiling, George patted my knee. "Better wait till you see the cottage."

George has a passion for highways; he praised Route 19 as we flew along. "Nobody thought it could be done—the cliffs were too high, too many rocks—but they did it, and now you can drive either direction, clear to Florida or straight to New York, without even a stoplight." He described in detail how hard it used to be to get to the lake. The countless streets and lights they had to cope with before even getting out of Pittsburgh, let alone all the little towns on the way. "Now it seems incredible that we'd go to all that trouble, but we didn't care. We often started out after my office hours at night, the kids and dogs asleep in the back. It was nothing to take off at ten o'clock or later, and get there sometime before morning. . . . You know, I'd like to take the old route once more, just to show you. How about it?"

"Yes, of course, if you want to," I told him, but I winced. At this point I was reluctant to share any more of other people's memories. Before leaving, I had found an entire set of drawers stuffed with my husband's impassioned letters to his wife. (Not one of them including jokes and cartoons.) It would take me a while to recover.

Nearly four hours of lovely landscapes—rolling hills and woods and farms—until at last in the distance, like a painted wall against the sky, appeared the proud blue lake. I refused to believe it at first. "Impossible! Water is flat, Storm Lake never stood up like that."

"Great Lakes are different," George claimed solemnly. "Their waters are very strong, they're held up by a special starch. You can't dive in, you have to climb them."

Strange wonderful George! I hit him.

Actually, at that point we were simply on lower ground. But in a little while we were passing the markets and docks and fishing places, where sea gulls swarmed, and on through charming villages and small towns with magnificent trees and ancient houses very much like those of my childhood. "This must be the old part of town," I said as we entered the shady outskirts of the first one.

George smiled. "They're all the old part of town. Little towns that time forgot, almost exactly the same as when we first came here over forty years ago. That's another reason we loved it—the peace and quiet after the city, no crimes or drugs that I know of, nobody in a hurry, just wonderful people that make you feel welcome, and as dependable as those trees."

The beautiful little towns flowed into each other. Sheep and cattle grazed on neighboring pastures, and grape farms were everywhere. The air was sweet with the ripening grapes. Their thick green vines looked like herds of elephants crowding the fence, reaching over with their long fat trunks.

The lake was now where it belonged on the banks of the road, glimpsed through trees and trailer courts and cottages. We came to a woods, where George turned in at the small sign marked "Portland Bay." "Our woods," George said as we drove by. "Seven acres—we haven't been in there for years, you could get lost." He turned again into a leafy lane of trees. Light spattered through their embracing tops, and bits of sky were blue sapphires sparkling among the branches.

It was like driving under a canopy to fairyland, for when we reached the house at the end of the road, it too was roofed by this jeweled gilding. It stood on a park-sized lawn, with stately trees surrounding, the lake a placid sheet of silver at its feet.

Hastily, George sprang out to grab and throw aside a huge PRIVATE PROPERTY, NO TRESPASSING sign. I noticed several in the ditch behind the cottage. "I meant to have somebody take that down." He grinned, wiping his hands. "I don't want to scare you off."

I gazed around, enchanted. "Well, don't try it, I want to stay here with you forever."

I hovered while George unlocked. A charming Cape Cod, slate blue, with white shutters, needing paint—and so did the garage, which matched and had an extra lodge for guests.

We'll fix that next year, George promised, do a lot of stuff. Things had been neglected since Carolyn's death, he explained. His sister had cleaned the place up, but it was too hard on the kids just yet to come back; they'd spent almost every summer of their lives up here with their mother—and the grandchildren did too later. "Thank God they weren't here when it happened."

"I understand," I said. "I love it, I can hardly wait."

The cottage smelled musty but of cedar, mothballs, and remembered life. George took my hand and led me through the confusion of the entrance hall, the ancient but modernized kitchen, groaning under its gadgets, the big timbered lodge room, with its captain's chairs and long pine table covered with a checkered cloth, the two bedrooms, and tiny bath. There was also a pleasant alcove where George's wife had her easel, and a bookcase, and several chairs for reading, resting, or painting. The lake was visible from almost every window, sparkling half hidden behind magnificent trees.

And here, as in McMurray, was the warm clutter of its treasures—dangling from the ceilings, crowding every shelf and windowsill and wall: driftwood, antique lanterns, ships and shells, mounted fish and birds, hats and shawls and baskets, souvenirs from too many years of trips to count.

George seemed dubious and a little wistful, assuring me, "Get rid of anything you want, it's okay, you're still lady of the house."

I hugged him—relieved but touched. "Honey, I'm not a demolition team—a summer place should be fun. I'm crazy about it already."

We decided to swim before supper. We didn't even wait to unpack, just got into our suits and followed Ben, who was already racing beside the bank with a stick in his mouth for throwing. We walked across the broad green lawn to a shady glen where a steep winding path choked with wildflowers led down to the shore. Deep in the gully frolicked a stream that spilled over the rocks until it became a saucy little waterfall at the end.

Rocks and boulders of myriad shapes and sizes lay at the water's edge and scattered along the beach. Many of them looking like huge gray turtles whose shells have been adorned by the swirling, sculpturing waves. "That's why they're called turtle rocks," George said. Others, brightly colored, look as if they had fallen from an ancient wall of mystical carvings. Above them rise the cliffs—stratified layers of multicolored stone and outcroppings, here and there arranged by some master architect to create a natural amphitheater of steps and seats and shelves from which to watch the constant drama of the water.

George enjoyed my awed amazement, but grieved at how much the beach, at least, had changed. "For years it was entirely smooth white sand, you could walk for miles. If you gave me a trillion dollars, I'd never believe it—I used to drive my jeep down here, we've got pictures to prove it."

Ben ran frantically along, mad to plunge into the water every time George threw his stick. Dodging both dog and the rocks even here, we waded until our feet found sand, then swam—George long and sure and graceful as a dolphin, me trying to show off my fanciest crawl. Suddenly he disappeared and came up under me, lifting me bodily to his breast. "Marj darling, you swim like a little bird trying to fly. You should reach out as far as you can, love the water with your arms, pull it to you." He took my arms to demonstrate, and a thrill of his maleness went through me, this magnificent body cold and wet against me, and the joy and privilege of being his wife. "Wow!" I sputtered. "No wonder those girls flocked around the swimming pool."

"It worked for Carolyn," he said.

"I know, I know," I stopped him. I shouldn't have said it, I didn't want to hear the story again—how she had flung herself into the deep end of the pool where he was lifeguard pretending she couldn't swim. It hurt too much—it wronged her memory somehow. In a way I admired her—I wouldn't have had the nerve. But that cry and George's rescue led to an incredibly happy marriage; one that lasted for a lifetime—and eventually led to ours. God bless her.

We kissed and swam and started back, the dogs bounding up the hill before us. But halfway there we paused to rest on one of the protruding shelves. A wind had come up, spreading long curling parallels that striped the water below us as far as the eye could see. And as we perched there, tiny whitecaps began to dance—looking like a chorus line, I pointed out to George.

"That's what they are," he claimed matter-of-factly. "Can-can dancers, we see them all the time, tossing their ruffled skirts to show their ruffled panties." He pondered. "But if you really want to see something we should come back at night. That's when the little people come out to dance and celebrate and watch the show."

"Little people?" I encouraged.

"Sure, the elves and leprechauns and hobgoblins—they sit right here in the moonlight. Some of them go into the water and dance with the mermaids, but most of the little people just sit and watch the little *water* people dancing, and they sing and clap."

"Did you ever hear them?"

"No, not really, but I'll bet you could."

"Why me?"

His eyes twinkled. "Because you're little too, and only *little* people can hear the other little people sing."

I laughed, delighted.

"Dad made our childhood magical," Diane had written, in a letter welcoming me to the family. Lucky kids! Lucky *me* now. Sometimes I thought George was part leprechaun himself. I was filling my notebooks, not only with his colorful stories and philosophy but with his whimsies and poetic metaphors.

What a mate for a writer. (Another treasure I hadn't even asked for.)

Rejoicing, we returned. I heated clam chowder while George made cold drinks to carry outside. We ate at a redwood table in the yard. The sun had moved far to the west, and was sinking, a ball of apricot fire between the trees. The trees held it in their swaying arms, which broke it into stars and gems of pink light flashing among the boughs and tossing leaves.

We went to bed early, we were very tired. But at the door of the little room, fresh and neat for our arrival, I halted, suddenly apprehensive, reluctant to go in.

Instantly George held me, speaking gently as to a child. "Don't be afraid, honey. Nothing happened in this room that might disturb you. Nothing's there."

I squeezed his hand. "Thank goodness—but look who is." The dogs had sneaked in, Ben already snoring and smelling at the foot of the bed, Tanjy reigning in triumph from my pillow. In the beginning, to please George, I had tried to accept them in our bedroom. He and Carolyn actually slept with their dogs, he had told me. "All six poodles, when we had them—they were miniatures, real cute and cuddly, no problem—two apiece at our heads, two more at our feet." (I was too shocked to ask, and it would have hurt too much to know: *"But how did you ever make love?"*)

I had tolerated Tanjy's hot furry body crowding mine all night until I realized he was trying to bunt me out of bed. The night he almost succeeded, I told George one of us had to go. Promptly, George scooped him up and ejected both of them for good. He did the same now, while I apologized profusely for the way I felt.

"Forsaking all others," he vowed again, raising his hand, "including dogs."

"We're not forsaking dogs, dear. Only in bed with us."

"Just so you don't throw me out," he laughed.

We fell asleep in each other's arms, but woke a couple of times at the plaintive whistle of trains in the distance, lonely and mysterious. Going where? we wondered. Seeking what? Like lost souls in the night. Yet comforting too, nostalgic. George held me even closer. "Good night again, my beloved."

I awoke the next morning to the fragrance of perking coffee, wild roses on the table, and a mild clatter outside. George was already loading the jeep with a miscellany of long-unused objects from the overflow in the hall.

"See? I've already started," he said proudly, when I ran out. "Wanna go with me to the dump?"

"Sure, if you wanna go with me right now for a swim." I had put on my suit first thing.

He shuddered. "Before *breakfast?*"

"That's the best time!"

"Well, I will not allow you to go by yourself," he ordered. "That lake can be treacherous, at least until you know it better. So wait a minute."

The waves, so docile yesterday, were now roaring giants trying to hurl us at the rocks, the dog, and each other; but we bested them and returned exhilarated, to eat mightily, and then be off on errands in neighboring villages and thence to the dumping ground.

We stopped first in Brocton, a charming town where old-fashioned light-studded arches span the center of Main Street and baskets of geraniums hang from the lamp poles.

Into the country store for eggs, the hardware store for light bulbs, the drugstore for a newspaper and a prescription. "Dr. Schmieler!" the pharmacist welcomed him back. "Are you still practicing, Doctor?"

"I certainly am," George declared. "Us old doctors never die, we just smell that way."

They both laughed, clapping shoulders. George introduced me to him and several others. Then on to the sunny meadow of the dump, where a truck with a hydraulic lift was raising the heavy loads of junk. George was enrapt. Together we stood marveling at its incredible power as it rose, whining and groaning under the tons of debris, like a creature forced to strain beyond its limits; the men in the cab tiny and insignificant by comparison, yet maneuvering this giant monster so deftly. Aware of our awed watching, they smiled, we applauded, and with a flourish, George gave them a snappy salute.

An old attendant, gaunt and sunburned, came to help us pick up the lengths and blocks of smooth shining lumber that were available for the taking; meanwhile, asking George's advice about his ailing wife. Sadly, cancer. George wrote something on his prescription pad, patted his shoulder, and signed him with the cross. The sun burned down, the machinery roared, the garbage stank, and there were flies. But in its midst the two men bowed their heads and prayed.

"Marjorie, what's the matter, why are you crying?" George asked when he joined me in the car.

"Oh, George, that poor old guy! Thanks for being so nice to him—his wife's going to die, isn't she? And so is he, pretty soon. But the sight of you two men standing there in the hot sun praying surrounded by *garbage!* was so *beautiful,* somehow. I could almost see angels looking down from that cab."

"So that's what they were? Well, I'll be darned."

"No, really, George—who are *you,* what's your secret? You're kind of a magician, you make things change right in front of our eyes. You just did—that dump, of all places, a public *dump,* you made it a kind of temple."

"Oh, come *on,* you've been out in the sun too long." He felt my brow, took my pulse. "I'm just a city-boy country doctor, with a wife I adore, and enough in the bank so we won't go broke, that's all."

No matter how lavish George's compliments to others, he found theirs hard to understand. He never considered himself extraordinary, perhaps because he was in such harmony with himself and the universe.

We drove home with our useful plunder, stacked it in the garage, George singing to accompany its merry plinking, and swam again before lunch. The mood of the lake had changed, even the water welcomed us now. We came out elated, to spend a quiet afternoon—George with his medical reports (I had no idea doctors had so much paperwork) while I addressed wedding announcements. A delightful thing to be doing at *any* age, but at mine such a rare treat I wanted to hug the world and dance.

It was Saturday night and we did dance to Lawrence Welk. George was an aficionado of the program, he could rattle off the names and talents of every member of the cast in a German accent as true and sweet as Welk's. He was surprised and thrilled that I even wanted to listen, let alone watch it with him. "Everybody else considered it cornball, I always watched it by myself."

He was not criticizing, he was always diffident and loyal in speaking of his wife. When we mentioned our previous mates, it was mainly to explain their differences, more than our complaints.

"A lot of people considered it corny," I said. "We thought it was fabulous, everybody so beautiful and talented and skilled —such pros, we seldom missed it, but we never danced."

"Well then, come on!" George pulled me to my feet, and we danced along with Sissy and Bobby and the band and dear Lawrence himself. And I rejoiced . . . Locked into the same patterns of George's life before, it was wonderful to discover something we enjoyed so much, that was entirely ours.

Sunday

One more brisk but misty morning, and a quick cold swim. George was a convert now. But we took mugs of hot coffee along. The damp woods and grasses were starred with buttercups—they seem to have been spilled there, a rootless treasury of little gold weightless stars. The sun shone fitfully and huge gray waves rolled in, moving eastward toward Niagara Falls. But the whitecaps scattered among them were small and dainty, appearing and disappearing as we watched.

"They look like a class of little white-capped nurses hurrying toward graduation," George said. "Look, they're doing the breaststroke. The little nurses have donned their caps and are *swimming* toward graduation."

"No, no, they'll ruin their caps!"

"Don't be so literal—you're supposed to be the poet, not me. Besides, dunking nurses is a secret rite of graduation—only doctors know it, so don't tell anybody."

He took my hand, and we too plunged in.

We returned exhilarated, and breakfasted to an inspiring religious program. Then George put some beautiful old songs on the record player. Songs we danced to in college (our separate colleges so long ago), and "Melody of Love," which made us remember our wedding; and we danced again and were so moved we went into the bedroom "to worship in God's church of love," as he expressed it. "The precious gift of sex. Two people who are totally united body and spirit, committed to each other, married—knowing it is right and perfect to dance or go to bed together when these unexpected moments come."

"That's what's so wonderful about you," I said. "You don't just wait till bedtime—"

"Not if I get the chance!"

"That's not what I mean—I mean all the sweet things you do to make me feel loved all day. How you fix those little bouquets, and call me from the office, and the notes you leave around the house."

"Oh, oh—"

"Yes, I found some more, and they weren't all mine."

"Well, they're all yours now—and I didn't *know* you then."

"Never mind, I'm lucky to be married to a man who can love like that even now, after so many years—"

"Love should be like wine," George said, "better with age, sweeter as you get older. If you don't get out of the habit of expressing it, it really never goes away. Actually, for true lovers the sex drive becomes more intense, maybe because we know life itself is slipping away. And if you're in good health and have found the right mate, it is the ultimate act of creation. Not to create children—you don't have to worry about that anymore—but if you love each other and love God, in those few moments of ecstasy you are creating something too beautiful even to understand. You become one with your own Creator.

"How terrible it would be with a stranger," George went on, "or someone you didn't really care about or trust. Someone who would be leaving you, or who hadn't been good to you in the first place. No, the act of love can only reach perfection when you have this combination, this commitment of total love based on the past, the present, and the future."

It had begun to rain and the sound of the wind and the rain was a part of our joy. As we rose I said, "I want to do something

I've never done before. Everybody's gone home, we have the whole shore to ourselves. I'd love to get up right now, just as we are, and go outside and run in the rain."

And he said, "Why not?"

And that's just what we did, and it was glorious!

CHAPTER SIX

Skyline Drive

Two more magical weekends at the lake—this time meeting a few neighbors and making friends now that the signs had come down. Then October, when George closed the cottage and his office, and we were off to the Blue Ridge Mountains of Virginia and the fabled Skyline Drive.

We left on a Monday afternoon, the Jeep piled to the ceiling with suitcases and gear and boots and wraps. We flew along Route 66 under a sky that was gray and overcast, changing to a buttermilk curdling of white clouds. The sun came out in patches of brilliance before hiding again. George decided to take the route through Warrenton, with its old homes and bridges and antiques . . . In the country, past big stone houses, white-fenced horse farms, cornfields tan-silver in the sun, the stalks still streaked with green.

Above and beyond us in the distance we sensed the Blue Ridge Mountains beckoning. Gradually their blue mirages began to emerge, take shape, the massive shoulders of the mountains undulant blue-violet waves against the sky . . . More and more little towns, and farms and roadside stands vivid with apples and orange pumpkins, offering their autumn wares:

honey, cider, crockery, shocks of corn, patchwork quilts, and gaudily painted velvet hangings.

Gradually we were climbing, and at last reached the famous highway that spans the mountains in the sky. A ticket from the booth and we were curving through the hills, riding their very summit, surrounded, almost smothered by the rioting colors of the trees.

We arrived at the long brown lodge of Skyland, where the family always came, around five o'clock. It would be their first reunion here since their father had remarried. I was a little nervous, waiting with the dogs while George went in to check our reservations. I knew that he was anxious too; afraid he might not have made them, or specified the choice locations they had every year.

Cottages and buildings were scattered all about, some in the woods, the finest ones with magnificent views and fireplaces and sitting rooms and kitchenettes—George had described them to me. But he had been in such a state of shock and grief when the children brought him here last year, he wasn't sure what he'd done about them now.

I prayed he would return smiling; I knew how much this trip meant to him—to all of them—please, God, don't let anything spoil it.

But George was disappointed. As he feared, there had been some confusion, we would have to accept other quarters. We drove through the parklike areas to a wooden building with accommodations for six people: three on the upper level, three below. And as we toiled up the hill after parking the car, we discovered we'd been assigned to the rooms below. Spacious, paneled, charming, but no kitchenette or cheery fireplace.

We agreed it didn't matter, as long as we were together. We freshened up for dinner, hung up a few things, and George, in his usual joyful, energetic way, went for a bucket of ice to toast our love before leaving. He was so happy to bring me here. He loves this place where he brought his dear ones for so many years. It was another adjunct of life for him; he was eager to share it now with me. I felt very grateful, thrilled for him and for myself.

We walked arm in arm down the now dark hill to the Jeep. Taking the dogs along, we drove to the lodge, telling them to "watch the car." The lodge was swarming with people in slacks and sweaters, casual outdoor dress; the dining room was full. The hostess, a small eyeglassed lady, thin and pleasant in her navy suit, greeted George effusively, but looked astonished as he explained about Carolyn, and a trifle miffed when he introduced me.

We were seated at a table by the window. Outside, in the distant valley we could see a bracelet of glittering lights that George told me marked the famous caverns of Luray. After giving our orders to the waiter, he excused himself to chat with the hostess a few minutes until we were served. "I was telling her how wonderful you are," he beamed, on his return. "And she said, 'But *you're* wonderful too, she's very lucky to have you.' "

"She's right, I am."

Then another old friend from the lodge came up, a man who reminisced about the days when the Schmielers made their annual pilgrimage here. "You were the people with the poodles. I can still see them, all six of them following you, looking so cute in those little sweaters and caps your wife crocheted."

To my utter dismay, I began to dig my nails into my palms. I felt so—*anonymous,* sitting there hearing them recalling a past I couldn't share. Ignored, lost, and alone. And then as they continued, a very little thing caught my eye and nearly broke my heart:

The *dishes.* The dishes on the table! I recognized those plates, those cups and saucers—their fond familiar pattern of brown and green leaves. *Our* dishes. Exactly the same as those with which I set our table every morning. They had followed me here; but they had been here all the time. They would be here forever for the people who always came year after year. Why this should hurt so much I didn't know, but I found myself sobbing, staring out the window, fighting for control.

The man excused himself, and George gazed at me perplexed, and very concerned. "Why, darling, what's the matter?" He reached across the table to take my hand.

"The dishes," I blurted stupidly. *"Our dishes."* I held up a cup. "This is where you got them!" It sounded like an accusation, which was absurd.

"Why, yes, we bought a set here a long time ago."

He didn't understand why this should seem so shocking, nor did I. But emotions I had fought so hard to conquer were torturing me again. The very dishes on the table seemed to be mocking, "We never *were* yours—and never will be."

I turned my back as the waitress served dinner, trying to hide the tears streaming down my face. The lady at the next table glanced at us, then away. I was stricken, appalled, but I couldn't stop crying. I poked at my food, barely hearing what George was saying, so gently, lovingly: "Darling, it's *you* I love, I worship you. I didn't dream it would hurt you to come here. We'll leave tomorrow."

I can't remember what else was said, but when we finished the pretense of eating and were walking to the car, he held me against him and said firmly, "We won't stay any longer. We can leave tonight."

"No, no, no," I protested, and wept in frantic apology when we got to our room. "I wanted things to be so nice for you, I wanted with all my heart to make you happy and be a comfort to you our first time here. I prayed to God I would. But to actually be here where you *were* so happy with someone else for so many years—it's hard, I can't help it."

"Darling, I *told* you we don't have to. We don't even have to go back to Lake Erie—we can go other places."

I came to my senses before morning, did my utmost from then on to make amends, and be happy myself. He was such a super companion, so joyful, so totally loving and eager to share his enthusiasms. But I was tested. Despite his many virtues, George was woefully short on tact.

Our very first day he took me on a beautiful hike through the woods, which led up a hill to the luxurious lodge suite he had thought reserved for us. "We liked this one best," he said, showing me through it. "We'd build a fire every night and . . . Look"—he caught himself—"does this bother you?"

I assured him that it didn't, but I lied.

The Clouds

That morning, as I peeked out the windows, the world was muffled in white. The clouds had claimed the cabins, the woods, the world, even the massive blue mountains. But later, after I'd gone back to sleep, then started my shower, George, who'd been walking the dogs, rapped on the door, calling, "Come see!" I hastily dried myself, hurled on jeans and sweater, and joined him on the stone walkway outside.

The mountains were reappearing in silhouette against the sky—undulant ridges and hollows folding against each other, soft-seeming amidst their scarves and drifts of pinky white. At their feet lay a vast white rolling sea—so thick and creamy there was no hint of the valleys and villages there . . . While near us, just beyond the burnished trees, bloomed one fat white cloud almost close enough to touch.

Above it coasted another, in the opposite direction, it seemed. But swiftly, even as we watched, it turned and bowed as if in greeting, then reached its filmy arms downward to touch and caress the one below. And the first cloud lifted its face—at least one of its many changing faces—for the kiss. Holding each other, we watched them merge and blend, become one—a lovely mass of white, shimmering in the sun. That's when George kissed me, and we went inside to get ready for the walk I just described.

Family Reunion

The family arrived the following morning, although we didn't expect them until late afternoon. While we were here in our warm wood-paneled room reading after breakfast, a long-limbed figure strode past our picture window. "George! George and Liz!" my George cried. They burst in, George Jr. and his stunning bride, bringing Debbie, his daughter from a former marriage. They had just moved into the unit around the corner . . .

And a little later, the Maryland contingent: Jeff and Tanya and their daughters, Lisa and Leslie. All three girls teenagers, bubbling over, and pretty as flowers. What hugging and kissing and laughing and loving.

They come bearing boxes and bags and bottles and ice chests of food. Jeff's family settled into the other unit, adjoining ours. Doors were unlocked, flung open; a stream of family and dogs flowed through. We cleared off space on the dressing table for an impromptu buffet. Paper plates and glasses, plastic forks. We opened cans and bottles, ate macaroni salad, and munched huge poppy-seed rolls stuffed with ham, turkey, cheese.

My George sings and dances and prances about, high on sheer joy of the morning and his own lively, ebullient tribe. What a vibrant, entertaining guy he is—like Danny, the hero of my novel *Saturday Night,* capricious, funny, fey, but, unlike that Danny, faithful.

Later, after much consulting, we pile into cars—Jeff's deluxe blue van with its wide windows, deep plush seats, gadgets, stereo, bar; George and Liz's sturdy Wagoneer—and drive along the brilliant roads to the place where we will begin our hike: a popular trail that descends through incredibly beautiful forests to a falls called Black Hollow.

The dogs tug ahead of us on their leashes. The path swarms with people returning. We meet green-clad forest rangers. The family outdistances us; we refuse to hurry. All this breathtaking color must be savored, tasted, smelled—this heady incense of spicy pine and mold.

A little brook tumbles over the rocks at the feet of these soaring pines—how it sparkles and chatters and dances in the light raining through their feathery branches. Among the pines are maples and elms, bonfires of gold and rose, whose falling leaves gem the outspread arms of the firs. The leaves lie upon them like glistening flowers. One pine near the path is strung with these colored leaf jewels, they hang upon it like necklaces of lights on a Christmas tree.

The path pitches and swerves down and down among the trees. The air here is quite lovely and cool, the ferns still green, the moss on the huge boulders a vivid deep green furring. At last we hear the roaring of the falls, both below us and yet plunging from the great rocks overhead. A quartet of furious white sisters pitching toward the dark pools beneath. Surrounding are cliffs and shelves and boulders, where a few people sit. Little streams bubble out here and there to join the mighty gathering of the waters. One pool is almost still, its edges paved with the fallen ruby leaves.

George begins to pick bright leaves for me as we move on. We marvel at their likeness, yet their variety. Even the maples have multiple colors. Some lemon yellow rimmed with rose, others of deep scarlet or purest orange. But all the same five-fingered shape, and at their center a pure yellow veining that branches out into golden candelabra, like the Jewish menorah . . .

We emerge at the end of the long path to the roadway where the van has been parked and the others are waiting. Rock and country music are blaring. George chimes in as we join them, singing and improvising comically as if possessed. He grabs an empty wastebasket and beats it like a drum, hoists it across an arm to strum like a guitar, sings into it for a megaphone, his voice rich and sweet even in comic satire, much better than some of the singers he imitates. What an incurable natural clown he is, funniest when his humor is spontaneous, as now.

He doesn't have to strive to be funny. He's been collecting jokes since childhood, and is always clipping new ones or buying books of jokes to tell. But he is really funny only when he is so naturally, joyfully himself . . . His grandchildren regard him with a look of merry adoration. They laugh until they nearly fall off their seats, and when he pauses for breath, they incite him to continue. Throwing down the prop, he begins to lead them in a chorus that rings out all the wayp back.

I love his whimsies, his clippings, the jokes and word games he's always saving to read aloud and share with me. But I particularly love him when he simply bursts out with these irrepressible fountains of fun, bubbling like those mountain brooks, or cascading as freely as those falls.

Saturday morning: The pink light, the soft pink chiffon clouds that film the sky. George, up early again to walk the dogs, rushes back in to call me. I peep out the door. A huge transparent shell of moon still lingers . . . and below, a long white plume lies across the valley, rising from the Shenandoah River, he tells me, tracing its course among the fields.

We lock hands to enjoy it together. I have never been so happy in my life.

Mountain Streams

George never ceases to marvel about the miracle of our meeting; and driving home again through the mountains, he found the perfect analogy. "Mountain streams," he said, pointing to one visible from the road. "Our lives are like those mountain streams. There are hundreds of them in there, far apart but running on their way, over rocks and hills and through the earth, heading without even knowing it in a single direction, the place where they will finally meet another stream and merge into the river that will take them to the sea. And oh, what a coming together when they do—like rapids pitching over a waterfall!

"How strange," he went on, "that there I was, growing up in Pittsburgh, and you a little girl way out in Storm Lake, Iowa, at the same time. Then to think of all the years you moved around after your marriage. How many states did you say you'd lived in before Washington, D.C.?"

"Oh, six or seven at least, it was the only way—"

"Good for you, I admire that . . . While I stayed right around Pittsburgh, mostly in a rather small orbit of the city, practicing medicine, raising my family. Yet there were these parallel lines of our lives. And gradually the distance between us began to narrow, drawing us closer and closer. You were finally in Virginia, not too far from Maryland, where Carol and I stopped every year going back and forth to Florida, and New York to catch the cruises, and Skyline Drive . . . To think that all those years we were driving back and forth, I was only a few miles from Manassas!" he exclaimed, rounding a curve. "You had no idea I was passing and I had absolutely no idea *you* were there. And it wouldn't have made any difference anyway," he added. "Not then.

"Yet when the time came for us to meet, the lines finally converged. Carolyn was gone, I was alone and nearly crazy with grief—good heavens, only a year *ago* at Skyline, I didn't think I'd ever go back. Oh, Marjorie, thank you for being with me this time, I can't remember ever *having* such a wonderful time there . . . What was I saying? Oh yes, how we finally met —the accident that could have killed me, but only kept me at Jeff's, where I learned you were alive and real on planet Earth. And the minute I heard your voice I knew our fate was sealed.

"Never mind Florida, I *had* to find you. And the minute you were ready, I was on my way. I knew you'd be there at the end of that country road. Someone I had to be with, the woman destined to share my fate and be my wife."

"You were shocked when you saw me," I put in. "You were looking for somebody else. You were expecting to find Carolyn again."

"Yes," he acknowledged. "You're probably right. There was something about your picture that reminded me of her—I don't know exactly what I expected, but I was disappointed for a minute. I found you very attractive—but you don't look anything like her. You are different, wonderfully different, I realized in just a few minutes. And as the evening proceeded, I couldn't believe how lucky I was . . . Seeing you climb the circular staircase ahead of me in that little restaurant—your pretty legs, that body you've taken such good care of. And sitting across from you, ordering for you. And how you urged, 'Eat your baked potato, George, it's good for you.'

"You were like someone I'd known in my heart all my life.

No wonder I didn't want to go home that night. Although I'm glad you didn't let me stay. I wanted to be with you forever. The paths we had traveled separately so long had finally come together. It was a miracle. It will remain a miracle the rest of our lives.

"And now here we are," he summarized joyfully. "Life has brought us right back to the top of the mountain, but we aren't *separate* anymore. Going downhill? What a stupid phrase for growing older. We've reached the heights! And the view is so beautiful from here. We can look back on our lives, on this remarkable century of progress, all the changes we've seen, and be thankful we've been allowed to be here on earth at such a time. We can look back at the work we've both done, how much we've accomplished, you as a writer, I as a doctor. All the people we've surely helped.

"And our families, our harvest of children and grandchildren, and our friends. All the memories and experiences that helped us grow into the people we are now. And that includes the mates we loved before. The very fact that we *were* both married before gives us a rich legacy, actually a great treasure of love that we can build on now. And we can look out so far beyond. Not as many years as we wish—if only we could be given another fifty years to start over! But we can't. But we can be thankful and relish the precious things we *have* together every day.

"Our breakfasts, the way you come running downstairs to greet me every morning. That we're both in good health and have so much energy—to swim and dance and walk the dogs every night. That we can drive to Lake Erie and do all those things at the cottage. And come to Skyline and hike right along with the kids. And we'll be off to Bermuda pretty soon. Look how much we've packed into these first three months. We're making up for lost time. And there's so much more to do and see.

"And we have the means to do these things, because we've both worked hard and valued what we had and God has been good to us. But the richest treasure of all, the thing we can thank God for most of all, is our love."

George parked before the roadside restaurant for lunch.

Helping me out of the car, he raised his hand, and stated like another avowal, "I love you with all my heart."

"And I love you with all my heart," I echoed.

"Good. That makes us just one big heart. And seriously, this is a priceless thing to know. That there will never be anyone else for either of us as long as we live."

CHAPTER SEVEN

More Adventures with George

The Love Boat

Even as we pulled into the driveway from Skyline, George was eagerly announcing, "Next stop Bermuda!"

"Oh, golly—already?" I'd almost forgotten. Inwardly, I groaned. George himself made every day an adventure, no matter where we were . . . And now that I'd almost finished redecorating our house, I was finally getting a little work done on my book. I was not tempted to run away again even on a glamorous cruise.

"Yep, only one more week," George rejoiced; then, as if reading my mood: "Why—Carol could hardly wait! We both looked forward to it all year—it was the absolute highlight of our lives . . . Oh, sweetheart," he assured me as we unloaded, "I'm so happy this time I'll be taking *you*. Talk about *The Love Boat*—that show should film an episode with us! We'll be real-live characters, bride and groom on our honeymoon."

As usual, he was right. The cruise was almost pure romance, from the first deep thrilling blast of the ship's whistle as we departed to the dramatic sight of the Statue of Liberty in the harbor, welcoming us back with her lifted torch on our return. But we were sailing on the *Doric,* their favorite ship, George told me. And in his sheer nostalgic enthusiasm and desire to show me everything, he forgot and kept calling me Carolyn. I tried to let it go—he was so proud to be my escort on my first cruise, and so pleased with his arrangements—where again I felt the effect of the couple's "forsaking all others."

George had ordered not only a table for two instead of with a group (which I secretly thought would be more fun) but even one of the most luxurious cabins, with a private deck . . . In planning, he had given me my choice about the seating, but was so obviously eager for the separate table, I told him to choose, he knew best. "Good, it's a lot more romantic. We'll just sit by the window and enjoy each other."

And the scene as we entered the dining room that first night was almost a replay of the one at Skyland lodge. "Dr. and Mrs. Schmieler!" The steward rushed up to greet us. "Welcome aboard, we've missed you, I'm so glad to see you, and I have good news—I reserved your usual table." Proudly he escorted us to it and pulled out my chair. "Exactly where you always sit, looking so beautiful." He halted, openmouthed.

Smiling, George put him at ease with the familiar explanation. But his attempt to explain to *me* only made things worse. "Oh, my precious sweetest Carolyn, it's a mistake, I *didn't ask for* this very table!"

He looked so miserable I didn't know whether to laugh or cry, so I exploded. "Wake up, George, you've been calling me Carol ever since we set foot on this boat. If you do it again I'm going to jump off!"

At that point, another of the weird coincidences that seem to trail us manifested itself. A couple was led to the table beside us. A pleasant pair from New Jersey, who leaned over and introduced themselves. And *her* name was Carolyn.

It seemed so ridiculous we told them our story, including my threat to George, and we all burst into laughter. Then the latest Carol took up my cause. "But don't jump off yourself. Tell him to get his wives straight or you'll push *him* off!"

. . .

George's most preposterous fantasies sometimes almost come true. As before, when we traveled in July, our role as newly-weds became known. (Never mind our not so tender age.) We dined one night at the captain's table, and a scriptwriter actually broached our private deck to discuss the possibility of basing at least one *Love Boat* episode on our experience.

We didn't spend much time on the little deck, but it was lovely to have coffee or cocktails there, and watch the sky and roiling sea. And one sight alone, after a storm the second day, was worth the entire trip. A fabulous rainbow, which must have been watching over us since our wedding, drifted down-ward toward us, drawing nearer and nearer until its misty colors actually surrounded us where we sat. "Why, it's in our laps!" I cried in great excitement. "But where's the pot of gold?"

"Gosh, where'd I put it?" George said calmly, although he too was awed. "It's here somewhere." He patted his hips, and then his breast. "Oh, I know, right here in my heart, where I put it in the first place, when we said '*I do,*' and you took your half and did the same thing, remember? So we already have it, *Marjorie,*" he emphasized, grinning, "and nobody can ever take it away."

Despite George's pretense of valuing exclusion, he really adores people, and is a born ham when encouraged. He sang to me as we walked the moonlit decks, hand in hand; and dancing every night, he was inspired as if by some divine afflatus. People applauded, men whistled, and one night, as in a grand finale, he danced me right out of the ballroom to what seemed an ovation.

Ah, ecstatic dreams of romantic love and never-ending youth. For a few brief moments *we* were Camelot—or better yet, Fred Astaire and Ginger Rogers.

All this, plus the wonderful shows on the boat, and the exotic tropical isle of Bermuda itself, with its calypso bands and shops and snow-white beaches. George knew every beach like an old friend and introduced me to a new one every day. The ocean intimidates me; after jumping a few foaming monster waves I would lie on the sand with a book, while he swam far beyond my courage or skills. And there, at his favorite, Tobacco

Beach—a bizarre place where rocks jut from the water like pyramids or giant gargoyles—I nearly lost him. The water was calm that morning, but the current was strong—neither of us realized. He was floating peacefully when I picked up my reading, but as time passed and he didn't return, I searched for him with the binoculars and screamed. He was almost too far out to find, and struggling.

A lifeguard roared off in a boat and brought him in, almost as ashamed as he was exhausted, lying on the beach.

"Don't you *ever* do that again!" I said furiously, even as I sobbed. "I have never been so scared. You could have drowned, I couldn't bear it!"

George had covered his face with one hand, blindly he reached out to grip mine with the other. "Forgive me," he begged, "I should have *known* better. Life is so precious, and I'm not as young and strong as I thought. God knows, I don't want to leave you."

It was the only significant flaw in our most enchanting adventure. No wonder George had described the trip in such glowing terms. Even this final threat drew us closer. My heart was singing new songs, my head spilling over with ideas. And to think I'd actually dreaded the interruption. How could I have been so stupid? Strange wonderful George. Any adventure with him would always be more rewarding than whatever I might have accomplished without him.

The Flower Show

I came home actually inspired. To my great joy the book soon began to sail right along—like that ship to Bermuda! But George decided to take Mondays off this month to work on his own papers, and he suggested we both play hooky and go to the Flower Show at Phipps Conservatory. One of their four major shows of the year. "They're all so beautiful. We never missed a one—and I just *can't* let you miss them either."

So we drove through the bright shining afternoon and the countryside that surrounds us, on toward the city—past the

myriad business places, and along the streets of Mount Lebanon, with its old but dignified houses crowded side by side;
through the Fort Pitt tunnel and across bridges, finally skirting
the city—its rivers ablaze, shining like satin in the sun, its buildings glittering against a cloudless sky . . . Around corners,
along streets of shops and neighborhoods filled with boyhood
memories for George, on into the vast green acres of Schenley
Park, where, as a student at Pitt, he used to run five miles a day
cross-country.

"Seems incredible now," he remarked, "after walking all
that way from Mount Oliver to get to class every day, across
the bridge, and back at night—at least ten miles. Never took a
streetcar, and carried my lunch in a paper bag to save my parents money." He'd worked hard and studied hard to get good
grades. "Had to, to get into medical school. But I wasn't an
especially quick student like my own children, every one of
them valedictorians. It took me longer."

Yet he was captain of both his track and swimming teams,
and had time for heavy dating, a lot of it right here in Schenley
Park—he'd have pointed out the very benches and secluded
spots if I hadn't stopped him.

We parked the car on an island in the street, and crossed
the graceful lawns to enter the vast glass pavilions of the Conservatory, its arched glass roofs shining bright in the sunlight.
Nearby, the tower of Pitt's Cathedral of Learning looked down
as if presiding.

Inside, a rich earthy smell, a sense of moisture and lush
growth. The acrid fragrance of chrysanthemums in brilliant autumn colors—yellow, burgundy, bronze; zinnias, asters, pop-
pies, daisies, mixed with scarlet barberry and orange pyracan-
thas. The colors blend, riot, become new hues to the eyes,
enhanced by fountains and pools and banks of white. White
blossoms spill over walls, plunge downward in foaming cascades, drift like beaded portieres from glassy ceilings . . .

Each room a new gallery of beauty to be experienced.
Whole rooms of cactus, palms, exotic jungle growths, a damp
and dusky world giving off its own heady incense . . . We
lingered longest in the orchid room, awed by the incredible
number of varieties. We examined a few closely, their open

pearly throats so daintily, exquisitely painted with identical purple designs. One kind, we discovered, has a tiny golden butterfly perched on its tongue. Another carries an open cup on its lips, as if eager to receive.

Finally, in another corridor just before leaving, we paused before two wax figures: the original Phipps father and son, the placard says. The father a shoemaker bending over his last; the son holding in his graceful hand some old-fashioned button shoes to be fixed.

What a handsome young man, I thought, vaguely puzzled: his mop of curly black hair, his strong cleft chin, the lower lip fuller than the upper, the corners tilted in a little whimsical smile. And the eyes, sweet, radiant, faintly flirtatious—excited and challenging eyes. I could hardly stop staring at this engaging figure. "He looks familiar," I told George, "I don't know why." Then suddenly: "Why, it's *you*. The pictures I've seen of you as a young man!"

George laughed. "Not really. It's a coincidence, though— my dad was a shoemaker too. But he never made enough money to endow a place like this."

As we left—to come home, I thought—George surprised me by turning into the tunnel that leads up to Mount Washington. "I want to show you Pittsburgh as you've never seen it before. We'll have dinner up there, the restaurants are great, and the view is fabulous. Carol and I always—" He caught himself.

"Don't worry," I told him this time. "I'd probably feel worse if you *didn't* want to take me to the same places you took her."

Our table looked down on the rivers, the stadium's huge orange cup, the highways across the bridge. And beyond all this, the teeming city as the afternoon waned, its buildings changing colors as the sun set, dusting or drenching them with gold. One had a column of gold, beginning at its towers, sinking gradually deeper and deeper across its windows, so that they stood at last like pillars of fire before the sun vanished almost as suddenly as it had begun its flaming task. By then other windows were donning their garlands of light.

Meanwhile, the three rivers below were turning pink, striped with the lights of buildings on their banks. (George named them for me—the Allegheny, the Monongahela, and the Ohio.) And in a gentle pattern just beneath us, boats and barges were gliding at their work. Anchored beside the island were long, enormous barges loaded with mounds of coal or sand. Beside them was a little white tugboat, looking like a floating cottage three stories high. We watched it being maneuvered into position to make room for its twin approaching down the river, slowly pushing ahead of itself one of these long, heavily laden barges at least fifty times its size. How gracefully these little boats move, are guided into their station, and then attached to the floating enormity they will nose ahead of them hundreds of miles of water to its destination.

As if this hadn't been enough to enthrall us, as dusk fell and the sky turned to violet, a huge rosy moon began to peer over the rim of the city, beaming like a proud father surveying his flock. "Pa Pitt!" George smiled, pointing. "He looks just like Old Pa Pitt. That was once a cartoon character very popular around here—a jolly symbol that seemed to epitomize the city of Pittsburgh."

But to me, I told him, it looked like my dad, Sam Holmes. "That's exactly the way my bald-headed dad used to look, grinning as if his face would burst, comical, half teasing, yet almost exploding with joy and pride."

George blew me a kiss, tipped the waiter generously, and presented me with a wilted little butterfly orchid he'd stolen from the flower show, but forgotten in his pocket.

The spirit of Pa Pitt, or Sam Holmes, beamed on us all the way home.

CHAPTER EIGHT

Doctor George

Doctor's Wife

I never dreamed I would one day become a doctor's wife.

I have always been a little in awe of doctors, and so was George from the time he was a boy. I think most people are. It's almost instinctive. The importance of the medicine man dates back to ancestral tribes. And with good reason. Medicine is the only profession on which our very lives depend. The men and women who enter it must be brilliant even to *qualify* for training; and medical school is itself so difficult that even some of them fail. Those who survive have mastered a body of knowledge and skills beyond that of most mortals.

Our daily language reflects their authority and prestige: "Doctor's orders." "Call the doctor!" "Is there a doctor in the house?" Personally, I was raised on a phrase from my mother, who had worked as receptionist for a doctor when she was a young lady: "Medicine is a *noble* profession," she would fervently assert. "Dr. Parker was a *saint!*" (Alas, however noble the calling, very few doctors are saints.)

In our little town, doctors' wives were gracious ladies who

dressed fashionably, spoke gently, and presided over clubs and teas in their lovely homes, where I was often invited to "give a reading" (fancy for "speak a piece"). They seemed to me charmed beings, actually married to these kind and genial gods, always so willing to help our whole family, day or night, but almost too wise and wonderful to walk the same earth we did.

They say we never quite outgrow the child within us. For me, this aura about doctors persisted even years later when, as a wife and mother, doctors and their wives became our closest friends. No matter how often we enjoyed each other and shared our problems at clubs, on trips, or in our homes, I still felt somehow honored to be in their company.

But none of this had anything to do with my marrying George. He was such a fantastic person I would have married him no matter what he did for a living. It simply didn't occur to me that I too would become a doctor's wife.

Actually I didn't qualify for the usual role. My doctor husband came to me whole, at an age when most doctors are retiring, or already have. I was not with him, as so many wives are, in the days of medical school, or the hardships of interning and getting started. (George's first office was two rooms and a hallway in a rented house.) I wasn't there when he rushed off in the night to save a life or deliver a child. I did not bear his own children, or work with him in the hospital, or take care of his office, as Carolyn had. I have great respect for such women, they have earned the privileged lifestyle they later enjoy.

But being a doctor's wife even for a little while, however late, enriched my life and added to the magic of our marriage. It helped me understand the special mystique that made this man not only "strange wonderful George" to me but "strange wonderful Dr. Schmieler" to so many others.

This was priceless to me both as his wife and as a writer.

By the time we met, George had given up his family practice for internal medicine. His skill was in diagnosis. Because of his passion for thorough examination, no matter how long it took, he often found a stubborn problem others had missed, and fixed it—or turned it over to someone who could. Most of his patients had been with him for years, so many of them living to such a ripe old age he had earned the reputation: "Go to Dr. Schmieler and you'll never die!"

I was never a participant in that side of his life. But rather his audience enthralled, as day after day he played out the fascinating drama of his profession for me, with a cast of characters I would never have known or imagined otherwise. Drawing colorful word portraits, sometimes of other doctors, but mostly of his patients, many of them from the ethnic surroundings of his office. I could not resist harvesting such a bountiful human crop; my notebooks were soon bursting with his brisk vignettes and detailed lengthier characterizations.

Actually, I met only a few of these people, sometimes in the supermarket when one of them would rush up to me singing his praises—or when someone died. Because, nature being what it is, no doctor can keep everybody alive forever. George was so deeply attached to everyone under his care, each death was a personal loss. He immediately sent flowers; and a part of our social life was to have dinner at a nice restaurant near the funeral home, and attend the viewing that evening. And oh, what a flattering and exciting reception. "Dr. Schmieler, Dr. Schmieler!"

The relatives rushed up to embrace him, and then open their arms to me. What hugging and kissing and laughing and little stories they told, even in their sorrow: "You'll never know how much your husband did for my father. Gave him hope, kept him laughing, stopped the pain. Just to see Dr. Schmieler walk *in* was a blessing—in a few minutes they'd be swapping lies about girls in the good old days at Mount Oliver."

The chatter hushed as George led me to kneel beside him at the bier. Rising, he would pat the hand of his now silent friend, kiss the cold forehead, and sign it with the cross. His eyes were always wet when he turned back to them, but he was also smiling. The sense of some joyous celebration prevailed. Their hearts seemed to overflow with wonder and joy at our coming to be with them.

I felt like the bride of a beloved king.

Doctor's Office

George's office was in Canonsburg, a largely blue-collar community, where he began. "There wasn't anything noble about it," he told me. "The priest just said they needed a doctor out there. Some of the guys downtown thought I was crazy, 'Oh no, George, you don't want to get stuck with a bunch of coal miners and people just off the boat. Come on with us, or at least a classier suburb like Washington or Sewickley, rents are high but you make a lot more money.' Well, I never wanted to make a lot of money, and my own folks weren't that long off the boat. Neither were Carol's. As I told you, my dad was a cobbler, hers drove a beer truck, we didn't care about country club stuff, we were perfectly happy out there."

He had built a commodious two-story brick building for the purpose. For years the family lived in a nice apartment upstairs (where George still took his after-lunch naps). It was convenient for his wife, who served as receptionist and bookkeeper as often as she could. During the summers she spent at Lake Erie with the children, George got used to doing everything himself.

"We never hired anybody else. Carol didn't like the idea of my being with another woman all day, just as I sure wouldn't want her spending that much time with another man."

Later their son George Jr., who shared offices for a while, had two nurses and a secretary. "Which would have driven me nuts. They'd be parading in and out while I was still on my first patient. I don't want to be that busy and I hate to delegate authority."

George's one-man, one-patient office created an atmosphere of friendly informality. He personally ushered everyone in (taking the arm of older people), examined them head to toe, and performed every task himself—from blood pressure to EKGs and X rays if necessary. He listened to them, joked with them, prayed over them, and saw them to the door . . . All this contributed to delays, interruptions, and sometimes confusion. Which he told me about in his fascinating, frequently funny daily reports.

Following is an account, as he described it, of a day he meant to get home early:

"Jack Anzalone, my first patient after lunch, has strep throat. I recommend tetracycline, and he says he has some at home. Two hours later, while I'm examining a heart patient, Lorenzo, on the table, there's a rap at the door—and there stands Jack with a handful of pills. 'Are these the ones you were talking about?' he asks me.

" 'No, those are vitamins,' I told him. 'You need antibiotics, which are orange and yellow.' I went to the cupboard and began counting out the capsules, my mind still on Lorenzo. How serious was his heart condition? Should I take another EKG? Meanwhile, also remembering that you and I were going to dinner at the Brown Derby, and if we got there by six o'clock the specials are half price! Weighty decisions over something *that trivial,*" he laughed.

Just after the pill patient left, George continued, Bud—another old friend and patient—dropped in with a platter of cookies. "A jovial guy who likes to talk. The cookies were a compliment from his wife. They both were thrilled at seeing us recently on TV. I had to smile and be nice to Bud, but my thoughts were still turbulent: what to do about Lorenzo? The older you get, the more you realize you can't be sure 'this one is going to be fine, this is going to die.' I've had people with normal EKGs, yet still suffering from serious heart disease . . . Bud himself is living on borrowed time. Other doctors gave him up ten years ago—couldn't operate because it's a three-vessel occlusion, carotid arteries in the neck, yet somehow I've kept him alive—another reason he keeps bringing me cookies . . .

"But back to Lorenzo. He's one of three Italian brothers I've treated for years; no matter what else may be wrong, all they ever worry about is sex. First thing they always ask, 'Doctor, can't you give me something for Upjohn? You know—Upjohn, *Upjohn!* Doesn't that company make a medicine that will help a man perform?"

"What do you tell them?"

"I just tell them not that I know of, no drug is actually

effective, although testosterone may help sometimes. I tell them not to play around, be true to their wives, get some rest, but they're not interested. Even poor Lorenzo today, here the poor guy could die any minute, yet all he's concerned about is sex. I had to get him off the subject long enough to ask, 'How do you feel generally?' The last couple of weeks he'd felt very fatigued and had squeezing pains in his chest. Very suspicious. His last EKGs were perfectly normal, but these symptoms made me very concerned. Oh no! I thought, still wanting to leave early, but knowing I had no choice but to take another EKG."

"And how was it? What happened?"

"He *was* having a heart attack. A coronary occlusion, no doubt about it. I had to call an ambulance and get him to Washington Hospital right away. Dr. Kay's a good heart man, they'll keep him until he's out of imminent danger . . . Well! Ready to go to the Brown Derby?"

"It's after six o'clock."

George kissed me. "It's only eight, I guess we can afford it. And I'm going to enjoy it all the more because my conscience is clear and you look lovely, and who cares whether we're early or late?"

George's stories and descriptions of his patients made them all very real to me. And as he painted their pictures for me, I began to see an even larger, clearer, more significant portrait of George himself.

Here are just a few from his colorful gallery:

THE GENTLE FAMILY

"I've never seen such a gentle family as the Shannons," George describes them. "They all are so gentle, they speak with a gentleness in their voices and in their eyes. The parents smile with their eyes, I have never seen either of them frown. Both are alike in almost every way—slight people, gentle, fair, and slim. They even look alike. The wife wears her hair in a beehive; except for that you could hardly tell them apart.

"Their eight children, all grown now, are just like them, except for one tall son who was in the Marines; the rest are slight, delicate, and small—if you put them all together they'd barely make three people. One girl is quite homely, but actually she is almost beautiful because of this family way they smile—gently, their lips slightly upturned. It's always nice to see them, a relief after the grim, plowing parade of other people. They are simple, ordinary people who make you feel warm just to think about them.

"They love dogs, and are always taking in strays. But none of them ever married. This seems strange for people who are so nice. Compassion seems to run through the whole family—a web of gentle caring. They all live in the same big house, and I don't think they ever had any problems, any real trouble. If so, I never heard any."

"What about their ailments?" I asked.

"Never anything really serious. Well, yes, they do have pipe-stem arteries, all of them, hard as rocks as long as I can remember. But it doesn't seem to bother them—no heart attacks as yet, although there's always that danger now that the parents are getting old. But they come in faithfully, and are the soul of honesty, and are so grateful for every little thing you do for them."

George laughed. "One girl, Rose, like her sisters, seems perfectly happy to stay at home and help her parents—I doubt if she's ever had a date. Well, this daughter came in very worried, afraid she was going deaf. 'You know, Doctor, how I love music, good music on TV. I can't bear to think of giving all that up.' When I looked in her ear I simply found a lot of wax, which of course I irrigated—flushed out. And when I finished she cried out, 'I can hear! I can *hear!*—as if I'd just performed a miracle.

"She was so overjoyed, in such absolute ecstasy, I too was almost overwhelmed. It was such a ridiculously simple thing, but for a minute I felt like Schweitzer, DeBakey, and Jonas Salk. The whole family is that way . . . And, as I said, they're honest, and proud, they always pay promptly, without waiting for a bill."

"Maybe that's because you never send any."

"Well, very seldom. Most people do pay before they leave. But a lot will take advantage, some families are oriented to be deadbeats, will come to you for years and never pay a cent. And if you remind them, they simply go to somebody else. If I collected on all the patients who owe me, I'd be a millionaire." He laughed. "But I'm of the old school; medicine is so *personal,* I could never sue anybody, and I couldn't turn anyone away. But the nice ones, gentle people like this family, more than compensate."

The Man with the Revolving Wig

Richard: "A dear little man," George described him. "Plump, jovial, about your height, four foot ten. One of the nicest guys I ever met, very kind and generous and prosperous—he could afford anything, but he wears a scraggly, ill-fitting wig. When he comes in and I say, 'Get on the table, Richard,' he always leans backward holding on to that wig. He adjusts it and grabs for it so often I call it his revolving wig.

"It looks like a thick brown rug on that little head. He could buy a dozen good-looking wigs any day, but he clings to that wig. And he's worn the same striped purple socks as long as I can remember. You can't miss them. But we have great talks. He's always speculating about life and world events. 'Doctor, what do you think about the end of the world?' he'll ask. And he gets very excited about destiny, and coincidences. He's been thrilled about how you and I found each other."

He told George that even before we were married, a strange thing happened which convinced him we were soul mates. He was a volunteer fireman. Incredibly, cleaning out his things one day, he found a book at the very bottom of his locker. "The very same book you found, Doc—*I've Got to Talk to Somebody, God.* Although I didn't know it then. I have no idea how it got there. I'd never heard of her and didn't even know you'd met her. But I kept thinking as I read it: Darned if that Marjorie Holmes wouldn't be great for the doctor, she's his kindred spirit!"

"Evidently his sister was a fan of yours," George went on,

"and maybe she left the book there, although they both swear she didn't. Anyway, when his sister told him, 'Have you heard Dr. Schmieler is going to marry an author?' Richard got very excited and said, 'I'll bet I know who it is!' He then rushed in to congratulate me. 'I knew it, I knew it, something told me!' Isn't that strange?"

Richard had been postmaster at his neighboring town for a long time, but he also made wise investments and became very well-off. "He had a big heart, helped a lot of people, gave money even to strangers, backed other people in business. And when his niece got married, he staked her to a fancy wedding . . . He and his wife had no children. In fact, they hadn't slept together in years. I never met her, she wasn't my patient, and Richard never complained, but obviously they *weren't* kindred spirits.

"He liked to dance, had an eye for the women, went to all the dances at the fire hall, enjoyed the other gals. But he sure loved dogs, and his wife did too—they were always taking in strays, hundreds of dogs over the years. They'd advertise, try to find the owners, or good homes for them. One time he found a poor starving animal along the railroad tracks, got him back in shape, and gave him away. A couple of years later, the new owner showed him and he won the state championship!" . . .

I finally met Richard. He came to an autographing party, hugged me, and bought twenty books. Then, carefully adjusting his wig, he sat beaming beside me while I signed them for his friends. What a delightful man.

MARY

Every few weeks when George came home with a pocket bulging, or a tiny sack in his hand, I knew he had just seen Mary, a plain little woman who always came bearing a gift, however small.

He described her as dressed very much as her mother had been years before: shabby sweaters, skirts almost to her heels, thick black cotton stockings, old-fashioned black lace-up shoes. "Her parents were people who lived frugally, had nothing, but were cheerful and I guess never expected more. Mary still lives in their poor little house perched on the side of a cliff, like so many there. Her brother lives in an almost identical one next door.

"Everything in Mary's house is spotless, so clean and orderly it hurts somehow, there's so little there—the furniture so sparse and drab and comfortless." She had never married, he said, and had always done housework for somebody else. All the warmth and color and luxury Mary had ever known was vicarious, enjoyed while cleaning homes for wealthy people in the community. "But I don't think she ever envied them, and she's never servile. She actually seems proud of their status and happy to be a trusted help to such nice people . . .

"I've been treating her for years for ulcers on her legs. Sent her to the best specialists, who don't know what to do either— they just won't heal. The only thing that seems to help is vitamin E. But she's always so grateful, she never complains, I've never heard her utter an unhappy word." Isn't that ironic? After the tales of woe I hear from people who have so much more."

She was of medium height and build, he said, about fifty years old. She wore no makeup, her face was almost unlined and had a fresh-scrubbed look. Plain as she was, she had a whimsical air, a kind of sweetness in her eyes and in her smile . . . She came about every six weeks, and always brought him something: peanut-butter cups, which she knew he enjoyed, a cantaloupe, a pink grapefruit, a couple of oranges. I never knew her to come empty-handed, she gets so much pleasure out of giving.

"She is refreshing to talk to, Mary has a good mind as well as a good heart, I really look forward to our visits. She reads and watches TV and has strong opinions about world events. But she seems to have no idea of how she looks, like she was put together by a committee. One thing sure, it's not a pose. Mary wouldn't know what a pose was." George paused to consider: "Maybe this is what makes her able to love people the way she does—honestly, straight-on. Out of nothing, giving what she can, asking nothing in return.

"She is just happy for people, and she is *so* happy about

our marriage—she had seen how I suffered before. I think that's one of the few things Mary ever did worry about." He chuckled. "And now these simple things are also for you. 'This is for Marjorie too,' she always reminds me. 'Be sure to take it home and tell her I love her.' "

JOSHUA

"Some people wouldn't smile if you gave them a million dollars. They always come in with new complaints, and are never quite willing to give up the old ones. They thrive on their misery, it keeps them alive.

"Others keep smiling, no matter how bad they feel." George named several, one of them Rogers, a wonderful old minister who had serious nephritis, was recovering from cancer surgery and suffering from other problems. "Yet ever since I've known him he comes in wearing his soothing smile—mellow, a kind of benign radiance like a simmering fire or a sunset's afterglow." George was smiling himself, in recollection.

"But the champion smiler of all is Joshua. He has this enormous watermelon smile, the kind you want to put a big slice of watermelon in. I've never seen it turned down, in spite of all his adversities. Josh is a born loser. He went into the Army smiling, and I'll bet he even greeted the Germans coming toward him with a smile. 'Those darn Nazis,' he'll grin even describing his wounds. Every time he's supposed to be promoted he's demoted. He lost everything in a hardware store, his children all have been divorced two or three times, one daughter was injured in an accident and can't walk, the whole family has tribulations. Yet nothing disturbs that cheerful grin . . . The county put a road right through his property and never paid him a cent. Even the lawyers couldn't help him. 'Those darn lawyers,' he'll smile. His own son is a mechanic but Josh's car wouldn't pass inspection. The only thing that seems to trouble him is that he can't make love to his wife anymore, but he's cheerful if a little wistful even about that.

"Josh has been running for office for over forty years, and always lost. He's run for mayor, supervisor, councilman, dogcatcher, and never won. Poor guy, can you imagine? Still he keeps on running. He's undaunted. He doesn't seem to mind. That man out-Jobs *Job!*

"I'll bet you if there was a contest for the unluckiest guy around Canonsburg and he entered, he'd *lose* by one vote. And even then he'd keep on smiling."

O SOLE MIO

"A tiny twinkle-eyed lady of ninety-two. Born in Italy. Her father was a wealthy grape grower, living along the ocean. She remembers the smell of the grapes, the festivities, the singing and dancing. Her stories are charming. She came to this country as a bride. Her husband worked in the steel mills, and died long ago. They lost a daughter to diphtheria, and one son killed himself, yet I never saw her dejected. She remains serene, whimsical, and life-loving.

"A few years ago she thought she had breast cancer. I tried to reassure her, but sent her for X rays to ease her mind. The X rays were inconclusive, but to my dismay, the surgeons wanted to operate. I disagreed—at her age it seemed folly, and she was so frightened. I increased her vitamins and gave her Digoxin and she recovered, her breasts are fine. After five years she's still with us—if just barely.

"She was always proud of being able to touch her toes well into her eighties. Now she comes in so feebly, like a delicate doll. Has to be helped onto the scales, it's like climbing Mount Everest. Her life is just ebbing out, it's like a fire flickering . . . Anyway, at ninety-two that dear little lady is still able to sing 'O Sole Mio' with me, we always have a duet when she totters in. Her eyes still twinkle, she even waves her hands and flirts with me as if she wants to dance." George paused, his own smile tender. "I'm almost tempted to ask her, but I'm afraid she'll die in my arms."

"At least she'll die happy," I said.

"She will anyway," he told me. "When her time comes, and it can't be long now—she has very high blood pressure—

she'll die just as happy and sweet, no matter what, as the way she lived."

THE RICH COAL MINER

Each spring, as we walk the dogs across the flowering hills, George quotes a former coal miner of Polish extraction who always exclaimed at this season, "Oh, I am so ensoosiastic! Everything coming back to life. How magnificent, how vonderful to be alife in the spring!"

He worked in the mines until he retired in his sixties, George says. But when he was a young man in his twenties he invested a thousand dollars in Reynolds Aluminum at a dollar a share, became a millionaire, and invested everything he made in the stock market. "He had mild stomach ulcers, nothing very serious, but wanted a complete checkup every two weeks. I had evening hours those days. I'd pick him up about six-thirty; he would sit in the office waiting his turn, visiting with patients, reading (he was an avid reader, though I doubt if he finished high school), figuring the stock market, and later he'd wait for me to take him home. He didn't even own a car."

Other miners envied him. But as he told George, "They spend their money in bars. They say, 'If I had your money, Pete, I'd quit, I'd go to Florida, live it up.' Sure they would, but they'll never get there anyway. They waste their money instead of investing it, they spend it on women and drink."

He was an honorable man, who never cheated on his wife, though they hadn't had relations in twenty years. They lived in a humble little half-house. His married daughter lived in the other half. "She and her mother were very close, his wife was always over there. She was a cold woman, Pete said, always had a headache. Yet in some ways she was a good wife too. Lived in that house that didn't even have a bathroom until the last five years of his life.

"Pete was very fastidious, however. When he got home from the mines he would sit in a big tub of water, and his wife would scrub him clean. Then he would put on fresh clothes, fresh underwear, and a plain brown suit. In the thirty years I knew him it was the only suit I ever saw him wear—except for his trips into Pittsburgh—but it was always well pressed and clean; and his shoes were shined so bright you could almost see yourself in them. He wore his hair slicked back like George Raft.

"Once a month he took the streetcar into Pittsburgh to the stock market headquarters. For this he really dressed up. Striped pants, a coat with a velvet collar, spats, a fine hat. A real dandy. He even carried a cane. You'd think he was president of the bank, a big financier, member of Parliament . . . Yet he never took a vacation. He died in the same little house with a stock market report in his hand. Died of a brain tumor, totally unsuspected, at seventy-four."

George paused, shook his head. "Leaving his wife and children about ten million dollars to fight over. The newspapers have been full of their battles. But every time spring rolls around I think of him and almost hear him declaring, 'Oh, I am so ensoosiastic! How vonderful to be alife in the spring!' "

MISS PRENTISS

One of the most distinguished characters in George's gallery of long-lived patients. A stately lady in her nineties who still swept into the office: "Like a ship in full sail," he said. "Always exquisitely groomed and dressed in the latest fashion. She won't let me take her arm the way I do with older women, she insists on taking mine, to be *ushered* in."

Miss Prentiss owned the most expensive dress shop in Canonsburg. All the best people went there. Her only rival was Hilary, another patient, who opened up later and was a few years younger. "Miss Prentiss has bigger display windows, though, smarter mannequins, and just more class. Her taste is impeccable."

Both had retired but still ran their shops backstage.

Miss Prentiss had come to him after a long parade of other doctors, when he first began. Mainly for a weak heart, though she'd never had a heart attack. She had never married; her fiancé was killed in an accident when she was thirty. People had been trying to match her up with somebody ever since. Which made her mad. *"I wish they'd let me alone!"* she complained, she wasn't interested in men.

She had fallen in love with George on sight, however. He was always well aware of it. Such a gentle, gracious, white-haired lady. "Like a cultured pearl," he described her . . . Her eyes sparkled just to see or speak of him.

It was evident when we called on her one night.

I went with some apprehension. George had warned me she had urged him not to marry me. (As I've said, tact is not his strong point.) She had the idea all writers are temperamental, she had known several doctors who'd married writers, to their regret. "Well, I hope she's worthy of you," she stated.

Yet Miss Prentiss was the soul of hospitality now. She kissed us both, admired my tailored suit (she herself was wearing a soft lavender flowing dress with a frill at its high neck that set off her pink-petal face and white hair like flowers on a florist's doily). She had lighted candles in our honor, and insisted we tour her exquisite Colonial house with its beautiful antiques and hear its history. She served wine and cheese and shortcake, and kept us until almost midnight, looking at old photographs and listening to her stories.

Finally, catching my desperate signals, George announced it was raining, and went to get the car. Miss Prentiss's eyes followed him to the door. Then, faintly smiling, she reached over to clasp my hand. "If you think your husband is handsome now," she said sweetly, "you should have seen him when he was young!" Sighing, she went on to describe him the day they met, even to what he was wearing. "His hair was so black then, and even curlier than it is now. That little mustache, those blue-blue eyes. This can't be the doctor! I thought—he looked more like Errol Flynn. He was so *tall* when he stood up," she exclaimed. "And his broad shoulders. He wore a teal-blue jacket —I'll never forget—an immaculate light blue shirt, and a deep blue tie. And oh yes, his cuff links! Blue star sapphires, I can see them yet." She laughed softly, in reminiscence. "I'm afraid I quite lost my heart."

Her bony fingers tightened, then abruptly released my hand. "But then I wasn't the only one," she declared, almost proudly. "Most of his women patients did. How could they help it? Even the married ones. Some, as he may have told you, were downright brazen about it. Not that it would do them any *good*. But I know for certain that more than a few were just waiting, all set to go after him if anything ever happened to his wife." Miss Prentiss hesitated, then plunged on. "And they're not a bit happy about your getting him so fast . . . My dear, does this bother you?"

I smiled. "I don't blame them. I feel very lucky to have him."

"But then he's lucky too," Miss Prentiss conceded, and suddenly laughed. "Thank goodness he found you when he did. At first I wasn't sure, but I certainly am now. I've never seen him so happy. In fact, I think you may be the best thing that ever happened to him."

A few days later George carried some old photographs of his own to the office to show her, one of them of himself as a curly-headed four-year-old. Miss Prentiss called it the most beautiful child she ever saw, and raved so about it I decided to have a copy made for her. I also clipped a lock of George's hair, now gray but still thick and curly, to slip in the envelope. We delivered it on Valentine's Day. George had already sent her flowers.

Miss Prentiss was enchanted. She laughed and cried and kissed it, and swore she would sleep with it under her pillow. "If you won't be jealous?" she twinkled pertly.

And she did sleep with it, George discovered later.

We called on her now and then (she got a little miffed when we didn't) and occasionally took her for drives on a Sunday afternoon. Meanwhile, she eagerly kept her monthly appointments with George, not only to be examined but to *talk*. All his patients looked forward to these visits; he was not only their physician but friend, counselor, and confidant. Sick or well, they made their appointments a year in advance. For many, especially older people, the time he spent with them was the highlight of their month.

Miss Prentiss usually ran way over her allotted hour, reminiscing, and scolding when George interrupted, "Now listen to me, no *buts,* I'm not *through* yet . . ." Sometimes the sessions included producing her checkbook and asking him to write large checks to various charities. Her eyesight was failing, and she didn't want anybody else to know how much money she gave away. (Over the years it had amounted to several million.)

She lived alone, but a friendly neighbor looked in on her and drove her places. One day there was a rap on the side door just as George was about to leave: "And there she was with a bloody towel over her head. She'd fallen in the kitchen, had a scalp lesion at least six inches long. I told them to get to the hospital, I'd call the emergency room, that's where she belonged. But she snapped, 'I *hate* hospitals, you're the only doctor I trust!' "

George finally relented, reminding her, "Okay, Priscilla, I'm not a surgeon, I'm not even a GP anymore, I'm an internist. I doubt if I even have the sutures to sew you up. I may have to use fishhooks, but if you insist . . ." And kidding her about having to charge for cutting her hair—"Barbers make more money than I do"—he did the job with good results.

Miss Prentiss thanked him profusely. To his dismay, on her next visit she tried to tell him where she hid her jewelry. In case of her death, she wanted him to have it. She had no close relatives, her only heirs were distant cousins who never did anything for her. "They don't even come to *see* me."

She also announced that she was leaving him the bulk of her estate. George was shocked. Oh no, he protested emphatically. While he appreciated her generosity, he could never accept it, she must change her will. It would only cause resentment and possibly serious trouble.

He was both touched and concerned when he told me. "We don't need it, it's the last thing I want. It would even be embarrassing professionally—people might think I had influenced an aging patient. Just imagine—*me* a gold-digging doctor!"

Miss Prentiss lived to be a hundred, still beautiful, if frail. Her heart gave out. George sent her to the hospital, where she revived but contracted pneumonia, and came home to die. One day, holding his hand, she pleaded, "Promise you won't let them keep me too long."

"Of course I won't, Priscilla," he assured her. "When a beautiful flower has faded it deserves to go back to mother earth."

Though he hadn't made house calls in years, George visited her every day to comfort her during the weeks of waiting. She always greeted him, "Here's my handsome doctor!" Then, with the old twinkle in her eyes, she reached mischievously beneath her immaculate, lacy pillow to bring forth his baby picture.

During this time her relatives had moved in. Elderly themselves, two very plain women and a dour thickset man. "Probably in their seventies," George said. "But they all look older than she does." In the adjacent parlor they kept what seemed to him a death watch, murmuring together and sometimes getting up to peek into the bedroom. George sensed a growing restlessness and hostility in them; and one day when he arrived they beckoned him aside to confront him: Were all these visits necessary? "Priscilla is not as wealthy as people think." They were afraid her money might be running out, it was their duty to protect her. They felt, in her own best interest, she should be persuaded to let them call in someone else. In fact, they had done so yesterday, a very nice young man, but she almost threw him out, saying, "No, no, go away, I want my handsome doctor!"

George strode into her room to find Miss Prentiss sitting up in bed, her usually pale face livid. "Why, the audacity of those people! How *dare* they interfere? It's my business, I need you, I want you, I refuse to die without my handsome doctor." . . .

Miss Prentiss was too weak to receive guests on her hundredth birthday, but flowers overflowed the house. And her employees sent her a greeting that reached from room to room, signed by the hundreds of people who would always adore her.

She died a few months later, leaving her dress shop to the people who had managed it so faithfully, and the rest of her fortune to the Salvation Army.

CHAPTER NINE

Doctors Great and Small

George created another fascinating world for me with his stories and character sketches of other doctors, going back to the giants who so profoundly influenced him in medical school:

DUCKY DALY

Professor of histology. His first doctor professor. "He was a short man, a little dwarf of a man who walked like a duck. He wore a white lab coat clear down to his ankles. It was always immaculate, crisply white, not a speck on it. He had a very keen look about him, seemed to shine, he was so crisp and clean, like a laboratory himself. Completely bald, silver-rimmed glasses, squeaky voice . . . reminded me of a penguin, but oh what a man he was!

"Their first day the new class would file by to be introduced. When students were presented to him, guys like me from Pitt would extend their hand and say, 'How do you do, Dr. Daly. Ivy League men, however, from schools like Harvard or Yale, would bow down from the waist, Japanese style, almost to the floor. With Ducky Daly it seemed appropriate—your first professor is like an emperor, the ultimate in bearing. Despite his size he fit the role. You knew here was a man who was a commander . . .

"I can still hear that squeaky voice: 'Think, gentlemen, think, think! *Structure and function.* Every structure has a function. Everything under the microscope. When you see the tissues, the cells, remember that everything has a *function.* Every cell, look at those islands of cells. Look at a blood cell; it is round but has a cavity. Why? What is its *function?* It has to be round but concave to have the most surface to carry the oxygen to the other cells. Look at the structure and ask: What is its function? Always remember that, gentlemen, never forget: *What is the function?'* "

Professor Stone

"An eminent surgeon. He had the face and bearing almost of President Lyndon Johnson. That type of man. Very powerful, strong. Expert surgeon, internationally renowned, not just at the University of Maryland. But his hands began to shake; when he was operating he was trembling. Had Parkinson's. We felt compassion for him, we knew his reputation, we were in suspense . . ."

Professor Pinkham

"Rugged, weighed about two hundred pounds. Tall, ruddy complexion, he had steel-blue eyes, a strong jaw, large hands. His eyes were like a beacon, they would range, as if seeking you out, looking directly at you. He had a precise, slow manner of speaking as if to each one of you. His voice was clean and sharp as a surgeon's knife. He would often tell us of a case where a man has just died. Convinced us we should know *why.* We were asked to examine the man's history and make a diagnosis. Then he would give us his own. We realized why he was outstanding among the giants in Baltimore.

" 'Be thorough,' he urged. 'Do a good job on everyone who comes into your office—the patient is more important than the clock on the wall. Don't think because you've weighed him, taken his blood pressure, and listened to his complaints you know what's wrong. *Go over him head to toe.*' . . .

"He advocated use of the ophthalmoscope to examine the eyes. Absolutely essential, the instrument he valued most. If he was on a desert isle and had only one diagnostic tool, that would be the one. In the eyes you can see evidence of so many things: diabetes, high blood pressure, hardening of the arteries, liver trouble, gallbladder disease. He also stressed the importance of looking in the ears—for wax buildup, inflammation, swelling. No examination is complete without careful observation of every part of the body, down to the last toenail . . .

"He had a plain office, drove old cars, looked like a farmer, you could almost see him in overalls. He was not a well-tailored man, his sleeves and his pant legs were always a little too short, his hair was tousled. But you forgot all that because when you looked at him the light of his knowledge shone through. He was earthy, rustic in appearance, yet every word he spoke was well chosen. No superfluity, direct, like a machine gun of words hitting each target. There was no fat on his speech, it was always bone clean.

"I believe, of all my professors, he had the most powerful influence on me. His advice became my credo."

DR. ULINHOOF

Professor of anatomy. "He was short and stocky, looked like a Russian wrestler. He had the head of a lion. His white hair never looked combed, it seemed to spray out of his scalp like a fountain. Or like a mane. He had a heavy German accent. He was kindly but tough, rather intimidating. He carried a little baton to point out things on the board, but he could also strike out with it.

"I was sitting on the top row of the amphitheater one day, waiting for him to arrive in the area below for his lecture. It was about thirty steps down. 'Hey, George,' one of the other students yelled, 'let's see you go down on your hands!' A lot of them knew I could walk on my hands, had seen me do it at parties. And they began to join in: 'Yay, George, go ahead, I dare you!' . . . *So I did.* Thirty steps down at least, and Ulinhoof due any minute, but I took off, with all them cheering me on: 'Attaboy, George, keep going!'

"But just when I got to the bottom there was a sudden deathly silence. When I looked up I could see two big feet. Ulinhoof had the biggest feet I ever saw, and they were standing right in front of me. Then, in case there was any doubt, I could feel his baton whacking me on the head.

" 'Mr. *Schmieler!*' he bawled out in that guttural voice of his. 'Just vat do you tink you are *doingk?* Do you vant to be a doctor or a clown? If it's a doctor, stay, go back to your seat. Othervise, *leafe,* go join the circus!' "

"What did you do?" I laughed. "What happened then?"

"Well, I slunk back up to my seat. Everybody was howling, of course. And those thirty steps seemed twice as far. Believe me, it was a lot easier walking down on my hands than climbing back up again on my feet!"

DR. PERRY

"He was always '*spitzboop,*' as my parents would say. Prankish, a rascal in college, the one to pull the practical joke on someone. Whenever you talked to him he seemed to have this spark of *spitzboop.* His eyes twinkled, he had a cute little smile, joked with the nurses, doctors, patients. Jovial, never saw him depressed, or worried, no matter how bad things were. He'd smile even if you told him, 'My wife just died of brain tumor.' He was well built, about five foot ten. He walked fast but proud, confident, he seemed to be always moving, even when he stood still. He was a very good surgeon, he operated the way he walked, on top of the situation.

"I almost never saw him serious, but he enjoyed hearing me recite poetry. He especially liked 'Ode on a Grecian Urn' and the one that starts 'The day is dark and cold and dreary' . . . He'd ask for them sometimes when we both were tired and taking a break in the lounge. For some reason those poems moved him. He'd listen with a kind of childish fascination, like a kid whose mother is reading him a favorite bedtime story. Then he'd smile and wipe his eyes . . . and goose me—and I do mean *goose*—before going on in his proud and happy way . . ."

"What happened to him?"

"Well, he had a drinking problem. Periodically he would take off, visit every bar in Canonsburg, and get so drunk they would have to carry him home. He would go to Steuvenville to dry out. Had a nice wife; she or a friend of his would take him there. Every three or four months he'd be back. His patients loved him enough to stick with him. So did his family.

"One time a prominent funeral director drove him there and talked to him on the way. 'Doctor, you shouldn't do this,' he said. 'It will be the death of you. I *know*. I've taken care of so many people just like you; they think they will live forever. They get cirrhosis of the liver or other alcoholic diseases. Or they wind up on a slab from an accident while they're driving.'

" 'You're right,' Dr. Perry told him. 'That's why I wanted you to drive me this time. I hope this is my last trip.'

"Ironically, after delivering the doctor there, and encouraging him not to give up, the *undertaker* was killed on the way home—by a drunken driver. Dr. Perry told me all this himself later. The whole thing sobered him up. He lived well into his seventies, still beloved by everybody. And when I was so broken up about losing Carolyn he tried to comfort me by quoting that poem I used to recite for him. The one that goes: *The day is cold and dark and dreary, It rains and the winds are never weary. But be still, sad heart, cease your repining, For behind the clouds the sun is shining* . . . I wish I knew the author . . . He'd memorized it too and it had helped him during his own depression after the death of that funeral director."

DR. MCCARTHY

He was about ten years older than George, and was in practice when George first came to Canonsburg. A thin, balding, cadav-

erous-looking figure as long as George can remember. "He was
the only doctor for the coal-mining company of Hill Station.
Hired by the company to take care of the workers. He needed
an assistant. I worked for him about a year; he was kind of like
a father to me, I really loved the guy. Even then he was so slow
and enigmatic he wouldn't jump if a bomb went off at his feet,
he'd just say, 'Weelll, let me *see* . . .' as the pieces were falling
. . . He still answers the phone the same way he did then. I'd
call briskly, 'Dr. McCarthy?' Prolonged silence, you'd almost
think he was asleep. '*Dr. McCarthy,* it's George, are you there?'
Finally he'll respond, 'Weeellll, hellloooo, George . . .'

"He prescribed aspirin for everything. Pink aspirin for
some reason. There was a big barrel of it in the back room. A
lot of medicines and other stuff there, but aspirin was about all
he ever used. He'd give it to everybody who came in. He'd send
me back to the barrel to get it for him, and oh what a clutter
. . . In those days he did everything, house calls, babies, surgery, you name it. I would send him my patients who had to
have their tonsils out, and assist in the operating room. He was
slow even there; any other doctor would do five or six tonsillec-
tomies while he was doing one. Eventually he gave up general
practice to specialize in eye, ear, nose, and throat." . . .

He was the kind of slow, homely, colorless guy you'd think
would be a bachelor all his life, didn't seem to *have* emotions,
but he married Bessie, one of the coal miners' daughters. Her
sister, Jessie, was his nurse. A big step up for both of them.
They all lived together, in a rather modest house, and both
adored him. The two were exact opposites, but very close. Jessie had jet-black hair, was plain, slim, and quiet, more like him.
Bessie, however, was a big noisy, fast-moving girl who liked a
good time. "A buxom redhead—the reddest hair I ever saw.
Her hair was like a red maple in the fall, almost aflame." She
was big all over, big smiling face, joyful, friendly, lots of fun.
She had a raucous voice, like a parrot's, you could hear her
across the room, her laugh would shake a house.

They joined the country club and played golf, went to all
the parties and dances there, and those given by the medical
society. It was almost comical to see them dance—Bessie so
fast, she'd be doing crazy steps of her own, jiggling all over, her

husband plodding along like a stick figure, smiling benignly
. . . He had a gaunt turkey neck, his head lurched forward, its
elliptical shape like a football balanced there. He became bald
as a skull, except at the nape of his neck, where a scraggly
fringe of gray hair curled up over his stiff white dress shirt
collar.

George and I saw them at many affairs after we were married. They always saved a place for us at their table. Spying us,
Bessie would stand up and bellow, "Here, over here!" Once,
during the band's intermission, she gave me a guided tour of
their club, proudly showing off its plush rooms and luxurious
facilities, urging us to join. She was wearing a low-cut flowered
dress that showed her freckled arms and back and enhanced her
bulging breasts. She sparkled with diamonds, and she had a big
girlish bow in her hair, which was now pinkish, like a fading
sunset. She was funny and loving and eager to make me welcome . . .

They had no children, no other relatives; but the three of
them had each other—and his practice. "Ed will never retire,"
she told me. "It's his life."

He was then well into his eighties and still slowly, slowly,
seeing patients. "You can't say he's slowing down," George
said, "he was *born* slowed down. But I'm afraid he's failing,
I've noticed the signs . . ."

Shortly after that, Bessie called us, sobbing. Her darling
had had a stroke, Dr. McCarthy was in a coma—in which he
remained for over a year. She and her sister Jessie took turns
keeping vigil beside his bed. George visited him in the hospital
almost every day, held his hand, spoke softly to him, thanking
him, always telling him, "I love you, Ed," before he left. "There
is a bond between us," he said. "I'm convinced he hears, sometimes I'm sure there is a feeble pressure in response, but I'd
know anyway."

George paused when he told me; sad though he was, he
couldn't help smiling. "Poor guy, he's slow even about dying. I
can almost hear God up there calling down, 'Dr. McCarthy
. . . Dr. *McCarthy,* are you *there?*' And after a while McCarthy drawling, 'Weelll, hell*ooo,* God.' And God saying, 'Hurry
up, we're waiting for you. Come *on!*' "

Dr. McCarthy finally died.

A few months later Bessie's sister, Jessie, followed him.

Bessie herself had shrunk to a shadow during the long wait. It would have been impossible to recognize her for the jovial buxom woman she had been. And one day, when she had finished closing her husband's office and disposing of his papers, she joined them.

"People often die the way they lived," George observed. "Dr. McCarthy took his time, as usual. But Bessie talked fast, walked fast, danced fast—and when it came her turn she couldn't wait. Wham! Away she went."

CHAPTER TEN

Physician's Philosophy

For me every conversation with George is absorbing, but especially when he expresses himself on the wonders of the human body. I feel privileged and sometimes awed to be his wife, sole audience for these discussions of a philosophy that has surely made him not only a fine physician but an inspiring, life-enriching human being.

Examining the Body

George says, "Examination. That's been my obsession since the beginning of my practice. To examine every patient thoroughly, from head to toe, no matter how old he is or the reason for his visit. That goes for everybody, from babies to people a hundred years old. Everyone, male or female, rich or poor, from the first patient that walked in to the last one I attended.

"And not just once a month or once a year. I mean on every visit, to make sure of detecting any early symptoms or signs that could be causing the trouble, or leading to something

worse. I could alert people, take what action might be necessary." He told of a man who came for his usual high blood
pressure check. "He had no pains, no symptoms, but I discovered an aneurysm that could have erupted any minute. If I
hadn't gotten him to the hospital it could have killed him . . .

"I start with the head, and feel it for any lump or depression; I think of the mechanism inside the brain and what could
be happening. A tumor, an aneurysm. I feel the jaws, the throat,
the thyroid. I examine the ears, the eyes, the nose, and the
breasts, even of old women. Some of the foreign women were
surprised, some of them reluctant; if they objected, I told them,
'Then go to somebody else, I have to examine your breasts
before you leave' . . . I examine the chest, the abdomen, the
legs and feet . . ."

For him the eyes and ears will always be the most fascinating. At times he waxes rhapsodic about them:

"When I look in the ear I marvel. Each ear is shaped the
same, outwardly simple, but inside so complex. I see the ear-
drum, thin as tissue paper. To think that this delicate thing
vibrates to all the sounds that enter. And behind it are three tiny
bones, the smallest in the body, to catch its vibrations and carry
them into the cochlea, a larger bone that looks like a snail, and
then on to the brain, which translates them into sound. The
whole design and process is so fabulous. How can this be? I
don't understand it, I almost don't believe it. How is it really
possible to hear? There has to be a Master designer working
miracles somewhere.

"And it's such a miracle that this ear is fashioned inside the
mother's womb, in absolute darkness, absolute silence. Impossible, it can't happen, but it does. God is in control, there is no
other explanation. When I see that, how can I be afraid of
death? God can do anything."

Another occasion—we happened to be in Florida—I discovered my watch had stopped; it wasn't ticking when I held it
to my ear. And as I rewound it, we talked about the wonders of
timepieces—and again about ears. That God should have given
us such a remarkable instrument to hear sounds, whether as
tiny as the ticking of my little watch, or the thunder of airplanes
flying overhead, or the fishing boat at the dock, its engines

throbbing . . . or beautiful music coming from a radio on the beach, or the harsh cries of gulls . . . or the voices of people singing, laughing, crying, anywhere.

George took up his theme: "None of us could create an ear. The whole remarkable system of hearing . . . Man can do a lot. He can make that watch, a lot of men probably, assembling the parts, the skill and craft of putting it together, doing whatever is necessary to make it work. But even a watch has to have a mind behind it. It could never create itself. Lay all the separate parts on the floor right now—the works, the crystal, the jewels, the hands—and never in a million trillion years could it assemble itself and start to work. And one sure thing, it could never reproduce itself and make another watch.

"Yet people say there is no God! That it's all an accident, the combination of the right elements and plenty of time, and the earth and everything on it came together to create itself. How ridiculous. If something as simple as a watch couldn't invent itself, put itself together and create another watch, how in heaven's name could it simply 'happen' that living creatures like us can have a single organ as complex as an ear?"

Reading the Meter

George has an insatiable curiosity and admiration for the seemingly ordinary devices on which we all depend. One day he took me out to look at the revolving electric meters which record the amount of electricity being used.

"Most people don't think about this, just dismiss it, the amount of energy it takes to run a home: electric lights, refrigerator, furnace, etc. But out here is this rapid little circle revolving. You can count the number of revolutions because there is a marker that goes back to the original start—here it is, whirling away like a merry-go-round; the more energy that's being used, the faster it goes. If you had nothing going it wouldn't revolve. Even a few light bulbs left on make it revolve more rapidly."

This was not an object lesson for me. He's very generous about such things.

Returning inside, he launched again into another of his favorite analogies: "In the human body we have tremendous amounts of similar surges, electric energy which motivates the heart, the brain, the liver, and all the 600-plus muscles, 169,000 miles of arteries, the billions of cells. It speeds through the nerves, spiderwebs of nerves, so many it's impossible to count. Superconnections, baffling and bewildering just to think of all the things that are going on because of it. Toes wiggle, eyes blink, bowels move, food is being digested and delivered through the bloodstream into all the cells. All these, performing chemical and mechanical functions depending on energy.

"Yet nothing records all this energy that's being used. The body doesn't have a meter, like a house with all its mechanical gadgets going at the same time, and the body is far more complicated than any electrical system ever devised. But there is no recorder or meter for you to read. Nothing to inform you of the energy you are expending.

"Even when you are resting it never stops. Your heart keeps beating, your lungs keep breathing, your glands go on secreting. You can't turn any of them off like you would a radio or a toaster or a light. If you *live* you are expending energy.

"No, there is no meter in the body. Only that vital Master Control in the brain which directs this master plan—the energy that generates the power to eat and sleep and move and even think!"

The Miracle of Life

For George, there is no miracle comparable to procreation:

"Man comes from the blood," he marveled, in just one of many discussions. "The umbilical cord takes blood from the woman and turns it into a living creature, a tiny person. From this blood comes everything in the body: the eyeballs, the heart, the fingers and toes, the nails. The blood nourishes the cells, the building blocks, the materials in the bloodstream, all in complete darkness and silence, forming this tiny human being that will emerge.

"And it's all *there*. Nobody has to send out for anything. Nobody has to order, 'Hey, get me a coil of nerves, about 100,000 miles, and a couple of arms and legs. Also I need some more arteries and intestines. No, don't bother about a plumber or electrician, I'm a master engineer, I can put them in . . .' No, no, it's all there," George repeated fervently. "Accomplished in absolute stygian darkness and silence!

"And along with this cargo of building materials, the blood carries the genes that will make that individual different from everybody else. His brain, his personality, his eventual achievements and failures. All this is *there,* everything packaged magically in the spermatozoa—one of those millions of tiny spermatozoa that start the whole process.

"You should see them sometime under the microscope, the head propelled by that tiny tail. They're so mobile, they swim so fast, they swarm like mosquitoes in their frenzy to be first to the egg. Each sperm competing—the first one there gets the prize. But sometimes it's a tie, sometimes two enter the same egg; if so, there will be identical twins. Or two might enter two eggs, and the twins won't be identical. Generally, though, only one is lucky—the one that gets there first and explodes into life."

George paused, eyes twinkling, on a flight of fancy. "I wonder. What if that spermatozoa could look up and see the potential man he'd become? And the man-to-be would say, 'Hi, Spermy, I'll give you a billion dollars cash to make me rich and famous. And while you're at it, make me healthy, so I'll have plenty of sperm of my own someday.'

"What would that little sperm think?" George grinned. "Maybe he'd think: 'What will I do with all that money? . . . *I know, I'll put it in the sperm bank!*' "

Nature's Blueprint

George said again, another time:

"Your chances of being President are greater than your chances of being born at all. The hundreds of thousands of spermatozoa which are vying to fertilize the one egg. Each one of them dashing frantically for their target, and only one can get there first. And in each one of these tiny, minuscule objects is the entire blueprint of a human being.

"They are so small you can't even see them, unimaginably small, but *you* are there. And you are there, of course, in another blueprint in your mother's womb. It is when these two merge that the miracle takes place. All the countless thousands of things that make you *you*: the color of your hair, your eyes, the size you will reach, your personality traits—your eccentricities, peculiarities, even your emotions—these are mixed together all ready to *become*. And what that combination turns out to be—is *you*.

"And your soul is there too, your very soul. We don't know exactly where or how or why, but it is, just as surely as the shade of your skin or the talents you have . . . In these blueprints are the geniuses, the artists, the musicians, the great mathematicians, and everybody else with the potential for greatness, as well as the mechanic, the nurse, the doctor, or whatever your gifts or leanings may be.

"And to think that these lives are being aborted every day! The loss, the appalling waste . . ."

I said, "But nature is wasteful too. Think of the millions of sperm you say are competing for life. Beauty and genius and talent and soul are in the rest of those sperm too, the ones that *don't* reach their target, and so they die."

"Oh yes, nature is profligate. Look at all these trees, every one of them is spilling seeds all over this place. And each little seed or pod or life form is trying to take root and grow. But only a few can survive. Yet those few, so to speak, also crowd each other for space and light. In nature there is always too *much* of everything. Too many trees and leaves and grasses and flowers and weeds. Usually far more than any of us can possibly appreciate individually, or consume. More than we can eat or use or even have time to admire.

"Yet even so, we shouldn't waste nature's gifts," he said fervently. "We should rejoice in all this abundance and protect it, take tender care of it. We should never use more than our share of it. It's a crime what we're doing to our resources. And all because of greed. Cutting down the forests, even the precious rain forest. Draining the swamps where wildlife feeds . . . Did you know they're planning condominiums in the Everglades? And the animals, what we're doing to the animals! Whole species are dying out." George reached into his vast pile of articles and clippings, read aloud a touching story about African elephants being butchered for their tusks, and wiped his eyes. He gets emotional about such things.

"God loves those elephants—and the birds in those swamps—yes, and the alligators and the mosquitoes. He loves even the heart of a rose or a weed. And he gave us the power to love all his living things too. But most of all, to love each other." Suddenly, laughing at himself, George leaned over and kissed me.

"Oh, how glad I am that your father's sperm reached your mother's womb."

Marauders of the Body

George says, "Human terrorists have a lot in common with cancer. One or two can get started and overpower an airplane, a ship, a communications system, a power plant, rendering the rest of the people helpless. A whole country! Sure, in the process the terrorists themselves may get killed, but on the way they have killed hordes of innocent people.

"Cancer cells are marauders of the body. Abnormal cells are like abnormal people, they don't respond to signals from the brain, or society. Independent, they just come on. They are the Hitlers, the Genghis Khans, or the nameless wild fanatics, killing everything in their path, even if it means their own destruction.

"There are fifty trillion cells in the body. But one cancer cell invader, if not caught in time, can destroy the whole body. That one terrorist cell begins to divide and multiply and becomes an army. All those other trillions of cells are helpless before it, once it gets started. They marshal their forces, the immunity system tries to drive it out, but unless the invader is caught early and stopped, it will overpower the whole system and kill it.

"In the process it's killing itself too, of course. But it just shows how dangerous one minuscule cell gone wild can be. And how even a few human terrorists, if not stopped in time, can pose a threat to the world."

The Magnificent Head

George is enthralled with the mystery and marvel of our heads. Any human head—he could talk about it for hours:

"Whenever I examine a patient I always hold his head in my hands with a sense of awe, almost reverence. Feeling the bone structure, feeling the ears, and behind them for clues, looking into the eyes. It gives me a sense of who this person is who's allowing me to examine him, and trusting me to do what's best for him. I realize I'm holding something precious.

"The head—what a wonderful thing stuck on top of your skeleton! Just balanced there by a neck, and adorned with a face. But more than adorned, the face is your portrait. It identifies you, not only by your features but by your expression. It reveals your emotions. With it you laugh and cry. You see other people with it, you talk with it, communicate with them, become a part of the human family. And oh yes, you kiss with it, and if you didn't kiss in the first place, the human family probably wouldn't *be* here!

"All this, toward the front of a skull with hair on it, curly or straight, blond or brunet, or sometimes bald. And the strange thing, despite the basic pattern, no two people look exactly alike. Except identical twins, of course, and there are differences even then . . . And I forgot to mention we breathe with it, without which we would, of course, die. And without a nose we couldn't smell our food and might die anyway, because we wouldn't want to eat, or maybe we'd fail to smell some poisons. Although almost as bad as that, for me at least, would be not being able to smell the flowers.

"And then, of course, the most remarkable thing of all—

inside that tough hard skull is the brain, which makes every function of the body possible. Eating, sleeping, scratching your chin as I'm doing now, or brushing your teeth, or making love, or performing a heart bypass. You couldn't move a muscle without it. And even more remarkable—just to realize that that brain records and stores everything that comes into the mind! No, no, it's too incredible, I don't believe it . . ."

All this led to the unlikely subject of beheading. Once a fairly common form of execution, especially for hated kings and queens, it seems. Evidently rebels like those in the French Revolution took special revenge in seeing crowned heads roll, I said.

George shuddered. "Horrible. Punishment by death is always horrible, but beheading is an outrage beyond imagining. Because once that head rolls, the body, for all its wonders, is nothing. It's the only thing a body can't live without. That's what they wanted, of course. But what an *insult* to the Creator —to sever that magnificent thing, a human head, from its body! Any head . . .

"No other creature has one like it," George went on. "Sure, all animals have heads, even eyes and noses and mouths. And when they feel pleasure or pain we know it. But animals of the same species all look alike. They lack the features and facial muscles that give us character and expression. Man is the only being with a face that can laugh or cry or smile or frown or speak.

"A human head is a treasure," George declared. "It's God's greatest sculpture mounted on his perfect pedestal, the body. I don't care who we are, whether we're rich or poor, good or bad, someone like Mother Teresa or the worst scoundrel alive—every one of us walks around bearing that most magnificent thing in all creation—our own head!"

The Incredible Brain

Not long after our discussion about the head, George sat me down and gave me an enthusiastic tour of the brain. Drawing a diagram to illustrate, pointing out the various centers where its remarkable activities occur.

"The brain is the boss of the body, the absolute commander, *nothing* can happen without it. Looks like a big cantaloupe, all curlicued with rubber tubes. Hundreds of tubes crowding into that space. Weighs on the average about three pounds. But oh, the astonishing things it can do!" he exclaimed. "It lets you move, think, feel, *be,* exist.

"Because it's so perfectly organized. The brain is like the most efficient house you could build, with all the furniture and utensils you need in the right place, its own area in which to function. And all connected with nerve fibers that keep exchanging signals, crisscrossing so the right side knows what the left side is doing—and vice versa. Every sensation the other side is feeling—cold, heat, pain if you cut a finger, fatigue—even itching. Amazing how it crosses over.

"In the front of this house or brain, speech is registered and coordinated." George clutched his throat. "Near the tongue, the throat, the larynx. It's all so incredibly logical and yet mysterious . . . And in the two sides, nearest the ears, everything we *hear* comes in. Talking, laughter, bands on the Fourth of July, babies crying, every possible sound. We literally hear with both sides of the brain." George demonstrated. "And not far below, at the base of the brain, is the center that controls breathing, the heart beating, hunger and thirst, things that concern our absolute survival.

"At the back of the brain is the biggest miracle and mystery of all. The invisible mind, somehow stored in the physical brain. Everything we think and feel, memories, dreams, plans, imagination, are all stored in this control center in the back of the brain. Our thoughts—whatever they are, or wherever they come from, nobody really knows, yet there they are, carefully stored away in this special mysterious room of the brain. Also information, what we are reading, learning. It's too much to comprehend. How can it be? But we know—*because* of that brain that it *is* . . .

"And as if all this isn't strange enough, near that same area at the back of the brain is the optic nerve that allows us to see. Maybe that's another reason people say we have eyes in the back of the head. But just imagine—sight itself is such a miracle I'll never really believe it! Everything we see brought to us through our eyes because of the unseen, almost magical controls in the back of our brains."

George shook his head. "Oh, the complex mental activities going on in the brain. Mental problems are such a terrible thing. Like losing your most valuable equipment. What if you went into your study to write and found everything you needed gone? Not just your desk and typewriter or computer—they could be replaced—but your very mind to think with! The computer God put in your brain!

"Doctors can spot the symptoms. Blood clots, for instance, or a tumor and its location. I have the utmost respect for neurosurgeons. Anyone who has the courage to open a patient's skull and operate on that delicate, most vital, critically important organ in his body, his brain. As every one of them would tell you, you could spend a *lifetime* just studying the brain and still find there was more to know than any of us will ever learn."

Cradle of the Deep

The lake, often such a ruffian, can also be quiet, soft-spoken, silken to the touch, its waves a graceful undulation, as in a dance. Soothing to the senses, despite the wind's brisk chill. As I swim with the waves, I wonder at the peace that seems to come from this gentle but powerful motion. It is like being in the arms of a strong but gentle mother. "Rocked in the cradle of the deep."

When I told George about this, he understood. "People instinctively need motion, or are rested by motion," he explained. "Before you were born you were rocked in the waters of your mother's womb. You are one with nature, which is always in motion—trees in the wind or simply currents of air, and those waves and currents we see and sense all around us now. The blades of grass, and all the little things stirring not only in the grass but below the ground.

"And the body itself is never still. Every nerve and cell is constantly in motion; the blood keeps flowing, the heart keeps beating. We ourselves must lie down and try to put the conscious body to rest—to sleep; but nothing in the body ever stops, it just slows down a little bit. During the day the motor keeps running hard, often at top speed, and at night it has to keep on running, but not so fast. It needs to rest. It needs to be calmed and comforted sometimes, even by day. To feel safe, to feel someone or something gently soothing and rocking you to sleep."

CHAPTER ELEVEN

Scenes of Snow and Spring

Snow Mystery

George is at heart a poet; his imagination and love of imagery thrill and stir my own. It's fun to see the world together, as if through a second set of eyes. Like me, he enjoys the change of seasons. Especially the beginning of winter and spring. To my surprise, he loves the snow—which Carolyn called "white hell," he said. "It's why we spent those winter months in Florida every year. But I enjoyed them too," he assured me. "And driving back north just as spring was coming on was wonderful. We got to celebrate spring in every state—at least three times before we even got home to ours."

Now, in McMurray winter is teasing us with its first sample of snow. A beautiful snow began falling early this week, soft, twinkling, the flakes forming a misty transparent veil. Before long, that first day, the ground was white, still soft underfoot as we walked the dogs at dusk. They bounded ahead ecstatically, little explosions of white at their tails. Ben far ahead, but Tanjy bouncing behind, a soft woolly white bundle himself, blending with the snow, his little belly half buried.

The world was all virginal white, our tracks making a
pleasant pattern, and we took the old childish joy in being first
to mark it with our trail. The tender little new snow kept falling
as we walked down the long hill, circled the big schoolhouse,
and began the steep climb back.

Meanwhile, the lights looked down on us as they always
do from houses on nearby hills. At this hour they are so bright,
many of them clustered together like yellow eyes peering at us
from some dark otherworld; odd little people from outer space.
Other lights are a bright scattering, and the twin golden headlights of cars race up and down a few distant streets, drawn like
slender black lines on a white map, leading people home.

The sky was fantastic, that first night. The horizon was
banded with that deep flaming orange my mother called "the
afterglow." ("The afterglow means hope," she always said.)
Directly above us, a gray-purple mountain of a cloud, literally
bursting with more snow. It kissed our faces lightly as it fell and
made little ticking sounds. But all around the cloud were vast
sky acres of gold and rose; while riding merrily on its side was a
tiny silver boat of a moon. Other clouds coasted over it, obscur-
ing it for a minute, then out it would sail. As George said (to
change figures), "Like a silver smile!"

The yellow lights of our own big house shone out upon us,
through the trees, warm and golden too. Standing guard as we
departed, welcoming our return. We stamped our feet and
brushed off our boots. The house was warm and fragrant with
the meat loaf in the oven when we came in.

The Blue Hour

Snow brings a blue hour, morning and night. The day breaks
with a dark blue sky that is only a little lighter, reflected on the
snow. The snow glitters as if ground jewels have been scattered
on a rich blue robe. The lights from our windows reach out,
enhancing this quiet blue morning brilliance; and the streetlight,
looking down from its pole beside the mailbox, gives it a special
fire.

Then as evening approaches, the blue hour begins again.

It's our favorite time for walking. Sometimes, if George gets home early, the sky is still the vivid color of a bluebird's wing. When we set off later the sky has a winey-blue look, and so does the snow. Blue shadows fall from the trees.

If he is very late, sometimes after dark, the blue is deeper, richer, as if to protect you from the cold. For now it is usually much colder, especially when the wind is blowing. Bitterly cold even when the wind is still. Yet always exciting, invigorating.

When it's too cold, we stop at the top of the hill and George calls the dogs back from their rollicking romp. Often calling me too, for I have usually forged ahead with them, just enjoying the blue hour with its brilliant cold, and almost bouncing on the thick white mattress beneath our feet.

Morning Jewels

George always gets up early, feeds the dogs, and goes out to get the two morning papers from their boxes along the street. I sleep until six-thirty or seven, but have been rising in time to see at least remnants of the sunrise, so beautiful, rosy behind the trees and casting a pink aura upon the snow. It sometimes looks like raspberry sherbet.

One morning it was still very dark at six o'clock. "The sky was still blazing with stars," George described it. "I've never seen so many. The whole sky was like a jeweled roof. And underfoot, all across the snowy yard, were a million stars too. The streetlight and the lights shining from a window turned that entire expanse into a diamond pavement.

"I found myself walking between all this brilliance—the diamonds overhead and the diamonds beneath my feet. It seemed unreal, it was like being transported along a path that must surely lead to a palace—or Paradise . . . And I *was,*" he declared. "Right here with you!"

Snowdrops

Each day for more than a week George has brought me snowdrops from the yard. "A snowdrop, would you believe it?" he
exclaimed, handing me the first tiny white bud.

"I've never seen them so early, but they're out there, scattered all over the yard. Like their names, like snowflakes, or
little pearl drops of snow in the grass."

We gazed at it in delight. Our first taste of spring. So small
and frail and silky, a closed bud with its secrets locked into
itself, behind that tiny point. Then it began to open a little, its
petals parted, like eyelids waking. We put it in a bud vase,
where it lifted its little head as if to look around, and opened
more. Within an hour it had revealed itself to us completely:
three shiny petals framing its shy white face.

"It looks like a French nun," George remarked. "One of
those that wear the funny white pointy-petaled hats."

And it did. Except that the snowdrop's linen headdress is
so floppy and fine, as if woven of threads too delicate to touch.
And the face inside is formed of white petals folding into each
other, trimmed with a circle of tiny green valentine hearts.
While deep, deep inside are gathered a cone of golden shapes,
like fingers drawn tightly together. And from the tip protrudes a
frail but firm white threadlike tongue. The pistil or stamen? we
wonder, from long-ago botany lessons. No matter, it reveals
itself to us, this miracle of morning.

Each day since, George has brought the snowdrops in, delicate bunches of them to grace the breakfast table. For the
weather has been springlike, buds straining, the ground spongy
underfoot. Yet a few days ago the whirling snow began. Things
stiffened, growing things went tight, holding back against the
swiftly dropping cold. And the snowdrops too were startled;
like frightened children who would have run away and hidden,
had there been anyplace to go.

Even so, this morning George brought one to me. The
same green stem and tender white ellipse he had first found. But

this one was so cold, half frozen, shrunk back into itself, stiff with its alarm.

"Taste its cold," he said. "Kiss it, bring it back to life." So I touched it lightly with my tongue. And in a few seconds, as it lay in my hand, the miracle began. I could sense rather than feel its awaking. It became fuller, softer, its tiny eyelids parted, its petals began to stretch. Until now, barely an hour later, it has lifted its head, wearing the pure white headdress of a nun about to shepherd children into the convent while the bells are ringing.

Falling Snow

After weeks of springlike weather, we awoke to another lovely snowfall this morning. George called my attention to it when I came downstairs, and we stood together at the window, marveling at its delicate descent.

"The flakes look like little white parachutes," George said. "See how some of them are circling, trying to find a place to land."

"Or maybe they're tiny angels trying their wings."

"Okay, baby angels. A few minutes ago they were all together, in a cloud. Snowflakes are really drops of water too cold to stay where they are," George explained. "Just one big happy family in a cloud. They take on this new form, these soft white garments, and become, as you say, like little angels that must take wing. It's as if a mother were telling them, 'It's too cold for you here, go down and cover the ground. Protect the earth. Tell the grasses and bulbs it's not yet time to come out. Tell them to sleep a while longer until the sun wakes them up.' "

We continued to watch as I was getting breakfast. Many of the flakes were circling, even rising a little with the wind, almost as if they'd changed their minds and wanted to return. They seemed to be searching, exploring, looking us over before they decided where to settle down. Then little bunches would gather, descend in a group, while a few stragglers followed. They continued to cluster, cuddling each other as they wove their white coverlet for the life that is stirring below. There they will harden, supporting each other in this task until it's time to vanish.

"When the sun warms them they will soften again," George continued. "They'll begin to change form once more, and return to being drops of water. Some will merge with the earth and grasses to soak the soil, then be absorbed by the streams, and flow into the sea. Others will be taken up by the sun and actually return to the sky to form another cloud!"

George poured himself another cup of coffee. *"Nothing is lost,"* he emphasized, branching off on a favorite theme. "Not *one* of them is wasted. Everything God creates has its special purpose to serve. Everything is planned and everything is used, no matter how beautiful or ephemeral it may seem, from a snowflake to a flower."

Visitor from Outer Space

The snow, which had melted to patches, came again last Friday —a wheeling blizzard. All day and all night it fell, muffling the world, furring the trees. George has been on vacation, and what a lovely time it is to have him home.

Saturday the snow was too deep, the driveway too slippery for me to drive to the hairdresser's, he insisted, so he took me in the Jeep and picked me up in late afternoon. The blue hour was just beginning—softly, softly claiming the sky; and the delicate twinkling veils of snow were still testing the air, tiptoeing down from the fat gray-blue clouds overhead. Like a ballet half seen through the transparent scrim that is used to create dreamy effects onstage.

When we set out on our walk, the snow was over our feet. We waded in this soft white fur, rippled by the wind into swirls and mounds and graceful blue-white patterns. And as the dogs plunged and plowed ahead of us, they created the first tracks. Ben leaps like a rabbit, there are spaces between his prints. Tanjy scampers with some effort behind him, trying to follow his trail. Sniff-sniffing his way through the soft white mass. His short little body draws a ribbon between Benjy's sets of paw prints, linking them like flowers on a string.

We notice, among the sweeping undulations of the snow, many little mounds, each with a tiny air hole. Like a baby's open mouth. "Moles," George says. "They must be air holes for the moles." And we envision the vast network of homes that lie beneath the earth; for the molehills are everywhere we walk, regardless of the weather. Darkish furrows that stripe and criss-cross the hills and are even encroaching on the school grounds nearby. But now they are buried in the thick blanketing snow. And the little creatures, the gnomelike fairy-tale beings that oc-cupy these streets and villages, have surely nosed their way up to the surface, then up, up, up even further to provide these passages and breathing holes through the snow.

I remark on the complete, untracked virgin whiteness of these acres that surround us. As if we are utterly alone on a white planet. But then, as we come up over the crest of the hill and look down, I exclaim, "Somebody has been here before us!" For there, below, is an enormous dark circle in the snow. Marked, it seems, with strange hieroglyphics. I gaze at it, mysti-fied. "Where in the world could *that* have come from? I don't see any tracks, at least of feet. But oh yes—look! See those parallel lines coming from the direction of the school."

"Funny," George pondered. "There wasn't any school yes-terday, all the schools were closed."

There were no footprints, and the ring itself was much too big for Fox and Geese, the game we played as children.

"I just can't believe this," I exclaimed. "It looks like a spaceship might have landed, like something made by people from outer space!" I ran on ahead to investigate, while George waded behind.

When we reached it, this vast magical circle, I cried out again. For it curved off in places to form a heart. A huge heart-shaped circle formed by car tracks—I could see them plainly now, the print of their treads on the snow.

"You did it, *you* did it!" I accused. "But *how?"*

Turning, I saw that the wheel tracks led back behind the schoolhouse and up its steep driveway. He must have driven the Jeep down here before picking me up, and drawn this merry, mysterious, enormous valentine by driving round and round. The hieroglyphics? His feet tramping out

I LOVE MARJORIE

in huge letters in the snow . . .

Strange wonderful George.

Laughing, and throwing snowballs at each other, we waded home through the loveliest blue hour of all.

Beauty Hurls Itself

At first spring comes so softly, so gently after the long gray winter—the tender haze, the prickling promise of buds. Then suddenly it explodes in a burst of color. As George exclaimed this morning, "Beauty just hurls itself into the world!" Suddenly we have this glorious landscape all around us: daffodils in the yard, a treasury of golden dandelions scattered across the hills. Trees proudly wearing their lacy new green gloves. Redbuds and dogwoods bursting pink and white among them, like brides' bouquets.

Variations of this picture, hundreds of variations, blooming and gliding and swirling all about us, wherever we walk or drive.

"It's so *alive*," George went on. "It makes me think of those fountains at the Conservatory, hurling themselves up for your admiration. Leaping and falling. This time of year beauty is alive, it's bright, it dances, it's so fresh and new and exciting after winter it wants you to applaud!"

It's also ephemeral, we realize. It won't last long. Gradually this cast of colors begins to fade and disappear. In such a little while the dogwoods will be curled and rusty, their petals scattered like snowflakes on the ground. The dandelions shrivel too, their gold turned to fluffy white globes—like white-haired ladies who've had their hair puffed for a convention.

But there will be replacements. An even bigger variety of summer colors. The roses and buttercups and clover, lilacs and daisies and iris, garden flowers and wildflowers—the lilies of the field. All to have their little hour, then vanish, bow out in favor of the gentian and the goldenrod and the gorgeous autumn leaves.

"We can't really keep any of them," I said. "We're just their audience for a while."

"That's right. You have to enjoy everything as it comes," George replied. "Beauty in its turn. We can't claim natural beauty in any form except with our emotions and our eyes. Well, yes, our noses too—fragrance plays a part. But whether we enjoy them at a distance, or have them near, bring them into the house for a little while, we know they have blessed us. Even when you throw flowers out, wilted, faded, finished, there is that knowledge. And the most marvelous thing of all is that the whole cycle will be repeated over and over, year after year!"

Whirligigs on the Doorstep

Whirligigs we called them as children. Those little single-winged seeds that come swirling down, hoping to find a spot of earth on which to grow. Meanwhile, covering walks and cars and porches with their golden clutter.

This morning our balcony was paved with them, glistening with last night's rain. The long wooden floor was grimy from winter's neglect; it needed scrubbing anyway, and the storm had given us a hand with the water. George volunteered, but I suggested we each take a broom and clean it as we swept the maple pods to the railing, then scooped or stuffed them through.

The sun had come out and was beaming as we began. The blackened floor began to yield its dirt, the water ran dark, the deep red paint began to show. But as we worked, more of the merry intruders continued to come twisting down and landing, as if trying to see what we were up to. Like children who always come running, getting in the way. Children eager to help!

As indeed they *were* helping, we both realized. These seed-pods gathering under our brooms were the best scouring pads we could have. Each seed, cleverly encased, was toughly pronged, sharp enough to pierce the soil. Each graceful wing was likewise tough and strong. They were a well-armed heavenly host descending!

Pausing to rest, we picked up a few and held them up to admire. What beautiful things. What artistry God uses to fashion even a simple seedpod. Each wing of palest gold sweeps upward, formed by tiny featherlike fronds branching from the central stem. Our fingers are holding a little airship, propelled by a single plume. Its nose is tough and sharp, the compartment for its passenger delicately but strongly protected. Peel open this sturdy cabin and draw out its precious cargo—an elliptical seed of vivid green, living, soft as flesh to the fingers.

All this exquisite artistry and engineering, we marveled, flung into the air in such abundance to land on field or forest—or our balcony. Seeds ready to root and grow—so many that even the few that survive will richly replenish the earth for us.

What treasures to land on our own doorstep!

Daffodils

The beds of daffodils have been greening for weeks, reluctant to bloom, but we see their tentative buds and one day their bright golden stars. The trees have been tentative too, their limbs a lacy fretwork against the sky. But now there is also a froth, a spume, a foam of green about their branches. A transparent scarf of promised leaves tossed about their shoulders, too tiny to be seen. Their fingers shine through it, they hold it high. While already beside the stream the violets swarm, whole villages of little faces bonneted in blue.

Then, this evening, walking the dogs, we discover that the daffodils have bloomed. A lovely golden spill of them down the hill like a river of light. How remarkable the vision, for yesterday this same spot was green. Yet somehow, while we slept, the buds began to unfold, the satin petals opened into these yellow stars with their deeper golden throats.

Coming closer, we scent their delicate fragrance. All exactly the same height, like children lined up for a performance at school. And George said, "Isn't it amazing that God is in such control, even of how things grow? Why don't these flowers keep right on growing—say, like lilacs? Or lilacs—why don't they keep on growing as tall as trees?

"And trees themselves. Each species of tree has a cutoff point; it gets just so tall and no taller. They don't go on climbing into the sky." He looked down fondly at me. "It's the same with people. We all vary in height, but for each of us there is a point where we *reach* our destined height. We simply stop."

"I stopped short," I said.

"I like where you stopped. You barely come up to my shoulder and that's just fine with me!"

CHAPTER TWELVE

Second Summer, Lake Erie

Opening Day

At last we're on our way again to Lake Erie. The new car purring along the highway swiftly, almost silently, to beautiful background music—Schumann, Chopin . . . I doze beside George as he drives, the dogs sleeping, Tanjy cuddled up against me . . .

A late start, as George had an extra-heavy day of patients, and an emergency at the last minute . . . Relaxing a bit with cheese and crackers and a cup of coffee before loading up the car . . . The cottage, closed all winter, would be cold and without water; as we were leaving so late, we decided to stop at Howard Johnson's in Erie for the night.

Dinner, fried clams, then to bed in a very dear room with twin beds, in one of which we cuddled, holding each other all night . . . Morning, tidying up while George is checking out. Looking around as I always do at any place where we've been happy, no matter how small. Loving it and wanting to tell it so, wanting it never to change, but just to remain there forever filled with happiness, waiting for us to come back sometime.

But meanwhile blessing it for its next occupants, saying a little prayer that they too will find joy and love within its walls—its beds, its chairs, its big sunny windows . . .

After breakfast an overcast sky as we drove, a light rain falling, chilly, misty, clouds drifting. "There's the lake," George announced, and as usual I told him it can't be the lake, it must be just gray-blue clouds merging with the earth. But he's right; the closer we get, the clearer the lake stands, for it *does* seem to stand upright, a soft blue-gray wall against the sky . . .

Buying groceries at the country store, then on past our own wooded acres, to tunnel down the dear familiar lane. The trees embrace to form a canopy above us. But spring is late this year. Their branches are mostly bare. Only the faintest froth of buds is showing, although the grass is already vivid on the hills, and bright across the lawn, even where the storms of winter have raged.

The last roadway is still filled with puddles of gray water, and wild winds have torn the branches and limbs from the trees and strewn them in our path. The cottage and its grounds look like a disaster area. Several trees have fallen and lay sprawled, their branches hurled about like slain bodies gray-white in the light. The whole place a battlefield.

I was astonished, but George says this is not unusual, in fact some springs it is much worse. "Opening up is always discouraging, it seems you never will get things done, but somehow in a little while you do."

He is right. We plugged in electric heaters, built a fire with some of the sticks and logs. And while George was working with pipes to get the water flowing, I went outdoors and began hurling a few of the large branches aside, or carrying them to the pile already begun. They are all dead whitish branches, easy to carry, and in a little while I cleared an impressive area. All day, on our errands, we picked them up, breaking them over our knees and piling them up, or bringing them in to add to the blaze in the fireplace. And gradually, what had seemed a task for a crew of workmen had yielded. The large sprawling yard, with its ivy, its picnic table and benches, was returning to normal.

While I was at it, I found myself working on the little entrance room that George had only begun to clear of its clutter last year. It was to have been a major project for the summer. Yet little by little, trekking antlike to the garage with my arms full, I achieved at least a semblance of order and promise. There is still work to be done. More hauling of larger objects, we will want to paint, put up some shelves, George agrees. "You're the lady of the house," he says again, as in McMurray. But I welcome his suggestions—maybe travel posters, new lamps, a screen to hide necessary tools.

Anyway, the insane jumble is no more; we now have a small but useful place that will eventually grace our passage from the kitchen to the outside door . . . So sometimes the seemingly impossible jobs are achieved within a fairly short time, if you just *start*.

The Letters

George and I worked very hard at these physical things all day, pausing, however, for cold drinks and to tell each other how much we love each other. Pausing too to watch the Kentucky Derby. I had stretched out on the couch for a little while before it came on, and George tiptoed up with a cover for me, and a more comfortable pillow. And he made his wonderful coffee for us to drink by the fire as we watched the race. A long shot came in . . . thrilling!

Then after a dinner of fried chicken bought earlier and heated, and some lovely sherry, about nine o'clock, after listening to Lawrence Welk, George went to bed (I insisted, he was really exhausted) while I washed up things in the kitchen. The mice had invaded this winter, and there was so much to be cleaned. Then I went into the other bedroom to put away some things . . . and discovered, to my agony, another drawer bursting with his cards and notes and love letters to his wife. Like those I had found in McMurray, which nearly killed me. And once again, to my own shame, I read them and allowed myself to be devastated.

I realize this is madness, but my emotions refuse to listen to reason. I *know* he loves me as much, if not more, but the fact that he did love so passionately, unceasingly, almost unreasonably for all those years—instead of comforting me, as it should —tears me apart. I *realize* I am the lucky recipient of a love that is unique; that he is a very unique man and it would be impossible for him to love except with that unique and intense passion. That he simply could not love any other way. But instead of blessing his past and releasing it as I promised myself, I found myself dissolved, disintegrating, wanting to run off screaming into the night . . .

In sober analysis later in the night, I realized why this is striking me once again, after nearly a year of marriage, when I thought I had overcome it. It is because I have allowed myself to believe that this absolute bliss we have shared *is* somehow new to him too. Ridiculously, the fairy tale come true for both of us: I was the sleeping princess awakened by the prince of my dreams. And we *are* living happily ever after. Only I had deliberately forgotten, put aside, or pretended not to know that the *prince* hadn't been sleeping all those years! He had been very much awake and already living his "happily ever after." Then, when the "ever after" was interrupted by the death of his precious goddess, his beloved, he nearly killed himself with grief . . . But revived, thank God he revived, enough to come riding into the forest to find me. And having waked me up, he would take up his life again and just continue his buoyant, fervent, beautiful "ever after."

I realize this is perfectly logical and right, yet it shocks and wounds me—my very soul (or is it my pride?)—that I can never be more than a *continuation*. The end of a beautiful journey of love he started long ago with someone else. I am just the last lap, the brief final portion. But better, far better even this much with him than never to have shared it at all . . .

I went into hysterics that night (to my present shame). I found myself weeping wildly; and he, so alert, so quick to compassion, sprang out of bed and comforted and calmed me, wiped my face, brought me a drink of water, helped me undress and put me in bed beside him, safe, safe in his arms, pleading, "Oh, my darling, my precious little girl, *don't* . . . don't do

this to yourself, or to me. *I love you.* It's you I will love forever." And he took me and made love to me . . . And in the
morning he got up very early and had the entire cottage swept,
a big fire crackling, his delicious coffee made, which he brought
to me in bed.

And I came to my senses and went on through the day,
continuing my sorting and cleaning, revitalized—it was such a
lovely day. But later an awful mood of depression came over
me, I had to keep fighting not to cry. George sensed it and did
everything to cheer me, brought more flowers from the yard,
sang to me, put records on the old player, held out his arms to
dance with me, the way we danced last fall.

Then, as I started dinner, everything came to a climax. He
had brought out a large basket of the letters; they were on the
floor beside him as he sat by the fire. I realized, partly in relief,
partly to my consternation, that he was going through them,
laughing at some, wiping his eyes at others, and throwing some
away. "Come, sit down, honey, listen," he called out to me.
And I did, bracing myself, puzzled, praying I wouldn't break
down again. But the ones he shared at first were from their
children, letters from camp or college, and cards and eloquent
tributes, especially to their mother. And somehow my demons
fled, a surprising peace came over me, a sense of sweet communion—almost as if in sharing this, he was somehow paying me a
tribute.

And then I said something maybe foolish—or wise, I
thought at the time. "Don't burn any of them, George, unless
you really want to. Even those you wrote to her. Don't be
afraid to read some of them too."

So he began, doubtfully, murmuring to himself, choosing
phrases from just a few, very tenderly, innocently, amazed at
some of his own excessive expressions, exclaiming several
times, "Why, this is exactly the way I feel about *you*. When I
say, 'I wake up in the morning thinking of you, you never leave
my thoughts all day, and I can hardly wait for your arms at
night,' that's exactly the way it is with *you* . . . Only *more*
so!"

I thought I could bear it—it might be just what I needed to
get over this—like surgery. But I found myself protesting,

"How can you top perfection? How can anybody be *more* than superlative, more than a goddess, an eternal soul mate?" . . . (What am I doing? I wondered, appalled. Do I actually want to convince him?)

He held my hand as I went on, as in a debate, a competition. (Who and what was I competing with? *Love should never be a competition.*) . . . But I had to try to make him understand. If I didn't love him so much I wouldn't go into such a frenzy. And it is *unlike* me, I am exploring an entirely new field of emotions.

"I've never *loved* anybody like this before," I pleaded. "And nobody has ever loved me like this. I know it seems crazy, but I'm not used to it—all this love I've inherited from somebody else. I respect it, am grateful for it. But I'm jealous of it too—the time you had together. It's my turn now, and maybe I'm scared, maybe I'm afraid I might lose it. Maybe it's too much."

He responded simply, "Well, a person can inherit two cents or two million dollars. Isn't it better to inherit a fortune than a paltry sum?" . . .

The fire blazed on, died down to embers. We forgot about dinner, the TV shows we meant to watch. Above us the carved white sea gulls kept turning on their wires fastened to the beamed ceiling; outdoors the live gulls wheeled in a kind of accompanying dance. The lake, gray all day, had turned to shimmering gold in the setting sun . . . So much beauty all around us for such torment—at least for me.

But it was somehow, I pray, a final purging.

And George said things I must remember: "*You* revived me, you brought me back from the winter of my despair, you gave me spring again. There *is* spring after the winter, and just because the roses bloomed once doesn't mean they can't bloom again, even more beautifully than before."

Oh, he is so wise and wonderful. We finally ate a bite in the kitchen and warmed up the coffee and went outside to drink it under the stars—it was dark by then, the stars were sparkling and dew had fallen and the earth smelled so sweet. We laughed and cried and kissed and came back in to catch the late news . . .

. . .

And now it's a beautiful new-minted morning, we are alive, well, still vigorous, attractive, more in love than a couple of teenagers and we're going to live forever . . . Please, God, let us! At least many, many more years to make up for lost time. Once, last night, he said, "I have made you so unhappy, and when you're unhappy I simply can't stand it, I want to die." We both wept and held each other, and I felt such a louse, a blind selfish terrible person, because it was all my fault.

Please, dear God, don't let me *ever* be so foolish again. Let me guard this precious treasure, no matter how late it's come. Don't let me ever again hurt or waste one precious moment of my life with George.

To Myself

NOW is what matters! Now, now, now. This beautiful life with George . . . His beauty of face, body, and mind. His high good spirits. His lovely voice singing to me. His attentiveness, his picking me flowers. His writing those crazy, delightful love things all over the morning papers . . . His kindness, his wit, his wisdom, his philosophy . . . The fact that he does ardently, totally, and intensely *love* ME.

What does *not* matter is the past. His past or mine. The contrast between his happiness, the floodlight of great good fortune that shone upon his whole family for nearly fifty years . . . and the hidden hell in which I lived for much of that same time . . . All that is

        OVER
            FINISHED
                DONE
                    GONE FOREVER

Never to be relived, changed by one word or thought. I cannot, *will* not, *must* not allow my mind to fasten upon that past, either his or mine. To do so is allowing the present to be damaged. To destroy or diminish the sunlight that shines so abundantly on this beautiful, wonderful, joyful life we two have together now.

ALL THAT MATTERS IS TODAY

Memorial Day

An early start for Lake Erie this Thursday. I had the car almost loaded when George got home at five o'clock. A beautiful drive, the days longer now. Trees that a few weeks ago were only branches, a hint of rosy buds and pale green froth, are now in full leaf, though the green is still young, golden, all the light hues blending. And the blossoming dogwoods like parasols in the woods; the poplars trailing their white grapelike garlands . . . All is new and expectant, fairylike, bridal. Even the blue sky was changing to the same petal-soft pink as my wedding dress.

How happy we are, sailing along the smooth broad highways beside the farms and fields—the hills undulant, rolling, new-green too, the pastures smooth as if painted, and the plowed fields stripes or blocks of rich brown-black . . . Cows grazing, a part of this bucolic scene, like a Dutch painting.

Sailing along so in love and comforted and rejoicing to be together. Reaching out to touch each other, cup hands, press our little signals of love. Marveling at this miracle, voicing it, thanking God for it . . .

I read aloud to George from some of the books I'd brought along—background references for my novels about the life of Jesus: *Summer in Galilee. Daily Life in the Time of Jesus. Sex and Love in the Bible.* He is just as fascinated by whatever I'm writing as I am by his stories. Ideas flash between us. Could Jesus have also been a shepherd? And surely he could swim—all those fishermen *had* to, the Sea of Galilee is very rough. "Jesus would be a very strong swimmer," George said. "And he could have had a dog. A faithful dog that looks like Ben—call him Benjamin, that's biblical."

"Why not?" I broke in, excited. "A dog that follows him everywhere and likes to swim!"

We were still discussing it as we pulled into the Edinburgh Holiday Inn for dinner. Never, before George, had I let anyone but an editor read my manuscripts, but with him I can hardly wait. I sometimes wonder how I ever wrote without him.

The place was quiet, uncrowded. We chose a table near the window—although you can't look out, it is stained glass in the manner of a Scottish inn. Dark beams, red carpeting, amber lights. A new musical duo was playing—an eager young singer and her husband fervently playing the organ. Their music was so inviting we danced, partly to encourage them, and our dancing was especially delightful, flowing together with a closeness and sweetness that seems new, a kind of silken flying.

A couple at a nearby table applauded. We chatted with them briefly as we sat down. Then as the music changed, they got up and jitterbugged. He was baldish and bellied, she thin and very plain, but they were so relaxed, vivacious, and skillful, so briskly in harmony with themselves and each other they were transformed—a joy to watch. Now we vigorously applauded them, George gave his famous whistle, and other people joined in.

Leaving, I had forgotten my jacket and doggy bag. George, the irrepressible, went back for them, pausing to chat with the couple again, and tell them about my books. The lady exclaimed that she had read them, and followed George to the car to meet me—both of us thrilled. I autographed her napkin, all we could find to write on, and we hugged each other like long-lost friends. As I believe perhaps we are. People destined to meet, if only to share one brief quicksilver moment of life.

It had begun to rain. I found more good music on the radio and cuddled down to doze while George drove, smiling to himself, reaching over occasionally to pat my knee. He enjoys this as much as I do, this cozy communion even as I sleep . . . It was raining hard by the time we turned down the lane to the cottage. Lights shining on the bowed trees, black silver, every-

thing glistening, slippery as we dashed to the door and unlocked . . .

The new carpeting smells toasty and feels soft underfoot;
it's still a little surprise to see it sweeping the whole lodge-
dining area into one unit now, like a broad beach before the
windows to the lake . . . Bathing, cuddling down, a beautiful
night together . . .

Friday was misty gray, showers, the trees bowing with the burden of water, the lake almost invisible in the fog. After breakfast I went to my desk to cope with the opening chapters of my
novel—the long-postponed sequel to *Two from Galilee*. Re-
reading what I've written, revising, happy at some scenes, at
others despairing . . . pondering George's suggestions. Once
he slipped up with a cup of coffee, hugged me from behind, and
disappeared. I sipped it, talking to myself. *The dog*—the swimming, such intriguing ideas last night—but I must be accurate,
not in the Bible, but possible—even probable . . . Jews didn't
keep dogs as pets, but *Jesus* could—a dog he'd saved from a
pack of jackals. His humanity, his love—Jesus broke many traditions. I wrote a few words and ran to find my inspiration.
"George!" I yelled. "Listen to this."

Later we drove to the neighboring villages through an almost blinding downpour. Cars stood hub deep in the parking
lot at the supermarket, customers huddled under the awning;
the lights had gone out. We joined the merry comradeship
among everyone waiting, or groping—then decided to pursue
our hunt for a place that sold wood stoves and fireplace equipment.

It proved to be a little one-story building, where we bought
an iron grate, curved and quite lovely, but the man said we'd
have to assemble it. A beaming, ancient pixie of a man with a
sporty hat perched on his head, eager to please. I talked him
into giving us the floor model. We lugged the curved thing together to the car, for it is very heavy.

The rain had abated a bit, but as we drove along the shore,
such a pure white mist was muffling the docks we could hardly
see the boats . . . Into the tangy-smelling fish market, to buy

pickled herring, a slab of crisp, deep brown smoked salmon, and a pound of just caught lake perch, small and silvery . . . Then into the Red Barn, where George ordered some hot fried mushrooms to eat from a tiny box, driving home.

The rain stopped suddenly, the sun burst out in splendor. Turning down the lane, we found it sparkling, bangled with brilliance, all the woods and trees that embrace the cottage flashing and mad with light. It streamed across the lake, transforming the silver-gray water into a great dish of gems.

We cleaned out the fireplace, gathered wood. It was still very wet but burned brightly with the papers on the new grate. It had been smoking, now it needed only to be uplifted, aired, the fuel able to draw, its energy released. How merry and bright it is, rivaling the sun!

We had cold drinks while I fried the fish, prepared the salad, which we ate while watching the news. The sky was becoming incredible, the sun going down beneath a vast lavender cloud, rimming it with fire, while leaving a brilliant golden trail straight to our doorway.

We went out and walked down the old rocky roadway to the beach. So much had been washed away we had to skid and scramble to get there . . . The sky was a rich sweet pink now, almost the entire sky, with little breaks of blue, and the water too was limpid, sheer soft pink, like the softest silk being rippled by unseen fingers, gently, gently, making silken sounds with its lips as well as it touches the sand.

We climbed over branches and trunks of a couple of huge trees that have plunged over the banks, torn up by the roots, great chunks of earth around them, the green leaves still alive but small, never to grow. (Or will they? There is still so much life in these mounds of wet brown earth.) There was a brisk yet soft winey fragrance to the air—wet woods, honeysuckle, soil, and the rocky marine odor of the water . . . Our usual path back had been washed away; water gushed down it over the layers of shale and rock, a white foaming waterfall, wet ferns bowing at its edges. We returned the way we came; skidding and grabbing for wet branches, we scaled the first few difficult steps up the road, so steep we have to brace ourselves to ascend, like goats.

At the top two men from a neighboring trailer called out, gave us a hand. One tall, gaunt, almost skeletal, but rustic and rosy, delightful. Merry, loquacious, funny. He and George embraced, began a volley of wisecracks and repartee, like a fast tennis game. It was pleasant to hear them, standing there with the sky such a heavenly pink beyond the cottage and the trees, and all mirrored in the silent lake. Their voices were like a downpour of showers, or the waterfall we have just seen. They don't *think*—they just open their mouths and all these bright, witty, outrageously funny things spill out! A merry music of the evening before we walked on, hand in hand, along the wet grassy lane toward the house.

This morning, Saturday, the lake was almost colorless, blending straight into the sky, with only a slightly deeper line of blue to mark the merging. George called to me to see a yellow boat sitting out there, like something painted or arranged on a flat blue-gray wall. And a minute later, after it glided away—a lone white sailboat, almost motionless, like a candle, a white candle duplicated on the water.

I went out to hang some towels on the line, and discovered a bunch of lilacs leaning over the redwood table. I broke them free, and arranged them in a jug on the mantel, along with a big purple tulip George has picked. Another tiny glass of lilies of the valley, frail and fragrant, sits on the coffee table. Now the whole house is delicately scented, as if the perfume of these flowers has been released by the atmosphere inside.

Before coming in, I stood for a moment with my arms full of the sweet wet lilacs, remembering how my parents used to gather them, along with peonies and other flowers, and carry them to the cemetery to decorate *their* parents' graves on Memorial Day. And I lifted my lilacs to the sky for a minute, dedicating them to Mother and Dad.

Next Day, Runaway Dog

The lake is entirely blotted out by a white mist. A thick white curtain which descended yesterday afternoon, blanking out everything beyond the green bank of the lawn. There is nothing there, absolutely nothing, neither sky nor water, no bird, no boat. To stand at its edge is like standing on a precipice to eternity. If you stepped off you would fall or fly forever, it seems, into this total white nothingness.

This morning the mists had drifted over even the broad lawn that surrounds the cottage. The beautiful trees reach through it like women draped in soft white veils. There is a stage-set feeling everywhere, as if transparent scrims have been dropped to blur the scenes. It is also dreamlike, a misty dream landscape where the ferns and flowers and leaves and swaying grasses are unreal. A sense of lovely mystery prevails.

Ben went off down the bank and disappeared into the water several times, returning sopping wet. We dried him off with big beach towels. Then toward noon we heard some children playing on the shore below, and he slipped away again and this time didn't come back.

George called and called, both of us more concerned as time went on. "He'll go off with anybody that throws a stick. A lot of strangers around on weekends, especially a holiday. He's a valuable dog, somebody could have picked him up." I could also see that George was hurt. "He's a very disloyal pet. And if he hasn't got any more sense than to go away with somebody else, let him. If he chooses strangers over us, I don't want him. I just hope they're good to him."

"Nobody could be as good as you are," I told him. "I've never seen a dog fed so often or loved so much."

We both were deeply troubled. Especially for Tanjy, his tiny white shadow, always trotting after the big retriever, leaping, nipping, trying to engage him in wrestling bouts; also using him fervently and shamelessly as a sex target . . . Tanjy began to miss him too, to share our dejection. At five o'clock feeding time, he refused his food, just lay there forlorn . . . Ben had been gone almost six hours.

We joined hands and prayed for his safe return. And finally, after dinner, I persuaded George we should at least go look for him. But just as we were about to march forth on our quest, Tanjy began to bark and rushed to the door. And there stood four little boys with Ben in tow.

We thanked them profusely, of course, and they said they knew how we felt, they had dogs themselves. They'd had a lot of fun with him all day, but he just wouldn't go *home.*

Ben came slinking into the house, obviously very guilty and contrite. We scolded him, lectured him about how dangerous it is to go off with strangers, while he lay with his head between his paws, cowed and shamed.

George refused to give him any dinner until about nine o'clock, when he relented. As he ate, George drew the sign of the cross on his head and blessed him. Then added, with a grin, "You better shape up, be more loyal, or I won't let Marj put you in her book. I'll tell her to use Tanjy."

We both laughed. "Don't worry, Ben," I told him. "Tanjy's not the type—I can't imagine Jesus with a poodle."

"Not that Jesus wouldn't *love* you," George hastened to assure Tanjy. "Just that he'd need a bigger dog."

We let Ben sleep by our bed. Thank heaven he's back. At least our prayer was answered—he is a member of our family, safe with us again.

Since it's his nature to wander, we'll have to be more careful about watching him. It seems cruel to pen him in or tie him up. The siren song of nature is so hard to resist. Especially here —for him, or for us.

Family Visit

Although we kept in touch with George's two brothers and his sister, who live in distant states, I hadn't seen them since our wedding. But yesterday, just as we finished breakfast, all of them (plus Chuck, Ann's husband) came honking up without warning, and trooped in.

George's sister Ann, radiantly motherly with her curly white hair, blue eyes sparkling behind her glasses, her sweet smile, and plump arms full of food. (A white ironstone pot of chili, a bowl of red beets, lettuce crisp and damp from her garden, homemade nut bread.) How warm she is, her voice richly melodic, bubbling over.

Brother John, a tall, sturdy, gentle-rough John Wayne. The same rugged features—handsome, restless, a mock cynicism camouflaging an innate tenderness and sweetness, a desire to be loved. Sharp eyes, a kind of fervent, endearing urgency about him.

Joe is the smaller, slighter of the brothers, but like them perfectly built, with magnificent chest and shoulders. In his swimming trunks he demonstrated his daily exercises, half modestly pulling in his stomach, bouncing about like a boxer, exhibiting his muscles. Animated, but more quiet and conservative than the others. The hair on his chest is pure white, like the hair on his head. When he swam, his head skimmed the water like a white sea gull among the waves.

We had all clambered down to go in, except for Ann and Chuck, who sat watching from a redwood bench on the bluff beside the cottage, high above the water. "I'd join you if I looked like *that*," Ann exclaimed sweetly, when I appeared in my suit with the men.

They were all champion divers, swimmers, lifeguards. (George's drawers are filled with his gold medals.) All very good-looking. A yellowed clipping from the Pittsburgh *Press* recounts their plaudits and achievements, along with their picture and the headline: FEMININE HEARTS FLUTTER AS SCHMIELER BROTHERS SWIM. Although George was the only Lothario in the bunch, his family claimed. Their eyes twinkled, they seemed to be proud of his exploits.

Swimming with the men, and dancing later, I felt like the belle of Lake Erie. George put some old songs on the record player when we came back, and we all danced barefoot. They're also excellent dancers. It was charming to see Ann dancing too, with her brothers. Then a joyful commotion of people climbing stairs to the attic to rescue things—china, statues, old toys, pictures, souvenirs, which had memories for most of them, or could be used. Meanwhile, laughing, telling stories, bursting into old German songs learned from their father, harmonizing. They even have good voices, although none as beautiful as George's.

Finally, we all drove to the village to shop for supper (we'd already eaten the chili). Past the grape farms, the flowers and ancient trees, the lovely antebellum houses. A detour due to a Firemen's Parade took us along the harbor at Dunkirk and to the fish market, where we bought smoked salmon, fresh clams, and some little fresh-caught lake perch filleted to look like double wings—crisp little birds when you fry them. And sweet corn from a roadside stand.

We ate on our new deck overlooking the water. They were friendly and fun, admiring the changes we have made in the house and yard, the painting and carpeting and redecorating, and cutting down most of the trees that had blocked the incredible view—such a forest we could hardly see the lake, except for sparkling glimpses. The view is now breathtaking—a vast 180-degree sweep of shining water, east to west . . . Although Ann seemed a bit wistful. "So many memories," she murmured several times, sighing as she looked around. "Memories, memories. It was *always* beautiful here."

Even so, I was glad they could see what we had done.

George had built a big fire on our new grate. We gathered around it a little while before they left, the family still reminiscing. Then they were driving down our lane, so beautiful lit by the falling sun, while we watched and waved until they honked and the red eye of their car disappeared around the bend.

The Fireplace Glowing

"I feel like that fireplace right now," George said, settling down before it. "Warm and rosy and full of joy and a kind of benediction. Those red coals, what a nice aftermath of a big blazing fire."

"Especially after a day like this," I exclaimed. "Wow! I really enjoyed it—I wish everybody lived closer."

"Yeah, me too—but this way makes it more of a treat when we do get together. We all light up and show off and have fun—like that fire when I feed it or stir it."

He got up to poke the coals, put on another log—and the flames suddenly blazed. "A fire is so beautiful and *alive*," he continued, "dancing and leaping, almost frantically sometimes, just like people. Then it begins to quiet down, burn more steadily, settles into that rosy glow we watch before we go to bed—it's going to bed too in its own warm bed of coals."

George studied the fire thoughtfully a moment. "It's dancing as if it feels good about itself and the pleasure it has given; later it will still be glowing—feeling the way the sun must feel after a good bright day of shining. Knowing it's lighted the earth, caused plants to grow, warmed the world and kept it going. Finally the sun sinks out of sight—but it too leaves behind those burnished streaks of light we can see out the window right now—the afterglow—a kind of hearth fire of peaceful coals."

I said, "That's why we feel so good after a happy day, isn't it? Satisfied with our work, what we've accomplished, learning something, or even just having fun with someone you didn't really know before. Like today, I learned so much more about them, and even more about you."

"Maybe too much about me," he grinned.

"Oh no, they're all so proud of you, George—they really adore their big brother, to them you could do no wrong—and I agree. I'm glad I married into a family like yours, even this late. I just wish—"

I caught myself, I couldn't say it. But George did: "If only we could have met each other first."

"No," I corrected both of us, "you wouldn't have wanted me, I was flippant and foolish, I couldn't have made you happy. We both had to go on growing and changing before we could really appreciate each other—the people we are now. And neither of us would cancel out our children or our memories—although I'd sure like to forget a lot of mine!"

"I don't regret one thing," George said, "except not having more time with you now." He held out his arms to draw me closer. "And the fire is getting tired and so are we, and I love you so much, let's go to bed and make the most of it."

CHAPTER THIRTEEN

The Jewels

George has always loved poetry. He often quotes one of his favorites, from a collection he'd begun writing down in a composition book in high school: "Some have too much and still do crave. I little have, and seek no more—"

I'm amused sometimes at the "little have." Because, despite his claim that he made less money than any doctor in Pittsburgh, saw fewer patients, sent fewer to hospitals, and prescribed fewer tests and drugs, he did very well in his practice, made wise investments, and has been richly blessed.

He never envied anybody, even as a boy. His family lived over his father's shoemaker shop. "We never had much, but we had *enough,* and we got along, I don't remember feeling poor." He once sold lamps door to door. "In some of the richest sections, Sewickley, Squirrel Hill. I'd ring the bell and servants would sometimes let me in—I remember one place especially, a mansion with a long staircase; the woman who came down it was wearing a gorgeous red velvet robe. But I never had the slightest wish to live like that or be anybody but myself."

He deplores moneygrubbing in any form, and the constant acquisition of possessions. To be comfortable is the main thing.

To have enough to meet your needs, and to satisfy your soul. (Another of his favorite quotes is the old Persian saying "If you have two pennies, with one buy bread, with the other buy hyacinths to feed your soul.")

"But go beyond these needs and you're surfeited, burdened," he said, in one of our many discussions. We'd been looking at pictures showing the excessive jewelry worn by the rich women of Egypt in biblical times. "Too much of anything is bad, even of precious jewels. Supposing a genie said to you, 'I'm going to give you all the jewels in the world.' You'd start putting them on, in your ears, on your fingers, around your neck, crowns of them on your head.

"They'd even dress you in jewels so heavy you could hardly walk. They'd begin to fill the house—"

"Like the porridge in *The Sorcerer's Apprentice*," I said. (And was secretly thinking: Or this house when I came.)

"Yes, only that was nothing compared to jewels. *Beautiful* jewels, so dazzling people came to see them in awe. Then the house can't hold any more, they fill the yard, and they are so dazzling, so brilliant they light up the sky. All Pittsburgh! The city becomes famous because of this enormous collection of jewels.

"But pretty soon you can't walk, you can't even move, there's no room for food on the table, you are starving for air and food and light. But you're still hemmed in by all the jewels. So they begin to take some away, more and more, out of the house, the yard. And finally you start stripping them off yourself. You get into some comfortable clothes. You take off the burden of that jeweled crown on your head—and how good it feels! All you finally have left is what you started with—a pair of earrings, maybe, a ring or two on your fingers, a bracelet, a pin. And how happy you are. They are more beautiful and dear to you than you ever realized before. Simply because you don't have too much. You just have enough."

I sometimes smile when he talks that way. But for him, at least, it's true, he is not self-indulgent.

Here are some more of George's concepts of life that for me are better than jewels:

The Universe in a Cell

Marveling at the wonders of the body:

"A single cell is a universe. And yet it has to work in co-operation with its brothers. No single cell can say, 'Let's go on strike.' Cells don't ask for benefits, bigger salaries, free dental care, free vacations. They ask for nothing, just do their job."

"How can they?" I remind him. "They have no choice."

"Yes, but every cell has an awareness of its own. It *has* to be aware, otherwise you couldn't move your finger. If I cut one nerve, my finger would be useless. The cells don't want to stop working, they do so only if they're forced to if a nerve is damaged or severely injured. If you had the optic nerve cut, you couldn't *see* . . .

"And these same cells are in the violinist or the laborer, the black man or the white. None of them feel superior to each other. They work together in unison, because they have a common bond, a divine Master, who is in control . . .

"The miraculous design of the body, human or animal! The incredible consistency. It isn't the *unusual* that amazes me, the occasional birth defect, but the *usual*. The fact that most of us are born perfect, and generally speaking, stay that way for years.

"Good heavens, just to create *one* person would be a miracle, just one human being. Or even one animal! All those billions of cells and miles of nerves and blood vessels functioning so perfectly. People should have more faith in themselves, for we are the demonstration of the Master Principle. A principle that is consistently followed all through nature—even in an orange, an apple, a flower, a bug, a bird, a tree. The limitless variety of products, but always, always the incredible consistency of design."

What Do We Choose to See?

On beauty:

"There is ugliness as well as beauty in the world; some ugliness we can't avoid, and are forced to see. But there is so much beauty available if we only choose to claim it for ourselves. A sunset, a walk in the park, a visit to the flower shows at Phipps Conservatory, the art galleries and museums, all of them free. Why not take advantage of these things? Yet there are people who refuse to budge from the same street, the same house; or who never go to anything but the most ordinary or mundane if they do.

"There are also people who deliberately choose the dark streets, dark clubs and bars—places where the sun never shines, night or day. People who feast on stories of crime and rape and perversion, in magazines and movies and on TV.

"What we choose to look at reveals so much about ourselves. What kind of a person are you? Do you want to see something morbid, or something cheerful? Something ugly or something beautiful? Would you want to go to a morgue and look at dead bodies? Or watch a ballet, a sunset, or children playing in a park?"

Electrocardiograms

George sometimes brings home a patient's electrocardiograms to study. He was doing so one morning while I cleaned up the kitchen. We had just finished our after-breakfast reading, which I usually find inspiring: something from the Bible, "Silent Unity," "Daily Guideposts," and/or a religious or medical journal; concluding with a poem, a beautiful picture, and a joke. He loves to read aloud (and I to listen). And this routine (which he says he always followed but never shared with anyone else before) actually seems almost more important to him than getting to the office.

But sometimes I disagree with the theme of some religious publications—that anyone who is truly close to God will always be at peace.

I'd had a hard week, and once again I protested. "If that's true, I'm failing. You know how happy I usually am, but also how things upset me. Right now that cruel attack on my book. In spite of all those wonderful, loving, beautiful letters I get, even one nasty one pitches me to the depths. I *can't* always be happy and tranquil. If only life could be smooth, if we just didn't have these peaks and valleys!"

In reply, George beckoned me to examine the electrocardiogram on the table. "Look at this—this EKG monitors one of the body's most important organs, the heart. The heart has the biggest job of all, it beats 100,000 times a day. It expands and contracts. When the ventricle contracts it sends a peak or elevation on the chart, then there is a line, then a larger peak which comes down, then there is another line.

"These elevations and pulsations fluctuate," he went on. "But the heart itself has to have these peaks and valleys. It couldn't *run* in a straight line." He paused to let this sink in.

"This is a fact of life," he said. "You're right, you can't always be on the mountaintop, there are bound to be descents into the valleys. So don't be discouraged when you react to things that don't go smoothly all the time. Your life can't be a regular, unbroken line.

"These peaks and valleys are natural," he assured me. "They don't prove you're not in tune with the Creator, they prove you're *alive*. Without them you'd be *dead!*"

Money

George says, "There's nothing wrong with money. Money itself has no conscience. It has no life. It doesn't care what you do with it, it's simply there—or not there. Millions or a few dollars, or nothing.

"But there is magic in the power and use of money. It can build palaces, beautiful cities, libraries, Disneyland—or the weapons to destroy them. It doesn't ask, 'What are you going to do with me?' It can belong to a criminal or a saint. It can buy a great painting or a tank. It can provide food for starving children or the assault rifle to mow them down on a playground.

"Your very life depends on money. It has the power of life or death—to feed you, pay the doctor, give you the medicine you need. But it is powerless by itself. It couldn't feed a single child or anybody else if the food wasn't there.

"Money has no ethics, it will do only what you make it do. And it doesn't care whether you earn it or inherit it or steal it. It depends entirely on the hands that spend it, no matter whose they are—doctor, lawyer, merchant, *thief*. Money itself is useless, and it can't buy happiness, no matter how much is spent. Sometimes the more you have, the more you want. And the more trouble you get.

"But money is wonderful if you have enough to take good care of your family, and still have enough to help somebody else. That's the best reward money can buy you—just being able to give it away!"

Steering-Wheel Philosophy

As we drove to Washington, D.C.:

"The government isn't bad just because the people who run it are bad. For instance, this is a wonderful car, but it's only as efficient as its driver. It's not the car's fault if I'm a bad driver, if I'm reckless, if I don't stop at stop signs but run right on through and wreck it. I've got to take care of that car, fill it with gas and oil and drive it properly or it will go to pieces, it won't perform.

"Also, I have to use the kind of gas the manufacturer says is right for it. And I can't give it too little or even too much, and I can't drive it too fast—the faster I go, the more gas I use, and the greater the wear and tear on the car . . . It's the same way with government. We've got a great system, but we have to have people in charge who know how to take care of it, and drive with some skill and common sense."

Other People

One day when I was fretting about the state of the world, as well as our own family problems, and scolding myself for letting such matters bother me when I should be writing, George said:

"That's only natural. Unless you are an absolute hermit, without family ties or television, you *are* affected by what other people do. Public figures like Ted Kennedy or Ronald Reagan, or Jimmy Swaggart, or writers and actors and football stars.

"But mainly people in our family, of course. Our children's marriages and divorces, your granddaughter's decision to leave the ballet, Jack's job problems, knowing that Melanie and Haris are safely back from Greece . . . We can't live apart or fail to react to other lives—even close friends, or sometimes even strangers. 'No man is an island.'

"But we must accept the fact that usually there is very little we can do about the events happening in other people's lives. We can't control them, prevent them, change them—at least not very often. Even the help we are often asked for doesn't always help very much, and may even do harm. We have to be reconciled to this and live our own lives as best we can.

"About all we can do is ask God's blessings on these others, and cover the whole situation with his love—and our own."

Getting Over Hurt

George and I both lay awake last night, we insisted at breakfast. Yet each always thinks the other is fast asleep. He claims I fall asleep at once; I'm positive he's asleep long before I am. I've sworn I'm going to get a little clock so we can take turns timing each other—when, of course, one of us is *sure* he himself is wide awake.

This led us to one of our discussions about controlling our thoughts. When I was a girl, I told him, I used to *deliberately* lie awake replaying the beautiful, exciting things that had happened—winning a contest, for instance, or a wonderful date. "But when we get older, why is it so often the worries and troubles that keep us awake? The things that hurt? And no matter how I try to stop them, they won't go away."

George says it is a choice. He insists we can *decide* which it will be. "Take those roses in the garden—pick a rose, you can see its beautiful colors, smell its fragrance, enjoy it. Or you can focus on its thorns, you can press those cruel thorns into your flesh until you bleed. You can make your very heart bleed with your thoughts."

We spoke then of how long it sometimes takes to get over pain. "It has to run its course," I said. "I learned that about myself years ago. Whenever I was terribly hurt by someone or something, there was no use even trying to slam the door on it, forget it. I couldn't, literally couldn't, so I finally stopped berating myself. All I could do was pray for deliverance, at the same time somehow no longer fighting the hurt. I had to just let it happen until it had worn itself out. I knew it would finally subside, but it was like a cold, it was an illness of emotions that would last about three days."

This George understood. "It's like that lake. It took a while for it to calm down after those storms. But gradually the winds stopped buffeting it, the waves lost their momentum, became quieter; yesterday they were just ripples, gentle again. 'This too will pass.' Both physical and emotional hurts take time to heal . . . You are human, when you hurt you hurt. Break a bone and it hurts. All the bandages and splints in the world may prop you up or help stop the blood, but they can't stop the hurt until it's ready to heal itself.

"It's the same thing whether your wound is in an arm or a leg or your heart. Prayer helps—as you say, deliverance from these storms that *can* be so destructive. And forgiving people, which is the greatest healer of all—but even that takes time, usually . . ."

The ultimate conclusion of this talk, like so many, is that the past should have no power to hurt us. It's over, we can't change it. All that really matters is *today*.

The Earth

Every morning when George goes outdoors for the papers, he brings back at least one flower. Sometimes a small bouquet. I often see him from an upstairs window while I'm dressing—a tender sight somehow, this rugged man so earnestly searching the yard, and bending to pick the first spring flowers.

For several days he has brought me a single perfect daffodil, golden yellow or creamy white—each blossom rich and crepey, the six petals surrounding a little ruffled bonnet; within its deep heart the tall golden pistils.

One day he surrounded the single daffodil in its vase with a cluster of tiny grape hyacinths with deep green serrated leaves. Yesterday it was the first tulip—this one pearl white, each petal striped with violet and its outer rims traced with loops of black. The outer petals are also rouged lightly with pink in places. Deep within its throat are three golden fronds whose base is black—and looking closer, we discover tiny black lines that reach out to make a delicate cross! We've decided to watch for other crosses hidden in the flowers.

The flowers are always still wet with dew or drops of rain. "And to think," George marvels, "that in each drop exists an invisible, miniature world."

But what really enthralls him is that all this color and beauty comes from the ground. A neighbor who raises baby orchids gave me some one day to bring home. George said then, as we studied their artistry, and again this morning, "How can anyone look at a flower—any flower, from a cultivated orchid to a nameless replica in the yard, and not believe in God? Such design, such colors, such perfumes. And not just to lure insects

—that is functional, it could be accomplished by other methods. But such incredible beauty *has* to be there to please man.

"And the mystery," he pondered, "what we will never understand, is how these multitudes of exquisite colors and designs could all come from the same dark formless earth. The black, gray, brown, almost colorless earth. All this sweetness, all this color from the *ground*. What makes daffodils yellow? Lilacs lavender? Why are roses pink or white or red? And why does each have its own special perfume?

"If I picked up a handful of earth I wouldn't find color in those clods; there would be no fragrance either. It would just smell like *dirt*. What a miracle, that God can create such beauty, such infinite varieties of beauty in every growing thing —from the *ground!*"

Water and Soil

At other times he's observed: "Isn't it remarkable that pure, clear, crystal-clean water comes from the soil? It flows for miles through dirt, earth, mud, yet when it emerges it's clean enough to wash clothes in, sometimes to drink. It shows no traces of its dark journey at all. Of course, it's being filtered all the time, through sand and rock, but even so, it travels for miles through sheer dirt. Dirt that squirms with billions of life forms that you might think were bad if you saw them. Yet the incredible thing is that it spills out of the springs and into the streams and rivers without color or flaw.

"Yes, water can be contaminated by the things that man so carelessly puts into the soil. Chemical wastes, fertilizers, detergents, a lot of things we wish weren't there. But the point is, no matter how much dirt the water flows through, or what it looks like, the water itself usually comes out looking so clear and clean . . ."

The Alphabet of the Earth

His fascination with the earth is endless. "The earth is an alphabet," he declared one day as we drove through the mountains and valleys to Virginia. "It contains everything necessary for man—it simply has to be properly arranged and read. Everything that exists came first from the earth. This car we're riding in, that dress you're wearing, that telephone pole and the wires above it, that farm, that school, that church. Not just the food we eat to keep us alive, not just the water we drink, but the papers we read, the TV we watch, the radios we listen to.

"Music, print, medicines, surgery, dances, plays—no matter how abstract these things may seem, they all come from the earth, right out of the soil. Man simply had to take the elements already there and arrange them in the right order. The most complex machine ever invented, the most beautiful music ever written, the greatest play ever produced would never exist except for the ability to first learn the marvelous alphabet of the earth and combine and arrange and rearrange its letters into their proper form."

"What about the sea?" I asked. "Does it have an alphabet too? We couldn't live without the sea."

"The sea is part of the earth," he said. "Every body of water has to have a floor—mud or sand. The earth supports the sea. And the sea holds some of the most important letters of the alphabet. All man has to do is to figure out how to put them together. We exist because we have learned to read the sea just as we've learned to read the land."

Silent Voices

George has been cleaning his study, the basement, and when he has time, the attic. He has been finding valuable papers—deeds, etc., along with the birth certificate needed for his passport before our trip abroad. He also keeps bringing other surprising discoveries down the ladder from the attic. Jewelry, favorite books, a forgotten coin collection, and to his delight some old recordings, including an album of Grace Moore's songs.

"What a beautiful singer she was," he declared. "And she died so tragically young. In that plane crash, along with the king of Sweden. I'll never forget the newspaper picture of them, their bodies lying apart from the others, looking so lonely lying there . . ." His eyes filled, he turned away to shield the emotion shaking him. "That poor girl, that beautiful woman!"

The next morning I awoke to some of the most heavenly music I ever heard: Grace Moore's rich sweet voice was throbbing from the speakers in the hall. I listened to it during my shower, and afterward did my ballet exercises to her songs, bending and stretching at the banister as I usually do; then dancing and jumping to them on my trampoline.

And George stood at the foot of the staircase looking up, loving the music and me with his whole being, with his eyes . . .

Later we discussed it at breakfast: the treasures that so often lie among the discards in a house. Forgotten, lifeless, unused. Utterly without life or meaning—until someone discovers them again. Rescues them from the long internment, sees and touches them again. Holds the coins in his hands, asks someone to wear the bracelet, takes a record from its album and hears a voice that has been still so long.

"*Ave Maria* . . ." the final song was throbbing from the speaker in the kitchen. Thrilling, heartbreaking . . .

"Especially a voice like that," George said. "Silent all those years. But now it lives again, we can hear it anytime we want to. What a genius Edison was—he revives the voices of the dead."

"And all those other great voices before he came along," I said. "If only he'd been around earlier to preserve them. Think how wonderful it would be to actually hear Lincoln or Washington or Shakespeare—even Jesus!"

"We could use them," George said. "The world hasn't changed that much. If we could hear them today their words would still fit." He pondered. "But thrilling as that would be, I'm afraid we wouldn't listen, any more than people really listened then. Unfortunately, the wisest, most beautiful words ever spoken are seldom appreciated until it's too late."

The Logs

Every fall day at the cottage, George splits logs to carry in for our fireplace. I gather up the kindling, dry branches and sticks for "starters." There is an abundance of wood from our surrounding acres of forest. Enough for the neighbors. One of them has a chain saw to fell the dead trees; we hear its tortured moaning, sometimes the crash. The logs smell fresh and fragrant when first cut. There is a glint of sap in them. And when George saws them into lengths, or splits them with an ax, they are a pale glistening golden color, like the freshly brushed hair of a blond woman.

Carrying the logs in one day, George remarked on their weight. "What makes a log heavy? What makes a tree firm and strong, so that the trunk and the limbs of that tree have weight? The tree comes from the earth, which is hard under our feet, but which is porous. It can easily be dug, or crumbled in our fingers. Have you ever tried to chop a log apart? Using an iron wedge and an ax, it takes a lot of human strength to split it. It is very hard and heavy. How can a tree draw such strength and weight and hardness simply from the ground?"

He lighted the fire, and as the flames sprang to life as if by magic, we watched their delicate dancing, and pondered this phenomenon, so familiar and yet so strange:

Logs are material; fire is immaterial. Yet both come from the same source: the wood from the tree that comes from the ground.

"A fire warms and cheers you," George said. "You can see its colors, you hear it crackling. As if it's trying to speak to you, tell you something. It must have an invisible spirit that makes it dance and glow and sing."

"A fire isn't all comfort," I said. "If you get too close, it will burn you. A fire has the colors of the sun—yellow and red and orange, they are two of a kind, mysterious and powerful. Enjoy them, respect them—they make life possible—but keep your distance, they can burn."

"The sun makes the earth habitable," said George. "Its light, its warmth. And it creates what we know as colors. Not only its own colors across the sky as it rises and sets, but as it shines throughout the day. Without the sunlight we couldn't see *any* colors. When the sun goes down, night falls, the most brilliant flowers fade into darkness; the entire earth is gray and black wherever we look."

"Not indoors," I reminded. "Not with candles and open fires like this, not with electric lights."

"That's right, but the light that makes things grow and gives us colors depends on the sun . . . Which takes us back to the logs. Logs seem so alive sometimes. Logs have so many possible uses. What if logs could talk? One says, 'I'll make a fire, burn brightly a while, and then dissolve into ashes and be gone forever.' Another says, 'I'll make a cradle, a chair, a church, a house.' Or 'I'll be turned into wheels to turn a mill for water, or to carry wagons across the prairie.'"

"No, they wouldn't," I laughed. "Not today, not now."

"Don't be so literal. My logs have imagination. My logs can be anything they want. Some say, 'I'll be a railroad tie, or I'll become a canoe, I could be a ship like Columbus sailed. Or maybe just a lot of little toothpicks. But I'll be useful, because I too was once part of a tree, a log!' "

"Don't forget paper," I said. "That's where most logs wind up."

"Yes, a lot of them could boast, 'I'll be ground up at the mill and turned into books and magazines and newspapers that keep people informed; or paper for people like Marjorie Holmes to write on in the first place; or packages, or grocery sacks. But whatever we become, the ultimate end for all of us will be like those logs in the fireplace. We will decay or be burned and vanish into ashes.'

"And so," George concluded, "all experience the same fate in the end: to go back into the earth where other trees are growing, nourished by the earth and drawn from the earth by the sun's light. To grow strong and hard for somebody's house or church or newspaper . . . or just to get people like *us* into discussions like *this* in front of a fireplace!"

Thoughts on a Windy Day

A cold windy morning at the cottage. The gray lake is roaring and raging, hurling great white-capped waves against the shore. All night we could hear it, like a thousand locomotives pounding by. At bedtime, as the fire was dying, we opened the door and stood listening and looking, and gradually through the darkness the long white curling mouths of the waves were defined. It was vaguely ominous and yet pleasant, making us feel snug in our little house high on the cliffs, warmed by the electric blanket and the carpeting and the last red coals of the fire.

By daylight the sounds and spectacle no longer threaten. We breakfast, looking out on it through the glass. Before, only glimpsed through foliage, the lake is now spread out for our view. Our friend the lake! It has clambered up over the beach where we walked only yesterday. It has swept away the sand. It leaps and foams and hurls itself against the hills. Yet it is still our friend, in a new and mighty mood.

The wind is whipping the trees. The golden leaves are spilling down. The bushes are tossing and bowing, a kind of mad merry roundelay. Even the grasses and ivy are dancing, their leaves silver-green along the ground. Sunlight is seeping across the sky, feeling its way with gilding fingers, illuminating the rim of the clouds. Gray, almost as gray as the water, the clouds have roofed the sky. Now they are breaking, shifting, a few of them turning white. White as the long curling hair of the waves. White as the gulls that challenge the wind, soaring alone, or in pairs, or in floating, flapping crowds.

George has built a merry fire and poured more hot coffee and read to me, and we have had one of our good long talks about many things. Among them, another discussion about getting over hurt, which has given me new insight. At least about George himself:

He speaks of the "mosaics of the mind." "In the mind we store all sorts of pictures, landscapes, beautiful scenes, places we have enjoyed. But also we have scenes of misery, futility, and pain. It is all there, painted or photographed on the mind forever; pictures that rise up unexpectedly, hold our attention for a few seconds or longer, then disappear, while others take their place. We are the constant spectator-participant, observing them, often with pleasure, but again with anguish. Many times we are simply bewildered by their appearance, and if they are painful, wanting them to go away. Again we deliberately play host to them, reviewing the same ones over and over, even when they hurt."

How strange, this vast continuing mosaic, George and I agree. Bits and pieces of dialogue, visual images of people we have known in the past or are about to see, along with bigger scenes . . . It is said we can pick and choose what we will pay attention to in our minds. George insists this is true; that if you don't like something you can simply turn the channel and switch to something else.

"Yet this is not so easy for people like me," I protest. The mind often persists in what it is determined we will see. "For instance, the times when I *still* lie awake at night, longing for sleep, yet absolute hostage to tormenting thoughts. Things I want to forget."

"You don't need to let them in," George insists. "They are like people in a waiting room, enemies you don't want to see and don't have to, if you are strong. Don't open the door to them; only *you* can let them in."

He insists that what is past is past. It needn't come back to haunt us. All that matters is now, today. And I agree. Yet it isn't that simple. We are the *products* of our past. And once a thing has happened it is imprinted forever on the mind. A part of that mosaic with a tape recording attached, able to play itself out for us over and over, however we try to resist. True, we sometimes invite these hurtful things, like a sore tooth we can't help biting. But just as often the repeat performance comes unbidden, the voices won't stop, the pictures won't vanish, however we try to shut them out.

"It's easy enough to say lock the door, don't let those people in the waiting room in. But what if they find another entrance, slip through another door, a window, down the chimney? You look up from your desk or your bed in the darkness and there they are!"

Wise as George's counsel is, and much as I value it—it has finally dawned on me: He simply doesn't *have* this problem. He is one of those rare people who seem to attract good fortune. But mainly, he has a positive talent for happiness *and a very selective memory*. To his honest recollection, his childhood was completely happy, his parents wonderful, his mother, particularly, a saint. He never quarreled with his brothers or his sister —or anybody that he can remember. Certainly not his wife. "Not once in all those years!" he believes. And there were few, if any problems, even with their children . . . He doesn't hold grudges. If wronged in any way, even now, he may fume a while, but is able to dismiss it as not worth worrying about. He doesn't remember hurts or slights, because—actually, I think— people have always enjoyed and respected him, and there have been so few. And he has this marvelous capacity to forget unpleasant things. He honestly remembers (or his mind has chosen to remember) only the beautiful perfection of the past.

"What do *you* think about when you can't sleep?" I have asked him.

"How happy I am," he says. "This comfortable bed, you beside me, all I have to be thankful for. Oh, sometimes—should I get the lawn mower fixed? Don't forget to order something, call the insurance man. Nothing serious. I actually enjoy being awake at night sometimes, just counting blessings, thanking God for my life."

I believe some people are born like that. Attracting good things to them by their sheer radiance of spirit. Not actually immune to misery and conflict, but able to deal with it when it comes, and then go on as cheerfully as before, the whole experience erased or blessedly transformed in the mosaics of their mind.

What a wonderful way to be! That is surely the best gift of all.

CHAPTER FOURTEEN

Love Songs

George is the most tender, romantic, funny, and fascinating man I've ever met. The finest character; and with only a couple of exceptions (which are in themselves ridiculous and almost entrancing—mainly his powers of exaggeration, his irresistible talent for hyperbole), the most honest. There is no guile in him; he has no wish to hurt, actually thinks himself incapable of hurting!

Even the things he told me about his youth, things that struck such depths of anguish in me I was appalled, not realizing I could feel such pain—at least this kind of pain. Even these were offered up in innocence and trust, wanting "to make a clean breast of everything." He *was* innocent, somehow, despite the many women he had loved. Loved just because they were women, tender and exciting and somehow noble, like his mother, whom he worshipped. He had always preferred feminine company to that of males—rough, foulmouthed, girl-mocking boys. He never swore or talked about sex, despite his joy in it. He simply loved women and women loved him.

Shocking though the details if I imagined them (and I did), the whole drama of his youthful sexploits had something fresh and spirited and earthy about it, with absolutely no sense of guilt or alarm. Even his foreign-born parents considered this perfectly natural—in some ways to be admired.

Yet now, he insisted, always, always: "Sex meant nothing, absolutely nothing. Not compared to what I have with you. Put them all together, every single sexual experience, not *once* did I ever have the pleasure that I have had with you. Not *one* meant what you do to me, or even approached it. The entire total would not begin to equal it. What you and I have, what we have shared, is the greatest love of my life. In even the short time we have known each other, I have experienced more joyous, genuine love than in the entire span of my life."

This was, of course, hyperbole. His zeal, his passion for language excesses. Yet I know he was straining to convince me because he quite sincerely believes this now. And because he believes this so ardently, somehow it makes it so. Even all the hyperbole he had used in writing passionate love notes to his first wife, all the fervent and excessive things he said to her, the one he had married and been true to so long . . . as they had been valid for that lucky woman then, they are valid now for me.

He does love me with the same blind overwhelming zeal. Or perhaps, if possible, in an even more dramatic and significant way.

And there was this to be said for his youthful affairs: He had gotten them out of his system, "sowed his wild oats." To him marriage meant total commitment. Despite the many opportunities of his profession, his continuing good looks and charm, the women who still threw themselves at him, he was never really tempted. In that one respect he takes great pride: He was completely honorable. He would not even flirt . . . He described incidents. One, a little nurse, very beautiful, who came to him to confess she had fallen desperately in love with him. " 'Honey, that's very flattering,' I told her. 'But I can't, I wouldn't. I'm married, I have a little boy.' . . . My children could never say that about me," he declared. "Never their daddy, not once their daddy."

So he had settled down and become happy, completely happy, satisfied, successful, not ambitious, for he had no real wish to make money, yet he prospered anyway. His only desire was to please his wife, and sincerely to help his patients. And all the people whose lives he touched have adored him, clung to him dependently like children. He was courageous and unselfish, he served them, worried about them, counseled them, prayed for every one of them, wept for them, and cheered them up with his antics and jokes. His laughter and his singing.

All the patients I've met speak of it. His laughter and his beautiful singing. "You could hear it every time you came into the office. Sometimes you could hear it clear across the street where he was making a house call. It was just beautiful, he healed you with laughter and his beautiful songs. He especially liked to sing to the children. I was just a little girl when my mother first brought me to him, and he sang to me, I'll never forget."

The nurses with whom he once worked in the hospital have told me: "He was our favorite doctor. We knew the minute he walked in, and we all got so excited. Dr. Schmieler was coming, we could hear him singing!" And a very old surgeon he often assisted: "I've never known a man with such a happy heart. George was always singing, even in the operating room."

And now he sings to me. He sings in the car as we drive, sings at his jobs around the house. And he's established a ritual: Every morning as I shower, and every night as I take my bath, he appears with a book of old love songs and sings to me again, to start and finish the day . . .

Strange wonderful George.

I love him, how I love him. For he is the most tender, romantic, funny, and fascinating man I ever met. And to think —of all the women he could have had this second time around, he chose *me*.

Affection

George was romantic and affectionate from childhood. Even as a little boy, he tells me, he had a sense of awe and respect for women. Not merely his mother, whom he worshipped, but womanhood itself.

He describes how among his toys when he was about three or four there was a mechanical couple who would dance when the toy was wound up. He would gaze in fascination at the figure of the tall handsome man holding the beautiful woman as they glided, even jerkily, about the floor . . . As a little boy in school, he retained this awed pleasure in the little girls. He doesn't remember ever teasing them or chasing them, the way some kids do, but rather he took joy in observing them, their ribbons and sashes and pretty dresses.

There was one in particular, Eileen Russell, whom he adored for years. She sat in front of him in first grade. He tells a story which I think very touching—how he trudged off alone and up the steps on his first day of school, excited but bewildered, especially when the teacher handed out papers and told them to write their names. His parents were German immigrants who'd never taught him the alphabet, let alone how to write his name. "So I leaned over the seat where this girl, Eileen Russell, was sitting, and carefully copied what she was putting down." He laughs. "To the teacher's surprise, she had *two* Eileen Russells in the first grade that day."

Another story that wrings my heart: That dear little boy climbed a fence one day to pick a peach for his mother. He was so proud of it, he could hardly wait to surprise her. But he'd torn his new pants on the fence, and his father gave him a licking.

He dreamed about Eileen Russell all through school, although they never dated. He also fell madly in love with one of his teachers. "Miss Sunshine—that was really her name. She usually wore crisp white blouses and simple blue skirts, and she smelled so clean. I cried when we found out she was getting married. I honestly thought she might wait for me."

He was very handsome as a child, with his intensely blue eyes and dark curly hair (as he remains to this day). And, his brothers and his sister tell me, he was much sought after by the girls. Oddly, he never thought he was good-looking, and sometimes made angry faces at himself in the mirror. He was also shy about his looks and physical prowess as an athlete at Pitt and lifeguard at the swimming pool. He often crossed the street or ducked up an alley to avoid attention when he saw people approaching.

He had many girls, of course, some of them married women who hung around the pool. Their advances were flattering. He had few qualms, they were all so bored and frustrated, so delighted with his company . . . And there were others.

But once married himself, during his senior year at medical school, he was utterly devoted to his wife. In all their years together he never stopped courting her, treating her like the queen of his existence. And I know he will never stop courting me. Our life is still a twenty-four-hour-a-day honeymoon.

Back in Washington, D.C., before our marriage, Frank Ball, my longtime friend and family lawyer, told me as he was making up our prenuptial agreement: "If that guy doesn't tell you three times a day how lucky he is, I'm going to hit him between the eyes!"

When I reported this to George, he regarded me with honest surprise and said, *"Only three times?"*

Actually, George says "I love you" dozens of times a day. They are his first words in the morning, his last at night. I believe I heard them more in our first year than in the previous thirty or forty of my life. And I respond. They are a part of our continuing dialogue, as natural to both of us as breathing. Nor have they lost their significance through repetition; instead they have grown.

"You wouldn't drink just one glass of water a day," George reasons, "or eat only one meal. The body has to be nourished often, and so does love. If you neglect your body, if you don't feed it enough or give it enough to drink, it will go hungry and thirsty. It can even die. That's the way it is with love. It needs those three little words to keep it going. The more it hears them, the happier it will be; it needs them even to stay alive."

Sometimes George will pause just to look at me, hold my arms, and state seriously, like an important pronouncement, "I *love* you, Marjorie."

It is important to him to declare what we both know. He

has this need for commitment and confirmation. And I respond in kind, enhancing the bond between us . . .

"If only more people would do this," I told George one day. "I honestly think there would be fewer divorces. At least there would be a lot more happy wives."

He agreed. "That's what I tell my patients. Not just wives. Men too. A lot of men crave affection, but don't know how to show it. That makes the wife think he doesn't care, and both of them are miserable. I see it all the time at the office. It's why a lot of people are sick. They're starving for love, and come to me for medicine, when what they need is those three little words *I love you.* 'They're cheaper than pills,' I advise. 'Say them! Don't wait till the poor guy is dying, or your wife is having a breakdown.' I sometimes put it on my prescription: 'Rx: LOTS OF LOVE. Sig.: Take on waking, several times a day, and always at bedtime' "

"You're kidding."

"I am not." George produced a pad and scribbled to demonstrate. "It doesn't always work, but they get a laugh out of it. At least it's a reminder. One patient stuck it on the bathroom mirror where her husband would see it."

"How did he take it?"

"I think it helped a little, she seems happier, doesn't complain so much. But then, unfortunately you can't change some people."

I shook my head, amused. Strange wonderful George. "Unfortunately, the trouble is, God didn't make enough people like *you.*"

Loving the World Around Us

His loving nature spills over into the world around us. He loves our dogs and tells them so. I will hear him saying gently to our golden Lab or the poodle, "I love you, Ben. I love you, Tanjy." He says it to the big gray cat that has adopted us. Holding it against his chest, cradling and caressing it, he murmurs to it words of affection, and the cat replies in kind, not only purring but emitting wordlike sounds and little moans. "He actually cries," George says. "I've seen the tears. And he drools, while his claws dig into my shoulder with little movements, as if trying to tell me he loves me."

This I have seen.

George also crouches to caress the tame squirrels in a park, talks to fish and birds, and refuses to hurt a living thing. Although not a vegetarian, he hates the very idea of hunting and fishing. Once, seeing a fish gasping and floundering as if dying in the water, he knelt to comfort it. I have seen him pray for little dead birds in a parking lot, then find a stick or tool to dig a little grave.

The family's previous dogs are buried all over the yard, both in McMurray and at Lake Erie. The loss of each one was a personal tragedy, with tearful services over every grave. George still remembers each pet vividly; he chokes up when describing their characteristics, and what happened to them. "Missy— what a lady. And Bobo and Gigi, parents of our poodles—how we loved those dogs. And Rags—he came hobbling to our door, starved and dirty, cruelly beaten, so bad he was almost dead. We nursed him back to health, and he was one of the liveliest dogs we ever had. But he ran into the street one day and got killed."

I tell a few stories of my own—about Spooky, the faithful black Labrador who was almost a nanny to the children. About Belle, the Dalmatian who was hit by a boat while chasing water-skiers and almost lost her leg. "The doctor said it was either put her to sleep or amputate. But I asked people who read my newspaper column to pray for her, and she got well! She lived five more years."

He listens with his heart in his eyes. When he prays for his dogs, past and present, Belle and Spooky get equal time. This is one of the bonuses of a good marriage later in life. Two people with a rich fund of experiences to exchange. Never mind that these experiences happened with somebody else. They are ours now to share through words. And to have this mutual love for God's creatures enhances our own.

After Sex, What?

"Life is designed in sequence," George says. "There is a law of progression. You must have the seed before the stem, the bud before the flower. A meal that starts with dessert is not really pleasant, you need to start with soup or salad and work up to it through the courses. A mystery story isn't worth reading if you've insisted on reading the climax first and already know who-done-it. Even Christmas and birthday presents are more enticing if you first have to unwrap the package.

"The mystery, glamour, anticipation of sex is surely the sweetest thing in life. The most exciting. Giving it to kids too early, without any secrets, is cruel. It's robbing them of the suspense, the aura. Saturating the media with it—seeing it every day even in advertising—watching actors having sex on the screen—treating it as an everyday thing for everybody destroys the illusion so precious to lovers: the belief that they are special. That this is magical and different, their love is unique, that nobody ever loved like this before."

Prescription for Counting Sheep

George is whimsical and tender in so many little ways. Even when writing prescriptions or dispensing medicine. This is what he wrote on an envelope of sleeping pills for my daughter in Virginia, whose two little boys have a new pet lamb named Marvin:

To our very precious Melanie for a restful, soothing sleep. Enough until Christmas.

Directions: With milk if desired. Take only if sleep does not come after watching Marvin jump over a 6 ft. fence at least 48 times . . .

This reminds me of something else he does when he takes his own afternoon nap. (So important ever since his cancer operation.) When I tiptoe into the bedroom I find him asleep cuddling something I've worn—usually a blouse or a nightie. He has never told me this, and I wouldn't have known—he always puts it back in the drawer. And for some reason, I've never said anything about it; but it touches my heart and makes me smile. It is *so—George*. Simple, natural, childlike—loving just because he can't help it, and expressing it in his own tender and honest way.

Love Must Be Used

George says, "Love is like an electric light. Or the blood in your body. All three must be used.

"An electric light not being used does no good. You can sit beside an unlit lamp and be in darkness forever. The lamp has to be plugged in, and you have to turn on the switch. Plugs are necessary all over the house, energy is stored in them. But unless it flows, you have no heat, no light, no warmth. And it must come from the sources—the wires that bring it into the house. And beyond that, the plant where the energy is actually produced. That energy must *circulate*.

"Blood must circulate too. A cup of blood has everything to sustain life, but it's no good unless it's *going* someplace. In a body, being used. The heart must pump it through 165,000 miles of blood vessels every day. Except in a blood bank, it can't be stored.

"And you can't store love," he declared. "Love has to be activated too, pumped, circulated, used. Love must flow. I have to hold you, tell you I love you. And that love has to be returned. Love can get discouraged and die unless it flows back.

"That's what's so great about us," he told me. "You respond. I can feel your love day and night, wherever we are. It's a part of me now, your own love flowing back."

Reading at Breakfast

We breakfast in our sunny kitchen (or at Lake Erie on the deck), with one eye on a news program, the other on our morning papers. George has already embellished their headlines with his merry greetings, and scanned their contents, picking out stories he doesn't want me to miss. And as we read we can't help interrupting each other with "Listen to this!" Especially George; his insatiable curiosity and fervent interest in almost anything in print make it harder for him to resist. Sometimes when I'm absorbed, I can feel him quivering, practically squirming, like an eager little kid trying to hold back.

"Would you mind if I read this to you?"

I sigh and smile. "No, of course not, go ahead."

For a few minutes I'm entertained by that vibrant voice sharing the piece, then launching his spirited opinion, and asking for mine.

George is also a true word hound. He keeps a huge dictionary on the table, which he lugs to Lake Erie with us, and would have taken along on our travels if I let him. On the shelves beside us are several editions of the Bible; a complete, if dated, set of *The World Books* to be consulted; a pile of magazines, joke books, and songbooks. But the real treasure of our breakfast table sits on the floor between us: George's canvas bag stuffed with today's sources for our usual read-aloud sessions.

He often reads from a very old book, which he discovered in college, when he was searching for answers: *What Science Knows About Life,* by Dr. Heinz Woltereck. George considers it a very important influence in shaping his own philosophy. After reading a portion of it to me one morning, he enlarged on the author's statement: that man has speculated about the male-female attraction from the beginning of time. The polarity of the male and the female, resulting in life, and that nature has a whole bag of tricks to bring this about.

George said, "Unconsciously we are practicing this bag of tricks all the time. When I met you—the courting, my taking you to dinner, the music, the flowers, the poetry I read to you— I would not think of doing that, reading poetry or singing, to another man. It was all designed by instinct or subterranean desires that are as much psychic as physical, to get you on that balcony and kiss you—the first step in eventually coming together, becoming one."

The Test of True Love

George says, "How does anybody know he's really in love and is marrying the right person? Somebody you're sure you want to be with the rest of your life? Nobody can tell you—marriage is such a mystery, every marriage is unique. You can read every marriage manual ever written and not find out. People just *are* the way they are, and sometimes it's magic, the way it is for us. And sometimes it's nothing special, and sometimes it's hell."

George paused to consider. "But it's strange—people can be so different from each other. Carolyn and I were extremely happy, as you know, but she was nothing like you, and not even very much like me. She was more reserved, aloof, she had to repress *me*. But she was perfect for me all those years— until she died. She worshipped me and I worshipped her, it's as simple as that. Neither of us ever wanted anybody else.

"But now I'm *sublimely* happy because you and I are so much *alike*. In some ways we're practically identical twins, our spirits recognized each other from the moment we met. I'm passionately in love with you as *the one person in the world I'd rather be with*." He came to attention, pleased with the thought: "Hey, I think that's it! That must be the answer—the real test of love: Would you rather be with this person than anyone else in the world? The most famous or beautiful, your best friend, your mother or your father or your child? Are you happier, more comfortable, more delighted, more contented with this person you love? If you are, then you have found your other half!

"It must be the opposite sex," George went on, "the sex connection. But when you are united in love, then it is no longer the *opposite* sex, but the *complementary* sex, the one who makes you whole . . . When you have that, you have everything, you are complete as a person, you can lick the world.

"The tragedy is—and I think it's far worse for couples who *have* this wonderful union—when there is quarreling and contending. Lashing out at the person you're supposed to love. Angry words that tear each other apart—hurt so terribly one of you may even threaten to leave. Sometimes this actually happens, and the suffering is worse because you did have something so rare and precious. When two people become truly one, you can't hurt the other half of *you* without hurting *yourself*."

Love Must Be Fed

In another discussion, George spoke again about the importance of nurturing love: "We need food every day to nourish our bodies. Fruits and vegetables, bread and milk and beans. We need fats and starches and proteins. We need minerals, we need vitamins, we need water. The heart couldn't beat without them, we couldn't breathe, our blood wouldn't flow. We couldn't do our work, or carry a child, or hug the person we love. But we need love food too. We need to be hugged back. We need the kiss on our lips, the sound of a voice saying tender words to us.

"Love is like a flower. We need its perfume, its beauty. It's not insubstantial, it too nourishes us, feeds the hungry soul, so that the life of the body is worth having . . . What a pity if a garden raises carrots, cabbages, and potatoes, but doesn't have a flower."

Why Do We Need Each Other?

There is a mystery I've wondered about for years: Why do most of us have this intense need for human companionship—especially when enjoying something? Why is a view more beautiful, the smell of flowers and woods and waves more sweet when they can be shared with someone else, hopefully someone you care about?

I asked George about this one day. "Why do you nearly die of loneliness, even after someone you've taken for granted disappears?" I described its first cruel shock for me when I was about nine years old. "My sister Gwen and I were vacationing on an uncle's farm. I was enchanted, but she was so bored and homesick our father had to come get her. I remember waving goodbye and running back to hunt the eggs, and jump in the haymow, and try to climb the windmill—only it wasn't fun anymore! The bottom had dropped out of my world, I missed her so much I couldn't stand it. I moped around until he had to come back for *me*."

I told George how, as a grown woman alone in New York, I lucked into a single orchestra seat during the opening of *Oklahoma!* "It was glorious! I wanted to laugh and sing and hug somebody, but there wasn't anybody—I felt deprived, almost bereft . . . And later, six weeks in Europe by myself, a misery beyond describing. Why? Why? I was doing interesting research and sightseeing. Don't these same eyes see the 'Mona Lisa,' whether somebody's with me or not? Don't my same senses respond to the highlands of Scotland or Westminster Abbey? *Why isn't your own company sufficient?*"

Before he could answer, I admitted, "It is, sometimes it is. There are times when we all need to escape—just withdraw from other people for a while, just be alone. I know I certainly do. But most of the time it really takes *two* to make any beautiful experience whole. Why two?" I asked. "Why always two?"

And George said, "Because it takes two to make you in the first place. A mother and a father to create a human being.

Every person on this earth came from the union of two. That's why you hunger so constantly for someone else when you're forced to be alone. You are incomplete alone, you are simply a *half,* striving to find the other half so you can be one. And that other half, for true and complete happiness, must be your mate. Someone of the opposite sex to join with you even in companionship, knowing that if you came together the two of you could create another *one.* It's part of the whole chain of life, this deep desire not only to procreate but to be one of the two who *could.* It may be unconscious, but it's there."

George paused. "Yes, you can enjoy a walk or a nice dinner or just a few uninterrupted hours by yourself. Or you can enjoy the play or walk or dinner or a trip with a friend—another man, another woman. But for it to be most significant it has to be with someone of the opposite sex. Especially if the person you're with responds to the same things that move you. And if you're deeply in love, as we are, there is no joy on earth to compare with it."

Lake Moods

Some days the waves come swaggering in, tossing up white fountains against the rocks and pounding the shore in rhythms. They are like a mighty army marching to insistent drums.

But again, as last night when we were finishing dinner on the deck, they come stealing quietly in as if reluctant to disturb us. The water undulates steadily, gracefully, like dancers on silken slippers trained to move soundlessly onstage, breathing softly, barely whispering, swaying to some lovely music scarcely heard.

"What a contrast," I said to George. "All day the waves have been acting like a crowd of noisy soldiers beating at our door. But now look—they've changed completely, the invaders have vanished, they're like a ballet instead."

Listening, we could hear the faint swishing of the dancers' feet as they came gracefully toward us in the falling sun.

George grinned. "Maybe they're trying to soothe us, maybe they're just being charming to make amends."

And gazing at it, we both remarked at the constantly changing spectacle of the lake. Of how we see something new here almost every day. There is a consistency about it, like a good relationship, yet it is never just the same way twice.

"It's good to keep coming back to the same lake," George said. "After a while it becomes *your* lake. A part of your own life. If you kept visiting other lakes all the time you could never develop this sense of union, this constancy. It's like being married to the same person," he declared. "You know that person is there in all his or her moods. Sometimes sunny, sometimes cloudy, even angry and raging—the way everybody is sometimes. But you make allowances, you are comforted by the knowledge of constancy and permanence.

"And you keep finding something beautiful and funny and delightful and fresh about that person, if you love her, no matter how often you see her or how quickly her moods can change. There is something wonderfully comforting about all this—the lake out there or a marriage like ours."

You Are Married

George and I had been talking about wanting to love God the way the Bible tells us to, trying to achieve the kind of emotional ecstasy the saints did, or that some Christians seem to achieve. But a little book he had found among his things, years old, written by a priest, stated it wasn't necessary to have this emotional manifestation. It's enough just to believe and serve God by doing what he would want us to. That too is a way to love him, certainly a better way than to weep with emotion and then go out and hurt someone, to be petty, selfish, mean . . . The main thing is the foundation, the deep knowledge that we are one with God, he is in us and for us all the time. *That* is loving him, even if we don't consciously think of it all the time.

This led George to remember a former neighbor and friend. "Reverend Cameron was his name. A large patriarchal man. He had big hands and strong arms. When he put his arm across your shoulders you felt reassured, safe. He had steel-blue eyes and dark heavy brows, a rugged face. His hair was thick and full, the color of pewter. There was something fine and strong and distinguished and yet down-to-earth about him. He had a deep male voice.

"He made me realize it is the same thing in marriage. He would say, 'Always remember this—*you are married*. That is the foundation, an ever-present fact, the commitment. Despite the emotional storms, the differences, the ups and downs, you love your wife and she loves you. The two of you are one. Committed. *You are married.*'

"It sounds simple, but the way he said it made it profound. And now"—George smiled and squeezed my hand—"that is the way it is with *you*. When I married you, you became one with me. We belong to each other, we have a foundation that nothing can really disturb or take away from us. Our love for each other is like our love for God. Even if we don't talk about it all the time or think about it all the time. We don't have to. It is there, a union, a bond, a foundation that is the most important, most precious thing in life."

Our Life Together

George says, "There is nothing in life so fulfilling as to be able to wake up with the person you love. And to know you are going to share the experiences of the day as one. To enjoy the same things, the sky, the birds, a good book, the same songs. This is so beautiful, so utterly satisfying, because the other one adds another dimension to your own enjoyment. Like when you and I were watching the dancer—what was his name, Baryshnikov? Or that singer that thrilled us both so much—we could thrill to her voice, we felt one with it, we practically vibrated to it together, exulting in the heights and depths she reached. It's not sexual, this feeling, but it is very close to it. It is another plane of sexuality, really, when a man and woman can come together in another emotional experience.

"And then to have all this when you have already lived so much of your life. When you're older you don't have to worry about sexual precautions anymore, or interruptions from the children—or worries *about* the children. At least you don't have to keep on working to get them through college, or married and on their own. And if you're financially secure, you're free to travel, go to the places you've always enjoyed, like Carolyn and I always went to Florida and on those cruises every year. But also new places you can discover together. Brand-new, like my first trip abroad with you. Germany and Greece—swimming in the Mediterranean, that cruise to the Grecian isles. I'll never forget riding horseback up the steep cliff to Santorini—it was Paradise! And we can go back, we can go to England, Scotland, around the world. Oh, we are so lucky. If you are in good health and have the right companion these are the very best years of all!"

We were having coffee on the deck at our cottage that evening. I joined in, and we both spoke of the futility of giving over so completely to grief after losing a mate.

"I was the worst example," George acknowledged. "I couldn't help it—some people can't. I was devastated. My heart was frozen—like Lake Erie in winter, utterly without feeling. I didn't *want* anything or anybody—I was cold, frozen, an absolute zombie, without life or warmth, like that lake. Remember when it was all ice? A solid sheet of ice and it affected the atmosphere; ice makes the air cold, makes other people cold. So I was like that, I affected others too, they could feel it, they too were depressed and cold.

"But the minute I saw you it was all over, as I've told you. The sun came out, everything melted! Well, no, not the exact minute, because I was so hopeful. I was a little crazy, I must have thought I'd find . . ."

"Yes, yes, I know," I interrupted. "Please don't tell me again—for some reason that still hurts, George."

"It shouldn't," he insisted. "Sure, you were different. So different in every way—face and figure and personality, everything—I was staggered. But then suddenly something burst inside me, like a great blast of sunshine. Something bright and new. I was *glad,* I forgot what I was looking for! I wanted *you.*

You flooded me with light and life and joy. The terrible cold was over, miraculously all those months of terrible suffering and cold vanished forever. I was alive and warm again, and have been ever since. You have been my resurrection. You have given me life and joy—more, far more than I ever had before."

We talked a long time about all this, and how lucky we were to have found each other when we did, at the time George was actually suicidal. "I can't bear to think of what I almost missed!" he said.

If only we could encourage other people not to give up to grief too long, we agreed. Make them realize there *could* be a bright new tomorrow dawning after the long dark days and nights. It doesn't seem possible, but it is—at least for the lucky few . . . "If only there were enough *right* companions to go around," I said. "Ah, there's the hitch. If only all of them could find each other."

Yet both of us have known a number of very happy older couples who had found their new mates after being widowed, often without too much delay. Not that anybody should rush into marriage just to replace somebody else. We've also known people whose second marriages were mistakes. But if you are lucky enough to be sent some bright new love whose character you admire, whose culture is compatible with yours, and whose company is truly a joy, don't wait too long. As George said when we first met: "We haven't got that much time!"

CHAPTER FIFTEEN

The Lovely Lake

Trains

It's June now at Lake Erie, where George always takes the whole month off to enjoy it. And oh, what a precious gift of extra time. Everything about being here seems more beautiful, exciting, to be savored. Even the sound of a train in the night, throbbing through the darkness, its whistle calling faintly, like a lonely voice hallooing as it passes on its journey—"Whoooo, whooo?"—as if it really longs to know. But our first night it seems to be exclaiming, "Hooooray, hoooray, it's Youooo, it's Youoooo!" I woke George up to listen—and he agreed.

Waking to a train on a summer Lake Erie morning is like hearing a distant orchestra playing—the low rhythmic drumbeat, the dimly sensed melody, the music of wheels and whistles blending with the chirping of birds in the trees outside our window, and the tireless soothing rhythms of the waves. It brings back memories of the waves and the trains of my own childhood, and my mother's singing out James Russell Lowell's "And what is so rare as a day in June? Then, if ever, come perfect days . . ."

This is such a day as we carry cups of George's fragrant coffee along through the woods and down the pathway for our early swim. Taking one last sip, we set our cups on a rock and wade in, hand in hand. The water is choppy, strong, so high it surges across the sand and stones to splash at our feet. The waves are fighters, wet-muscled wrestlers, reaching out before you can take their measure, wallow in them, swim through them or beside them, or turn on your back and let them heave you up and down, a liquid hammock, or maneuver you side-wise along their silvery floors.

The sky is blue above our uplifted faces, white clouds coasting, and a layer of others, gunmetal gray. Invigorated, we wade out, back into the wind, and pick our way along the rocks to the place where the stream in the glen makes its tiny water-fall. Then up the path, fragrant with pine and ferns and name-less little wildflowers—purple spikes and bells and the froth of white Queen Anne's lace—which George pauses to pick for his usual bouquet.

After breakfast and dishes and hanging out of wet things, we carry more coffee to the deck, along with another slice of kolacky, the poppy-seed roll like George's mother used to make for them as children, and a copy of *Walden* George found on the cottage shelves. A worn copy, still marked with his pencil. He begins to read aloud from this book we both had read years ago; we rediscover its treasures together.

How happy we are. The emotions that unite us never seem to dim, they radiate all around us, like the sun on the leaves or the water. Sparkling. We feel so at home with each other, yet so refreshed by the other, stimulated, full of rejoicing and constant wonder.

The Rabbit

Bouquets of wildflowers and lilacs were all over the cottage this morning, including the bathroom . . .

"I had a wonderful time getting them," George beamed. "I walked a little farther than usual, down the road and into our

woods. And there beside the path I made the acquaintance of a
dear middle-sized rabbit, standing there so still I thought for a
moment he might be a statue. But I spoke to him anyway,
'Good morning, don't be afraid, I won't hurt you.' And he
didn't respond, just stood there, with his tall pointed ears erect
as an antenna and his almond eyes staring back without expression.

"Gee, maybe he's dead, I thought. Maybe he just died
standing up! But I knew he wasn't, I sensed his aliveness, and so
I spoke to him again, quietly, knowing he couldn't answer,
didn't even understand, but the God part in him understood the
God in me, and it was delightful. 'Goodbye,' I told him, 'I love
you.'

"Then, as if that wasn't enough, I walked on, and in front
of me was a tree alive with birds, like a big condominium or
convention center, swarming with these tiny little yellow birds
chirping and trilling, then suddenly exploding into flight. Ten,
fifty, hundreds, shooting up suddenly like a fountain, a spray,
like a baptism of little golden birds, giving me a blessing for the
day."

Shared Memories

As I've said, there is an ancient record player here, and a vast
stock of old familiar albums. Big bands, jazz and blues and
Dixieland. Paul Whiteman, Duke Ellington, Tommy Dorsey,
the Ink Spots, the Andrews Sisters, Vincent Lopez, Guy
Lombardo, Benny Goodman, Lawrence Welk—dozens more.
And George's adored personal friend, Lang Thompson, who
was so popular, especially in Pittsburgh before the war. I don't
remember him, but the rest are old friends of mine as well.

It's fun to share them. George plays some of them every
few days, and holds out his arms for a dance. Both of us remembering the emotions they evoked when we were young. Yet
how can anyone be younger than we are now—feeling the same
delicious joy in dancing, singing, or just enjoying the music as
we move about the house?

"Do you remember how it was?" George sometimes asks. "Holding somebody close, feeling romantic and full of excitement and dreams. It's still like that for us, only it's better now. We have the same feelings of sexual romantic joy, but we have realized most of our dreams. We have earned the right to be happy.

"All those other people have disappeared, melted away into our past, stopped being important to us. Today if we met some of them we wouldn't even know them. Yet here we are, two people of the same era who lived so long ago so far apart. We had to come almost to the end of the road before we found each other. Yet somehow, despite all the detours and stop signs and barriers, we did find each other as we were meant to, and it's the grandest event of our lives."

Our conversations often go like that, with me chiming in, expressing some of the same thoughts. The most cogent theme of this particular conversation—how lucky we feel to be of the same generation, almost the same age.

There are so many things we don't have to explain. We respond to the same stimuli because it is so familiar to us both. Enhanced by the fact that we are so much alike in our tastes, especially our fascination with words and ideas. And our intense love and wonder before life itself. The endless mystery and marvel of nature. Of everything about us in this incredible world, large or small.

We are both so grateful for it. If only it could last forever. We can't imagine life without each other anymore.

Lake Erie Summers

June went too fast—summers here drift away on swift but silent wings; before you realize it another month has passed. It's now July, but we have long weekends here, and make the most of every precious day, each with its own surprises.

Yesterday morning, to our amazement, we found the usually rocky beach miraculously transformed, swept clean. As if a giant broom had risen up in the night to sweep away its boulders, shale, and fallen trees and leave this unexpected gift—a long smooth stretch of sand. "It's hard to believe," George exclaimed. "This is like the good old days! Let's hope it lasts."

But lo, this morning our hopes were dashed. Not only more rocks but more logs and driftwood had been deposited for us to clamber over, while the waves rolled and foamed at our feet. "The lake giveth and the lake taketh away," George laughed.

Nonetheless, we enjoyed the water, quite warm though the air was cold. Ben eagerly chased the sticks we threw in, Tanjy making his usual terrific racket . . .

I love writing here. It's much easier now that I've equipped the little office space available beside the water. Duplicate desk, typewriter, even word processor. It was a rewarding day—six pages of rough draft, which is pretty good for me. I keep revising—spent almost two hours on *one* transition which I may not even need. George read the pages while I got dinner, making nice little murmuring sounds—and one excellent suggestion. It's wonderful to have someone with whom I can actually share my work; I never realized it could be so rewarding.

After dinner, while I cleared up, he stood on the deck applauding the sunset. "Super-magnificent!" he shouted. "What a spectacle, come see it."

"I can, from the kitchen," I called back. But as soon as possible I joined him.

On the horizon a freighter was silhouetted, slender and black against the burning rose of the sky, gliding slowly toward the faintly discerned towers on the Canadian side. We can barely see them without the field glasses, but with them they are quite distinct, thin black fingers pointing.

A few clouds drifted, turning to pink and gold as the sun sank into the water, a glowing disc of molten gold. And from it streamers of light splayed up from the water, spreading out like an enormous fan. "Or like the crown on the Statue of Liberty," George said. "She's wearing a jeweled diadem." Flakes and gems of light sparkled from it. And a jet plane climbing high and far away sparkled too in the glow, trailing a fiery comet.

And all the while the gulls kept soaring, from east to west, in groups of ten or twelve or twenty, like whole families or clubs of people deciding to go out for a joyous ride on the wind. All of them headed straight into the sunset. Winging into some rosy Paradise where mere mortals can't follow. But meanwhile we stood on the deck with the wind whipping our hair and marveled at its beauty with them.

Sky Serpents

Jets and their vapor trails striping the sky. Boats and their wakes striping the lake . . .

The sun is sinking, a ball of fire, into the silver-blue water, the sky fading from blue to golden shades of pink. And overhead, as we stretch out on our bright yellow deck chairs, the sky becomes alive with snakes breathing fire. Tiny heads of serpents, more sensed than seen, their tails lengthening as they rise and curve across the sky, still half aflame with sunset, arching, curving.

They seem to be climbing—even as they merge into the distance they are achieving across the great globe of earth. Some moving west, toward Chicago, Colorado, the coasts of California. Some lifting straight up, drawing a brilliant line skyward toward Canada, and arching on, curving as they strive with all their soaring speed toward Alaska, Greenland, Europe. Serpents swimming in space, driven by some fires we cannot see.

The trees frame this incredible panorama, indifferent to its wonders; the sea gulls wheel and cut their own arcs unconcerned. While below, the gently overlapping waves are calmly changing colors—blue, gold, flamingo—layering toward our feet.

But I watch fascinated, excited and curious. "What's going on?" I exclaim. "They can't be fireworks, or even vapor trails. And they're certainly not Northern Lights, the Aurora Borealis —I've seen that a lot in Iowa."

George was delighted. "They aren't," he said. "This is a miracle I ordered just for you."

"Stop kidding, George, what is it?"

"It's the way the sun is hitting tiny particles in the air. Transforming them into little ribbons or snakes of light. They really do seem alive, like they're swimming or flying creatures on their way to somewhere."

"Have you seen them often?"

"Only a few times in all these years. But I do know what it is when they appear. Call it a miracle of sunset, a miracle of light—it's a very rare sight. I was hoping to show it to you sometime. And there it is! So you see, I *did* put in my special order, and it came tonight just for you."

Runaway Dog

Ben's stick addiction seems to grow worse as the summer progresses. Worse than usual this August. We almost lost him for good. What a joy it is to wake up knowing he is safely home. He had disappeared again—gone this time for four days. We had called and called in vain, sought him on foot and by telephone. Driven down adjacent roads, lest he be lying in a ditch. Rumors were he'd been seen playing with some children throwing sticks, and later getting into a strange car—evidently visitors here for the weekend. The police offered little hope—dogs are often stolen. He was probably miles away by now. We'd be lucky to see him again.

We were heartsick. George especially—torn between the familiar hurt and exasperation, and our mutual sorrow at losing a pet that was so much a part of us. Yet we both were praying for a miracle. And the other day, even as we consoled each other over the inevitable, the telephone rang. Somehow I knew—even as I dashed to answer it. It was our veterinarian, Dr. Wood. "Still want Ben?" He laughed. "A lady from Jamestown just called. He's been wandering around her farm."

"Jamestown!" I screamed. It was thirty miles away.

"That's right. All you have to do is go pick him up." He gave us her name and directions.

Astonished and elated, we set off to meet that precious lady who'd be waiting for us at the public library. Her farm was six miles beyond, she told us, along a difficult road. "Too hard to find, and you've been through enough." Her grandson had discovered Ben's name and Dr. Wood's number from the tag on his collar, she said. "He deserves all the credit."

The boy stood beaming proudly, holding Ben on a leash. We hugged both of them and tried to pay them a reward, but they refused. "It's reward enough just to know he's safe with his family," she said, stooping to pet him. "He's pretty thin— we fed him right away, but I don't think he'd eaten for days. Anyway, here he is."

We all were petting Ben, so his tail was wagging. But he didn't seem particularly glad to see us; or even Tanjy, who pounced on him at once, wild with reunion. Ben just scrambled onto the back seat, and lay there phlegmatic, half sheepish, not meeting our eyes, unresponding to our excited chatter about how much we loved him, and why did he run away with strangers who might not be good to him? "Darling, where did you *go?* How did you get so far away from *home?*"

Questions nobody will ever be able to answer. We just know we're lucky to have him back . . . And that it could very well happen again.

In fact, only two days later Ben sneaked right back down to the beach and was gone all afternoon. When we finally missed him and George went after him, that darn dog was having such a good time chasing sticks in the water, George actually had to wade in and *drag* him out.

There's no understanding such a creature. For a dog like Ben it must be like drugs or alcohol or sex for some people. He has a craving more important to him than food or family or security and love. Just as some men can't help drinking or chasing skirts, Ben can't help chasing sticks.

September Swim

Lake Erie is more beautiful than ever in September, when the trees are turning. We leave for the cottage as early as possible every week, and stay as late as we can. We won't be closing until late October—maybe even early November, George says. "Just one jump ahead of the snow."

This past week we started after George's final patient Thursday evening. A lovely experience during dinner at the Holiday Inn. We ate in the Garden Room, with its many green plants and glass ceiling where water cascades. Three women at the next table fell into conversation with us after George rose and drew a big heart inscribed with the words "George Loves Marjorie" on the misty window. He's like a big kid, he does this no matter where we are when the impulse strikes. He told them about our romance and my books (he's also a born press agent!), which luckily two of them had read. They all had followed "Daily Guideposts" and my "Woman's Day" column. Fans! Fun, instant friends. Exchange of addresses. They were "escapees from routine," they said, housewives fleeing Zanesville, Ohio, to visit Eastern cities. They promised to watch for our program coming up on *PM Evening Magazine* . . .

George enjoys these encounters and so do I.

The wind was blowing, trees swaying and lashing about as we drove down the final lane. All the cottages were dark, deserted. No flag was up to signal the presence of our dear friend Mary Downs . . . A kind of lonely, joyful midnight with a few stars prickling through the clouds . . . Shivering in the wind as George unlocked, house cold, but snuggling down warmly together, holding each other close all night . . .

Friday morning was still cold but bright. George built a blazing fire, perked coffee. Clutching warm mugs of it, we ventured out for our swim. Sunlight flooded the trees, which now seem resting after their lively night; painting the trunks and gilding the leaves. Pouring through the vines and tall leafy branches overhanging the glen and the steep-sloping path to the water. The steps cut into the earth have almost washed out. We descend carefully, sometimes reaching for a branch or vine. The stream racing down the hill is flaked with sunlight and cobbled with twisting golden leaves. Its tiny waterfall pitches over the long rock ledges that rim the beach. The rocks overlap, and at their base are round flat rocks, wet and glittering in the sun, or slippery, moss-grown.

The beach is wider than it has been all summer—areas of

rough pebbles and stretches of soft pale sand. We walked along the edge of the lapping water to a place where the big flat rocks reach out like platforms on which to step. The sky is silver-blue, the lake now a placid expanse of rippling silvery silk. Softly, gently, it laps the shore with liquid murmuring sounds, like a baby going to sleep.

I waded carefully in, yelling at the cold. "Holler, it helps to yell!" I called back to George. This softly nibbling stuff is bitter against the legs, blazes up fiercely cold against your body as you plunge in, begin to swim. But within a few seconds it is your friend, tingling warm, lighting up all the unsuspected fires in blood and flesh and bone. You are one with it, merging into a bright tingling joy. "Thank you, God!" I cried out to the sky and the bright blue morning. Hooray for life, for energy, for strength and the peace of this beautiful day out here alone. Alone except for George, who was now plowing through it too with his long beautiful stroke.

Back on the beach we rubbed briskly with big towels, pulled on our robes. We had gone so far down the beach we decided to return by an even steeper path—so steep we had to run, scramble, climb, feeling like mountain goats . . .

This morning, Saturday, we found it had stormed in the night. A strong wet wind was blowing; all the grasses and bushes were dancing against the windowpanes. And waves were rolling in below, wild and gray, maned with foam. We could hear them roaring when I tested the air by opening the door. It was tempting to stay by the fire, but habit and morning's call were too strong. Again braced by George's fresh hot coffee, we set forth, crossing our open parklike lawn where the great trees were again lashing and bowing, some of them squealing as if in pain.

We were afraid the path would be slippery from the rain, but the wind had dried it. Though the mild little downhill stream had become a torrent, as if to compete with the turbulence below. Again we walked the beach, seeking the best place to go in. The water is high once more, the rocks and formations always changing; some of the biggest boulders submerged or swept away, new ones appearing.

Undaunted, we charged in, again yelping and shouting a
challenge to the waves themselves, bashing at us, hurling us
about, tipping us over, knocking us down. But we fought back;
jumped them, dove through them, rode with them, these wild
horses, and finally emerged, battered but sound . . .

The clouds are gray-white overhead, rolling low over the
water, as if wanting to join the rodeo, become one with the
waves. Yet along the horizon a pink streak begins to glow, to
widen, to tinge the clouds with its faint blush. The distant water
is winey, gray-purple beneath the clouds, then a pale turquoise
as it nears the shore. And all of it host to the leaping whitecaps,
which no longer seem to threaten, but rise and drift and fall like
bridal veils. They are now like brides on the way to the altar,
trailing their skirts and veils.

We returned by the usual path, climbing through the bow-
ers of green—trees and boughs and tall feathery grasses, and
goldenrod spurting like delicate flames. All now bangled with
light, for the sun has broken through and is hastening to spill its
treasures. A few monarch butterflies wing through the vines,
though not the swarms we usually see. Gulls dip and wheel
above the water, when we pause to catch our breath and look
down. And far out, against the horizon, we see a white ship so
enormous it looks like a building afloat.

We had slept late, and swam longer than we expected. It
was ten o'clock before we had breakfast. Through the windows
which surround us we can see the water—now looking friendly
and festive as we eat before a crackling fire.

The Dandelion

All summer George and I enjoy the dandelions, scattered like
jaunty yellow cushions across the lawns—at home or here at
the lake. But now it's October, and last night he called my
attention to the beauty of these same wild weedy flowers gone
to seed. And plucking one, we studied it. The once flat shaggy
golden head has faded, exploded, become a perfect fragile white
globe. Round, transparent, airy as a balloon, made up of tiny

white starbursts, centered with dots like tiny pearls. Each supported by a silvery thread of stem, rooted in a cluster of dark brown seeds.

Turn this frail globe in your fingers, peer through it. It is soft, light, faintly seductive—like the hats women used to wear, with dainty dotted veils . . . It is a universe of loveliness in perfect balance, a sphere of infinitesimal stars.

George breathes on it, blows it softly, and on the instant it disperses, each segment airborne, floating, lightly falling like a delicate parachute, to rest on the earth or the very tip of a blade of grass. Thus to propagate, renew itself . . . They are like spermatozoa, George says, only a trillion times larger, life-filled, seeking to create new life . . .

Gulls and Ducks

A lovely sight this bright October morning: The lake, silver-gray, is combed with long waves, each perfectly spaced and formed like one old-fashioned marcel.

Above them dip the sea gulls, white and shining in the sun. And riding the crests below, along with a scattering of gulls, we are surprised to see hundreds of *ducks*. Great flocks and herds of these smaller, darker visitors, guarded and shepherded, it seems, by the gulls!

No, no, impossible, we must be imagining things. Yet even as we watch, more gulls are flying off as if to greet the other flocks of ducks we can see approaching, and escort them in. Yes, here they come, descending together, the gulls leading to less crowded places on the water. Then, as the noisy strangers are settling down, a few gulls move about among them, as if getting acquainted, making them welcome. "Rest a while," they seem to be inviting. "Do some fishing, it's very good here." Now and then another gull will wing down to join them, like a belated host to see to their comfort and pleasure.

For hours the arrivals dive for fish, or rock contentedly on the long silver waves. Masses of small brown bodies quacking and glinting in the sun. Then, toward late afternoon, the ducks begin to flutter upward, revealing the unexpected white flashing of their wings. Flock after flock they rise, to resume their journey into the sky. And although most of the gulls pay no attention (it's suppertime now, they're diving for fish themselves), a few join their departing guests and soar with them briefly, as if to say goodbye and go with them a little way.

How amazing. Such hospitality and generosity. We always thought wild things were selfish, treating any strangers as intruders, guarding their own feeding grounds against them, driving them away. And true, most of them do. Yet *our* gulls, the lovely birds that soar across our cottage, so familiar they seem like family, have treated the ducks like long-lost friends!

It has warmed our hearts to see them. For some reason we actually feel proud of them, and inspired by them. They have set us a beautiful example.

Visiting Geese

Sunday, another surprise. It is misty outside, drizzling, with drops that finally form a brief dancing crystal shower against the glass. The lake lies gray and almost placid, heaving slightly, undulant. And on its surface this time are little groups and scatterings of geese.

We hear them crooning their delicate, lovely music as we open the door. Geese do not *honk,* they *sing* in voices plaintive but light and sweet. Tremulous. In tremolo this sweet flutelike quavering.

We know these indeed are geese from their voices and the swanlike necks. They have not come in hordes and droves like yesterday's ducks, but in groups of ten or twenty or a dozen, neatly spaced. There are couples, floating a little apart, and a few alone, scattered like grace notes on the water. All do not make an identical sound, we discover. Piping or singing in unison, some are sopranos, some altos, and they harmonize in lovely song. *Honking,* indeed! Whoever coined that term must never have listened to the sweet songs of the geese.

The gulls fish among them, indifferent to their presence,

giving them neither welcome nor farewell. The geese fish too, a whole group will dip their heads and simply disappear below the water. Unlike the ducks, they don't come up at once. We wait and watch for them for a minute or more before they reappear, again in unison, like some well-trained dancing or swimming troupe.

What entertainment! As George says, "It's like having box seats in nature's theater on the water."

The Lights and the Leaves

I must throw them out at last—this big brown jug of scarlet leaves, George's substitute for flowers. "All I could find this morning," he said, when he first brought them in from the cold. A flamboyant explosion, more vivid than roses, their deep red colors streaked and splashed with gold.

I set them on the long wooden table flanking the lake, a brilliant bouquet. They were silhouetted against its silver-blue for two weeks. No, three, for I could not bear to part with them even when they became brittle and began to fade. Today they are crisp to my fingers, and the color of old dried blood. But I have put them in the wood box. They will burst into brightness again when George builds a fire. They will crackle and have their hues restored as they dance in the flames . . .

No day passes that George doesn't present me with something that lives or blooms. This morning a fistful of tangy marigolds as I showered. I laughed and held them up to drink the cold water. To share the fresh invigorating assault of water on my skin. Their yellow petals glistened, and their deep green ferny leaves. I put them into a little copper kettle that sits on the windowsill.

About the house are scattered little bunches and remains of marigolds and geraniums and gentians and wild daisies and ferns and graceful weeds. Glasses and jugs and vases holding these love gestures, tangible symbols of love. I am continually sorting them out, disposing of the fading to make room for the fresh, for he constantly replenishes my supply . . . And when there is nothing at hand to pick, he buys a bunch at the grocery store. Or slips into a flower shop, as he did the other night at the mall, and emerges with a crisp green paper filled with rosebuds. Their tiny red faces peered out at us, and I cradled them in my arms like a baby as we went to the car.

On with the Show

"On with the show!" George said this morning as we admired the sunlight flooding the trees. "Every day here is like a stage play, with a crew of experts controlling the lights. Backlighting the scenes."

What an apt description. The theatrical arch of trees overhead as we drive down the lane. The thickets beside the road, and the tall swaying trees that encircle the grassy parklike area where the blue-and-white cottage sits. Always the light plays through this leafy backdrop, creating effects so perfect, so lovely it's hard not to stop and cry out, "Look, look!" Whether the trees are green in summer, or golden as now, or even barely budding in the spring, yet the light is striping or gilding or drenching them with life and beauty. Even on a dull day when the sun doesn't shine, they have a shimmering quality of their own.

This is true even at night. Last night the moon was almost full as we arrived. A light mist had risen, blurring the lake, softening the outlines of the cottage, clouding the trees. But the moon made everything opalescent, unreal, a cottage in a fairy tale, a mirage . . .

And now, this morning, another mirage, it seems. A tall pink floating castle, a half-seen, half-sensed Taj Mahal. George called me to come see it, and through the field glasses it appeared, drifting smoothly, swiftly to the west. A ship—probably just a barge hauling coal, with only its living quarters rising visible and touched with the miracle of sunrise, yet from here a vision out of *The Arabian Nights*.

Sunset and Sticks for Ben

The lake on this autumn night is rimmed with fire. Deep red bonfires are simmering on its borders, while below the water roars, blue-black all day, and still wind-driven, but now the color of tarnished silver.

We finished dinner before our own fire—steak and fresh sweet corn from a neighboring farm—watching a football game. But the world outside was becoming too lovely to miss. The sky turning a vast expanse of gold that seemed to curtain and claim the world, shimmering on walls and windows, drifting into the very room.

George suggested we take the dogs down for Ben's promised swim. We'd kept him home this morning while we were in —he comes chuffing and clawing and pressing against us in the water and must be shoved away. Much as he loves it, and we love him, he's sometimes too much trouble. So we bundled up in sweaters, I put on a little hat to protect my hair, and away we walked across the broad lawns, now gilded with this dancing burnished light. The trees around the glen were frantic as we descended, roaring with a mighty voice as if to outshout the waves.

Waves, wind, and trees are all shouting as we press ahead along the beach, George tossing sticks in the water for Ben. His fawn-colored coat is golden in the light, burnished as he goes leaping after them, bouncing over and through the breakers, pursuing the prize. Little white Tanjy trots along the water's edge, barking in a frenzy, dancing to avoid the water that surges in gold and silver arcs at his feet.

Above us the tall cliffs stand, many of them like bereaved women, still clutching their fallen trees. "They look sad, somehow," George said. "They don't want to let go." Their sons, enormous giants, lie all about us, on the banks or prone across the sand, felled by the gouging of wind and water and underground streams. Uprooted, wrenched from the breast of the earth they have gripped so long, their leaves dying; though a few still sprout brave little flags of green. These too are limned and gilded, bathed in this russet light.

Ben's stick has been lost in the rushing waves, they nearly submerge him as he leaps and bounds or wheels in desperate search. Finally he yields to George's whistle and comes dripping in, but passionately barking, pleading for more. "No, Ben, no, that's enough," we both protest. "Not tonight, it's time to go home." Reluctantly the dogs trot ahead of us to the path by which we return, and up the steep hill. We follow their climb, turn down the road leading past the small white cottages of our neighbors.

We're the only ones here this week. All are empty and still. Yet every window is aflame, as if lighted from within.

The Waterspout

An exciting, roaring, rioting day of wind and waves. Very cold for this time of year; even the electric heat and the fireplace don't succeed in warming the house. The wind keeps trying to push the doors open, a bold intruder determined to shove or sneak its way in. George puts a heavy chair against the door facing the lake. Yet we are cozy and happy, thrilled by the churning, roiling water. The waves are snarling and foaming, molten lead, gray and heavy, and so are the clouds.

All day there is a constant spectacular of clouds. Gray-purple on the horizon, hanging down to the water's edge. Then they separate, thrust each other aside, like dark velvet curtains parting, and in their center a boiling gray mist appears and begins to move directly toward us "on little cat feet." Soon it has enveloped the house, as in a shroud. We are veiled, muffled in softest fog.

Then it drifts away. Another formation glides toward us, dark this time, and armed. It releases its ammunition: Tiny bullets of rain at first. Then hail, rattling on the roof and bouncing as it pebbles the yard, turning it white as a crazy snowfall glistening in the sun that peeps down through this madness.

The trees toss their gold and scarlet heads—like the waves,

driven before the wind. "They look like they're trying to run up the hill," George says. But it seems to me the trees are dancing in place.

The World Series is on. We watch it, torn between the drama of the game and the incredible performance outdoors . . . Toward late afternoon a preposterous monster, snarling fire, shoulders its way across the sky, a dragon breathing sparks and smoke. For the sun has somehow gotten into the act to enflame this creature, and lay before it a broad red band of coals.

Then suddenly: "Look, look!" we cry out to each other. Grabbing wraps, we rush outside, to stand on the bank, marveling at what is happening below. For now, bursting suddenly onstage, like a lovely ballerina leaping and dancing, is a pure-white waterspout!

The Rocks

Two evenings ago, after the first assault of these heavy waters, George and I picked and skidded and grabbed our way down the muddy path, not really expecting to be able to walk on the beach. From the hillside glen the stream had become a small torrent, and along the ledges at the bottom it was a frantic waterfall. We stepped over it and waded through it, for we could see that the beach was no longer drowned in waves as it had been the day before. But now what a sight: The former sandy stretches where we had walked before were entirely paved with big flat stones. Almost as if a big truck had dumped them there, load by load. And along with these wet, shiny gray-black stones, round or elliptical in shape, were scattered enormous boulders. Huge, heavy rocks scooped up by the mighty hands of the water, as if a heaving giant had hurled them there.

In the process, the water had also grabbed all the great-trunked trees that had fallen on the beach, snatched them to itself, and swept them away.

"Maybe the lake made a bargain," George fancied. "Maybe it bought the trees and paid for them with rocks."

"But this is terrible," I protested. "It should be ashamed, we'll never walk this beach again!"

"Don't worry, of course we will. The lake always cleans up its own mess, nobody else could. It's too strong. Unless you're used to it, nobody can realize how mighty and powerful Lake Erie is. But it always makes amends, you'll see—in a few days every one of these boulders will probably be gone, the lake will have grabbed them back and left us big generous loads of sand instead.

"That's one reason we like this lake," he said as we struggled on. "It's exciting, temperamental, it keeps changing. Like a woman who keeps moving the furniture in the house—you never know what to expect. No two days are ever quite the same. But it's fascinating, it keeps you coming back. You don't want to leave because of what you might miss!"

October Morning Moon

Almost daybreak. George gets up to let the dogs out, and comes back to lean over the bed, saying, "Honey, get up if you're not too sleepy. I have something to show you. Better put on a wrap."

Pulling on my big white woolen sweater, I follow him groggily to the door. The house is fragrant, winey with the smell of grapes ripening on neighboring farms. Their sweet perfume seems to be released with the falling of the dew. All night it rises, drifting through windows. Now, nearly morning, when the grapes are drenched, their purple sweetness is thick and heady, intoxicating on the air.

We breathe it in as we stand in the doorway, gazing toward the west, where the moon is full. We see it shining behind a clump of trees, its brilliance reflected on the waves curling below. They are splashed with silver coins, flaked with gems; and each wave is crested with silver fire as it breaks upon the shore.

"Let's go on out to see it better," George suggests.

We cross the wet sparkling grasses to the point where the

moon reigns round and full, like a monarch over sky and water. Here its lane of diamond light stretches pure and uncluttered across the lake. The sky is a silver-blue moonlit color; the grasses and trees are silver-etched. Although it is nearly morning the moon still claims the world.

Yet in the east the sky is faintly pink. Intensifying even as we stand there, deepening to a blushing rose. And the moonwashed water responds. Delicately at first, oh so faintly, like a young girl almost afraid to try her rouge, she brushes color into her cheeks.

"The sun is rising," George says. "It wants to get into the act. The moon keeps insisting, 'Look at me, see how bright and beautiful I am.' 'No, it's my turn,' says the sun, 'I'm even more beautiful when I come out. And I wake the birds, I get people out of bed, I keep them warm and give them life all day.' It's like a beauty contest," George declares. "They're competing for our admiration. And it's wonderful to stand here with you like this. Just you and I, like a couple of judges trying to decide who wins."

"You decide," I tell him. "This judge is going back to bed!"

The Butterflies

A cool gray autumn morning, the world to ourselves as we set off for our swim. Ben mouthing his treasure, a frayed old tennis shoe, Tanjy looking skinny after his trimming, with little chops of chin whiskers, his tail a pert flag . . . Ivy underfoot, and beds of heart-shaped violet leaves. And in the glen the trees soaring skyward, flaunting their vivid colors—though some are leaning, almost buried beneath masses of wild grapevines. Unlike the vines in adjacent fields, George says, none of these bear fruit.

There are other vines too, spilling, looping, roping the branches; and among the tall ferns and grasses, a few laggard daisies are scattered like stars, and frail white doilies of Queen Anne's lace. And today, returning as the sun came out, we spy flakes of gold flying—twisting and dipping and swirling in a delicate ballet, or coasting down to rest on twigs and leaves.

"Monarch butterflies!" George exclaims. "They must be migrating, they usually do this time of year—travel clear across the continent to California—we often see them, they seem to love this spot."

We pause to marvel—so delicate, so frail, these small bright creatures, to undertake such a lengthy pilgrimage.

"How long do they stay?"

"Usually only a few hours to rest. They lie quite still, with their wings closed, you'd almost think they were praying. But after a while they open their wings and lift off—if we watch we may see them, little wheels of them together, flying off in the direction of the sun. By evening most of them will be gone."

We got busy with other things, however. The golden horde blended with the changing trees, I completely forgot they were there. It was after supper, when we'd taken our coffee outside to enjoy the sunset, before we thought of them again. A beautiful sunset, reflected on the water that was moving toward us, like lines of people paying their respects. Bowing and speaking to us in some rhythmic throbbing language on their way to Niagara Falls.

"Because that's where all that water's really going," George informed me. "All the Great Lakes except Ontario flow into Lake Erie and pour over the falls. They join Lake Ontario there and form the St. Lawrence River, which carries them on to the ocean."

"Gee, what a long journey," I said. And suddenly, looking up, remembered. "Like the butterflies!" For now, flitting above the water were a few strays. Not the flocks we'd seen in the glen, but wanderers, loners, so vividly yellow and filled with light and tender life, but coasting witlessly along the shoreline, obviously lost.

"Oh, the poor things," I cried. "They must not have waked up in time. Look, some of them are going the wrong direction!"

George sprang up and we both began to wave and call out to them in some foolish need to help. "Hurry up, you're late, the others have left, they're already far ahead. No, no, turn around, you mustn't go back, go forward. Go west—California's that way!"

Others, we knew sadly, had already given up, were still lying in the glen. "Lots of them fall by the wayside," George said, "they can't make it, we often come across their little bodies after the others have left."

And gazing helplessly after them, we wondered at the sustenance of such fragile creatures; what hidden strength impels them, what enables them to survive at all?

"And why do we *have* butterflies?" I asked as we sat down. "They're beautiful, yes, like the flowers. But flowers provide nectar for the bees and butterflies. The bees are useful, they turn the nectar into honey. But the butterflies don't produce anything *I* know of. Not even food for other creatures, do they? What are butterflies *for?*"

"Food for the spirit," George replied promptly. "Butterflies provide a symbol for us. The symbol of life. Even a schoolchild is familiar with the miracle: how a common lowly caterpillar can go to sleep in a dry gray cocoon, and when he wakes up, emerge as such a beautiful colorful thing—what's more, free, able to fly!

"Butterflies remind us that an ordinary person, no matter how humble his beginnings, can rise up to something better," he continued. "But even more important to a lot of people—they're a symbol of life after death. Escaping the tomb. The body is left behind, a useless shell. But the spirit that leaves it will be beautiful and free beyond anything we can imagine. Butterflies illustrate that miracle for us."

We sat for a while, holding hands, aware of the sunset, the gulls, the waves, the dogs at our feet, and each other.

"This is so beautiful," George said. "This is perfect, the dogs lying there, the light through the trees, and to have you here with me. So wonderful that we can be together to see the monarchs as they migrate, those dear butterflies stopping here on their way clear across the country. And the water . . . listen to it right now, so patient and persistent—maybe it's trying to tell us something on its way to the Falls and the sea. And knowing that life does go on, and on . . . If only it could go on forever for both of us."

"Or that when we do leave, we could go together," I implored. "Don't fly off without me, George. Wait for me. Wake me up, take me with you, I don't want to be late and get lost, and not be able to find you!"

"I promise," he said, "if you'll do the same for me."

We hugged and kissed and both laughed to ease the awful eventuality.

"It's a deal," I said. Then, not wanting to, I asked, "But one more thing: What about after we get there? Will the two of us still be together, somehow, just as we are now? Do the butterflies have a symbol for that?"

George couldn't answer that question. And I try not to let it bother me. But the butterflies added to the wonder of another precious day with him.

CHAPTER SIXTEEN

Talks with George About God

The Religion of the Body

George and I have a lot of conversations about God. His faith is fervent, rooted in his never-ceasing awe at the miracles of creation—especially the body.

"Jesus kept reminding us that God isn't just a fairy tale," he stated. "Jesus made us realize that he is *real*. As near as your own heart beating. Not just something that preachers talk about, or to be found only in the Bible—but indwelling. An ever-present reality, a force that you breathe in constantly if you are only *aware* of it.

"We breathe 25,000 times a day. The main difference between animate and inanimate objects is that one is dead; the other is alive and breathing. The process takes place in your living body. Your heart keeps beating, your liver keeps functioning. The liver, that remarkable organ. It's an enormous manufacturing plant for most of your enzymes, your bile, the juices to metabolize sugar. The liver has about thirty functions. God is a great chemist, they should portray him standing in a lab coat creating all these chemicals to be disbursed just by the liver!

"We don't have to worry about oiling the heart or the kidneys or the liver," George marveled. "All that takes place twenty-four hours a day, without any effort on our part. Our organs are designed to last a lifetime. You don't say after a few years: The old ticker is wearing out, time to trade it in on a new model."

"Some people do," I reminded him. "They have to have bypasses, or sometimes get a new one."

"Yes, of course, in case of disease, but that's the exception that proves the rule. You don't have to have your body put on a rack to be cleaned and oiled. You do have to have it checked, but you don't automatically add a new motor, air filter, or spark plugs. We have a Master Mechanic who sees that if we take care of it properly, don't neglect it or drive it too fast, and obey the rules, it will last seventy or eighty years. And sometimes more."

Alphabet of Blessings

Every morning at six o'clock George begins an hour of prayer, which consists simply of thanking God alphabetically. His "A–Z's," he calls it, an alphabet of blessings from A to Z. Here's how he explains and illustrates it for me:

"This morning I was on the *S*'s. I always enjoy the *S*'s, there are so many wonderful, really important things that start with *S*. As you know, I don't look them up in the dictionary—if I did, I'd be on one letter all day. I just let my mind focus on the letter following the one I did yesterday. Well now, just listen to some of the marvelous things God gave us that begin with *S*:

"Starting at the very top, the *sky*. The roof of the world, the vast expanse all around us every time we lift our eyes—the sky with its changing colors and its beautiful *stars*—one of them, the *sun* that heats and lights the world. Why, just thinking about the sun and sky alone is enough to make a man fall on his knees.

"And add to that the *sea*, the very place where life began. In the waters of that sea, those *salt* waters, were all the elements essential for life. Those first cells, our ancestors, did start life in the sea, and there are vestiges of them in our own bodies—we are three-fourths water ourselves, *salt* water, if you please. We couldn't live without salt (not too much, of course). And the water in the womb cradles the fetus, the new human life. And that fetus, if you could see it under a microscope as I have—at one stage it actually has gills and a little tail.

"And *skin*—that baby has skin, of course, as we all do, that fantastic package we're wrapped in. It's a joy to thank God for our skin. I look at my own and marvel at it, I touch it as I thank him, I feel it with my fingers, all those marvelous muscles and tissues composed of trillions of cells, thinner than tissue paper and in different sizes and shapes, but layered like bricks, so carefully fitting into place exactly where each one belongs . . .

"And other parts of the body—the *sclera,* whites of the eyes, they look just like egg whites, they really do, but so important to *sight,* the ability to *see.* One of our major *senses,* critically important. But eyes are so much more—they give us expression, we call them 'windows of the *soul.*' So as I thank God for all this I include that thrilling mystery, the soul . . .

"And the *skull* which molds the face, with its openings for those eyes, and holds the brain which gives me the ability to think about these things. And the *scalp* which covers it . . . and on and on.

"As I think of each one, I pay it tribute for all the things it does for me—and stop to write it down. Not the details I've been telling you, of course, just list it, and before you know it, my hour is gone."

George paused, studying the small leather-bound notebooks he uses, scribbled with these enthusiasms underscored. "Take a look at this list for just the past few days. Just look at all those S's—*sleep (especially with my Marjorie) . . . silence, swimming . . .*" He handed it over. "And I've still got a lot more to add before I start on the *T*'s—they're a rich *treasury* too. See, I've already got one. And when I finish the alphabet, I just start over. And each time I find more things to appreciate and marvel about and thank God for . . .

"Especially you," he added with a grin. "I didn't even start writing my A–Z's until I met Y-O-U."

The Holy Spirit

It's always been hard for me to understand the Holy Spirit. Father, Son, and Holy Spirit, we're taught—the Spirit, third member of the Trinity. But just what *is* the Spirit? I ask George. I know it exists, I can feel it within me. Sometimes, in a moment of inspiration, I can "feel the Spirit upon me." But I can't even imagine who and what it is . . . I still can't comprehend.

George tries to explain: "Think of air and water," he says. "So important we couldn't live without them, and everywhere from the beginning of time. What's more, they are eternal, they may change form, but they never die . . .

"Every drop of water that ever existed still exists. Take a pan of water, heat it . . . it goes into the air as steam, becomes invisible, merges with the clouds, becomes part of the clouds, condenses, falls as rain or snow—maybe on the tallest mountain miles away, maybe on the valley or your own backyard— merges with the earth and becomes part of a stream. But it's *still the same water.*

"Take our humidifier. You can't see any air, it too is invisible, but it takes in the water, condenses it, and it becomes buckets of water, heavy to carry. You can see it, feel it, it has weight . . . Air and water are like the Spirit—everywhere. Even in the desert, water is there if *you* are there, because *you* are seventy-five percent water!

"You can show doubting Thomas water, which he can taste, touch, feel. But you can't show him the Spirit, which is far more powerful and just as real. *That* he has to accept on faith."

The Eyes of Love

One evening at Lake Erie, as we were drying ourselves after a sunset swim, we marveled at the age-old mystery that intrigues most of us from childhood: Why is it that the selfsame sun or moon will beam down on you, and seemingly you alone?

We had left the cottage together, but I could hear the telephone ringing. Telling George not to wait for me, I ran back to answer it. The sun was sinking into the water by the time I got there—and spread diagonally like a sash across these shimmering skirts was the golden pathway that follows the sun. To my delight, it lay at my feet, I could step right into it and swim.

"Look, look, come join me!" I called out to George, who had dived in a little farther down the beach. "I'm swimming in the golden path!"

"So am I," he called back. And when I swam to him I found he *was*. "You can't avoid it no matter where you swim," he laughed. "Didn't you know that?"

I laughed too. "Of course, I just forgot." How could I? I really thought I was lucky and special, embraced by all that radiance. But George was in that same blazing pathway too. And so were the children leaping joyfully into it from a distant rock.

This was demonstrated for us again later as we walked down the road to visit some neighbors. The moon had risen, and tagged along. But when we arrived the moon was already beaming down on all of us. And as we came home it followed us, framed by the trees; then presiding over the water, where it had flung down its own sparkling path of crushed diamonds, as if to rival the sun. If we had stayed in the lake a little longer we'd have been bathing in the *moon's* radiant path.

And it occurred to both of us that this beautiful, almost everyday phenomenon is like God's love. "They're like his eyes watching over us," George said. "The sun by day, the moon by night. Even when we can't see them they are there. And when they are visible in the sky they seem to prove it. They're a confirmation of his love. You can't get away from it. God won't let you go. He created you, he is in you, and he *is* watching over you from the day you are born. Following you wherever you go, no matter who you are. And that means everybody, even an atheist.

"I've had this concept ever since I was a boy. And it always made me happy—to think God keeps his eyes on us. And he must love us, because those eyes are always shining."

God's Hiding Place

As I've said, George reads to me every morning after breakfast, and again at night. For us this is a wonderful way to begin and end the day. And whatever we share like this, inspires George to discuss.

He often returns to his favorite book, Dr. Heinz Woltereck's classic, *What Science Knows About Life*. Yesterday, the portion he was reading talked about man's curiosity, his passion to solve the mystery of his own creation, and why he is here at all; his need to look for answers in philosophy and science and religion.

"Nobody knows everything about *anything*," George declared. "The more you learn, the more you realize how little you really know. It's a vain search. Man will look for the answers to all these questions about life forever, but he'll never find *the* answer until he looks in the right place. And what a wonderful place God has chosen to hide it—the answer to everything.

"He doesn't put it under that cup on the table, that plant on the windowsill, that tree waving out there." George pointed to his own brow. "God has hidden it right in here, the most secret place of all, in your soul, your mind, in what is inside. You have to look *within* to find the answer.

"Most of us don't realize that," he went on. "We try to find it in books or sermons or science or nature, but the secret is where God himself lives—in your own being, inside!"

George smiled, remembering. "It's like one year when the grandchildren were trying to find their Easter eggs. They ran all over the place filling their baskets. But when we told them that there were still a few they hadn't found, they were baffled. They raced around again in a frenzy, looking behind curtains, under chairs, they picked things up and put them down, they boosted each other up to explore the shelves. They didn't know we'd hidden those last few eggs in our pockets.

"Whenever they got near us we'd encourage, 'You're hot, you're hot!' and if they got farther away, 'You're cold, you're cold!' But they didn't know the prizes were right there on us, close enough to touch."

"Did they ever find them?"

"No, we had to tell them. We all had a good laugh . . . It takes a long time before you learn to look in the right place," he concluded. "It's easy to forget the clue that Jesus gave us—that the kingdom of God is *within* us."

The Master Switch

We had just watched a documentary about funerals in the former atheistic Soviet Union, where brief nonreligious services were held before the cold assembly-line disposals of bodies. Yet the faces of the mourners seemed even more distraught and grief-stricken than we commonly see here.

"How awful for them," I protested. "To think: Well, that's over, they're gone forever, the body is all there ever was—just a body living out its time until the end."

George nodded. "The body is a marvelous thing, the most incredible marvel God ever made. Life itself is a miracle," he declared. "But the body *has* no life without its Master Switch."

He told me how in medical school he was handed a just amputated leg. The surgeon ordered him to take it away and dispose of it. "The patient was still on the table, alive but sleeping. It came to me then: As part of that body, that leg had lived. Now it was dead, it had no life of its own. I could burn it or bury it, and yet the *man* would live on. You could cut off his other leg and both arms, yet the man would live. You could take out parts of his body—a kidney, a lung, his spleen—even remove his heart and transplant another, but the man, that vital life, would continue to exist! And I wondered: Where is the spark of life that controls it, where is the Master Switch?

"Every cell in the body is controlled by a Master Switch.

Like electric power—there must be a source. There are thousands of lights in a city, and countless lights and switches in every house, but all must come from a Master Switch in that city. You can find it, it is visible and real, you could see it if you cared to look. But in the human body where is the Master Switch? That little spark—touch it and boom!

"The brain is the only thing we can't live without. It must be in the brain. But we can operate on the brain. People have had parts of their brain cut out and still lived. Neurosurgeons know which spot controls the left eye, which the right arm, but the finest surgeon in the world has never located that Master Switch.

"It came to me very strongly that day with the leg, and has haunted me ever since: The life does not lie in the body, it simply resides there until the body is entirely gone. The body is nothing of itself. When you have worn out the body, used it up and disposed of it, it's nothing.

"No, no," he said fervently, "life is something else, with a powerful force of its own. Life is in the spirit, the power behind that Master Switch. Life is in the soul."

"So that's what Jesus meant by eternal life," I exclaimed.

"Exactly. I feel sorry for atheists, no matter how smart they are in other fields. Whether they know it or not, their life depends on what they deny, their eternal soul, the Master Switch."

That Still Small Voice

We have been reading Leviticus, one of the most incredible books in the Bible. Boring and bloodthirsty, with its incessant details about sacrificial offerings to please God or make amends for human sins. Some of these rules are obviously for hygiene, simple sanitation to keep disease from spreading. But most of them, about butchering animals and poor little innocent doves, just don't make sense. It seems incredible to us, especially George, who is such an impassioned animal lover, that the Creator would want to have his own creatures destroyed like this, and even dictate the methods.

What an awful job for those priests to have to perform. And how in the world did Moses have time to write it all down? Where did he get the necessary parchment if they were still out in the desert far from the Promised Land? Who preserved these records? I'll have to ask Dr. Roy Blizzard, adviser on my biblical novels.

But the point here is not Leviticus itself, which is only a part of our morning reading, but *the business of God talking to Moses.* In fact, God's talking to *anybody,* especially today. Oral Roberts is always quoting what God told him. Also Jimmy Swaggart. And lots of other sincere Christian people.

I personally have heard that special voice only a few times that I can remember—and be reasonably sure of. Primarily when I got that strong message about George when I first saw him: *"You will marry this man before Christmas."* And a few weeks later it came again, over and over: *"Don't wait! Don't wait!"* This proved remarkably valid. But at other times—several times before, when I felt quite certain, I was mistaken; the words I heard in my head did *not* prove to be true prophetic words, far from it. One message that I took literally and tried to follow, makes me uncomfortable whenever I remember it, even now.

George, who is very devout, has questioned this too. He is so open and trusting, not cynical, but kindly marveling. And wondering sometimes, as *I* do, why this just doesn't seem to be a manifestation for us. This morning he told me, "As you know, I wake up early every morning and spend about an hour going through the alphabet thanking God for things. But today when I finished I decided to just lie there waiting to see if God would reply.

"Lord, I told him, I know you healed those growths on my face the other night just because I asked you to. I tested you the way Thomas did when he asked to put his hands in your wounds after the Resurrection. I put my hands on those two growths that were small but seemed to be getting worse, and told you, 'Now this is simple, compared to the rest of me. But if you will heal them, as I know you can, I will have faith in your power to heal the really serious things that could be going on in my body: a return of the cancer, or those ulcers on my feet. So please, I ask you humbly, as I lay my hands on these two small growths, take them away. I trust you to do this and I thank you.'

"And you know," George went on, to me, "it happened! When I was shaving the next morning both of them had vanished, without a trace."

I certainly remembered. A tiny lump on his nose, but hard as a BB; another strange brown "caste mark" on his forehead, which his son, also a doctor, had said should be biopsied right away. Both of us were astounded at such a quick, undisputable answer to prayer.

"So this morning," George continued, "when I'd finished the alphabet and thanked him again for that miraculous healing, I asked him, 'Lord, are you there? If you hear me, please answer. I will lie here and wait patiently on you, as the Bible tells us—to wait patiently on the Lord. I would love to hear your voice sometime.' . . . Nothing happened. There was just silence, except for the train—its whistle that sounds so plaintive and old-fashioned here at the lake, and the pounding of the waves.

"But as I lay there listening, a strange peace came over me, and a wonderful feeling of assurance. I don't need to hear God's voice saying things to me. He's already in me, taking care of me. I couldn't breathe without him. I couldn't even swallow. He provides the air, he provides the saliva. My body depends on him, even my thoughts, my whole life . . ."

In the discussion that followed it came to us: God doesn't need to give us explicit instructions for everything the way he did through Moses for those priests. He gave us brains, minds to think with, we have to make our own decisions. Yes, we can ask him for guidance, pray that we will make the right choices. But it's not necessary to stand around waiting to be told by some inner voice what to do.

People who claim God talks to them may be right. People like ministers, particularly evangelists, whose entire profession is dealing with God, may indeed have a special line of power which results in such outright orders or confrontations. The rest of us just have to love him and trust him, thanking him for all the miracles, large and small, that he provides for us.

The Spider

"Come look at this," George called from the dining room the other day. "We have a visitor."

I ran to join him and we gazed at it in wonder, this tiny spider dangling from the ceiling, with nothing we could see to support it. It was simply *there,* alive but absolutely still, so motionless we thought at first it might be dead.

George reached out an experimental finger just above it, and sure enough, the tiny body swayed back and forth on its invisible thread. And yet it did not stir. I too touched the delicate strand, careful not to break it, and watched the seemingly lifeless body swing. "He *must* be dead," I decided. "If he was alive he'd be scared and do whatever spiders do to get away."

The telephone rang; we went about our other activities and forgot it. But later, eating lunch, we both realized our little visitor had disappeared.

"Did you sweep it down?"

"No, I thought perhaps you did."

We both realized then: The spider had indeed been living. Simply waiting, trusting that we would not harm him, and when we turned away, scampered back up to the ceiling, drawing his lifeline with him.

"He had faith in something we couldn't see," George said. "Invisible to us, yet real and vital to him. God gave him something he knew he could depend on. All he had to do to be safe was to be patient and hang on."

"At least until we left," I said. "Then run like the dickens. Wouldn't it be great to have faith like that?"

"Yes, because real faith *is* like that," George insisted. "Faith is a secret lifeline. Never mind that other people can't see it, or that the storms of life sway it and even try to knock it down. If you have that kind of faith, you'll be okay. Just have patience, like that little spider, trust God, and hang on."

Don't Cut Off Your Lifeline

We often talk about getting closer to God. George expresses it this way:

"God is transmitting, speaking to you, sending you pictures, keeping you going, giving you life, but you have to be able to receive. You can't feel his presence if you cut him off.

"Hate, prejudice, resentment, ego, self-pity—all these cut off your line to God. The same as if scissors cut off the telephone wire that lets you hear a voice, or cuts off the wire that plugs in your TV set. Or in your body—if you cut the optic nerve you are blind, you can no longer see. If you cut off the nerve that goes to your leg you can't walk. Or if somebody gives you directions and you don't pay attention you can get lost; or warns that your house is on fire but you don't listen, you can lose everything.

"It's the same with God. You've got to at least try to be the kind of person he can reach, otherwise he can't help you. If you cut off the line, he can't come in."

"But we're all human," I pleaded. "We all get worried and angry and make mistakes, or even just forget."

"Sure we do. But all you have to do is fix the line, plug back in; he's still there ready to be close and ready to help you whenever you're ready to listen."

That's the Way He Made Us

This morning George read aloud from a book about trusting God. If you're aware of the love of God in your life, it claimed, nothing can hurt you. Neither failure nor disappointment, not sickness or even death. When you know God is looking after you, nothing can really upset you or go wrong.

I contend this simply isn't *true*. This would reduce us all to zombies or automatons, or people seemingly as devoid of emotions as rag dolls. "We were made with feelings, we can be hurt, worried, angry, upset. We do react to our surroundings, the stimuli of people and places, and things that happen to us. We would not be human otherwise."

George pondered. "I guess you're right. We would be rocks or sticks."

I said, "You and I both feel the love of God in our lives. We live in his presence, otherwise we would not be so aware of the wonders of his world, or thank him so constantly for beauty and nature, and the very humblest things. And the blessings he's showered on us. Above all, our wonderful fortune in finding each other, our love.

"But you have been hurt by death, and I have been hurt by life. We both have suffered. God wouldn't prevent it or make it different for us. That's the way we are designed—to endure, to go through a lot of things, some of them terrible, almost devastating. Even knowing God loves us, and never doubting, there is still the pain."

George agreed. "That's right, it's not only spiritual, it's biological. Even a tiny cell in your body responds to stimuli—let something prick it and it reacts. Knock your shin or your elbow, and you can't help yelling—it's instinctive, the whole body screams. Have somebody hit you and there's a double reaction. This is an outrage not only to your flesh but to your very soul. Both scream."

We are shaped by our experiences, good or bad, we concluded. Everything, even suffering, can help us to mature and develop, grow stronger, tougher, more courageous, and yes—more trusting in God's continuing presence and love. And just as important, maybe even more so, to grow in understanding and compassion for what other people are going through.

Miracles in the Morning

George and I have a kind of coalition of awareness. We are always pointing out sights to each other on our walks: the contrails that stripe the sky at sunset, the treasury of diamonds sparkling on a tree after the rain, or the many little unexpected wonders in a house.

Yesterday George called my attention to the stoppers in two blue glass bottles that stand in our kitchen window.

"Look, just look at them, how they catch the light. They're like crystal balls. Look into them and you see reflections of clouds and trees and even Margaret's house next door. A little miniature world. And in their very middle you'll find a perfect cross."

I looked, and all this was true. The cross was a reflection of the window frame.

Then we began counting the crosses all around us, never noticed before. Each window held four distinct crosses in the bars that held the glass. The top half of the Dutch door held four more. While below, in the closed wooden half, there was another cross made by the panels; plus two larger white crosses in the other door leading to the hall.

Then we noticed the crosses made by the Carrara glass walls and ceiling; where each square met, it formed a cross. The same was true of the tile blocks of the floor . . . Simply too many crosses to count. Yet it was a lovely experience to discover them there. Surrounding and supporting us . . .

This morning he summoned me from my shower to witness a strange vision in our bedroom. "Look—over there, what do you see?" He was pointing to the light streaming through a high window. "No, a little more to the left, toward that picture."

The painting was one that had been there for years, a scene of the ocean at sunrise. But now, incredibly, poised just above the water, a shadowy yet clear figure had appeared. A robed figure with a nimbus around his head.

"Why, it's Jesus!" I gasped. "It looks like Jesus walking on the water. But where has it come from?"

"Step over here and look up at that other window." George guided me in its direction, tilted my chin. "See how the light is coming through it too, picking up something on your dressing table."

Yes, now I could see another soft banner of light drifting toward the seascape, passing through a little crystal knob that held a lampshade fast. Just a tiny, inconsequential fixture that had been transported by the miracle of sunshine to the painting, where it became the silhouette of Christ.

As if that weren't enough, later, just before he left for the office, he called me again to come to the basement stairway and look down. I did—upon the usual confusion of old paints, furniture to be fixed, things nobody's bothered to clear out for years. And maybe a good thing too. For there on the ledge below the landing was a very old thick faded Christmas candle in a tin holder shaped like a star. And again the miracle of sunshine had made that star its target, so that it was now ablaze, its five points rimmed with fire. Never mind the clutter, all else lay in shadow, bypassed and ignored by the dazzling laser of light.

And once again I cried out in wonder. Two visions in the space of an hour. "Maybe God's trying to tell us something," I said. "Maybe it's a sign."

George sighed. "Let's hope so, I think we both could use one." He lost a patient last week, and has been very worried about another woman.

He also knows how troubled I am about my novel. I work on it all day and wrestle with it half the night. I feel so unworthy sometimes, so inadequate to deal with what I have begun. The material itself is so important, and in places so painful there are times when I don't see how I can go on. "Yes, you can, honey, God will help you," George encourages me, and I know he's right. I have to trust in that. If I didn't I'd be lost.

One thing sure, there's no turning back; I've swum halfway to the opposite shore and the water's deep, but I've got to get there or drown. I wrote yesterday in pure torment. There can be no freedom until it's done—to travel, to rest, to just escape into my life with George. *When the book is done, when the book is done . . .*

Yet now, suddenly, the past two mornings these incredible "accidents" of light. A simple painting turned into Jesus walking on the water. A battered old stump of candle transformed into a dazzling star.

Later, when the dishes were done, the beds made, and some urgent letters mailed, I went back to my desk with a new feeling of peace and promise, and wrote simply but well for hours. Inching the book a little bit forward, knowing it *will* proceed and one day be finished. Finished to the best of my ability, which is all I could ask of myself. Or that the Lord himself has asked of me.

Or of George, who is so understanding, content just to be with me, wherever we are. I'm very glad he is still going to his office, taking care of all those dear people who love him so much and have depended on him so long . . . And this evening I rejoiced with him when he got home. He'd had a good day too—the patient he's been so concerned about is better; and he had merry tales to tell of two more. One of whom sent a fresh apple pie for our supper.

How alike we are. Those little morning miracles must have been a bright omen for him too.

Look Up

This morning as George went out for the papers, he looked up at the sky, he told me, thanking God for another day of life. And he began to wonder about how many religions look up in worship. "I'm not sure about Muslims and Buddists—I think they prostrate themselves, we must find out. But for most people, including the American Indians, there's some instinct that tells us the source of creation is out there."

I joined in, we began to discuss it, with both of us contributing to the following reflections:

This planet is so small—the astronauts look down on earth from their incredible heights and see it as a tiny thing, really just a speck among all the other suns and stars and planets. But we're down here, we live here, earthbound unless we fly, and even then we can't see the earth whole. We look down from a plane and see parts of it rolling out beneath us, but mostly we see only the blue space around us and the clouds, those wonderful clouds!

When we're on the earth everything seems to draw our eyes upward toward the sky. The sun, the clouds, the stars at night. It's a mystery to us, drawing us out of ourselves, leading us to imagine, to speculate, and to feel a sense of awe and worship.

I said, *"Here* we're limited when we look down. All we see is our own feet walking. All we see is the earth, the ground. The place where, as you say, we're trapped, we can't really escape . . ."

The earth is wonderful too, of course, all the things that grow from it—trees and flowers, the grains and other things that feed us. But even the life of the earth depends on the sky. Nothing would grow without the sun, or the rain that falls from the sky. Come to think of it, some of our most significant sounds come from the sky: thunder, the sound of rain falling, birds singing from the treetops. We look up instinctively to hear them.

"And planes flying over," George said. "Somehow, whenever we hear something unusual, even something unimportant, we can't help looking up . . ."

And we remembered the psalm: *The heavens declare the glory of God and the firmament showeth his handiwork . . .* And what Jesus said: *"I, if I be lifted up, will draw all men to me . . ."* He *was* lifted up bodily, and the results are history.

The very word "uplifting" tells us a lot about human beings. Looking up is natural to worship. It makes us feel closer to God.

Flying Through the Fog

I don't have to coax George to fly anymore, although he still prepares for a plane trip with some anxiety as well as anticipation. But once in the sky he exults in the experience. In some ways it becomes for him another form of worship. To think that God could create such miracles as the Rockies or the Grand Canyon, and give us not only the eyes with which to marvel but the means to actually coast above them, gazing down on those snowy peaks and into such magnificent depths.

But bad weather is a test. On our last trip we had a rough ride in a small commuter plane. Much of the time bucking and pitching as we flew through clouds and then a dense fog to our final destination. Even I was nervous. But George gripped my hand and said firmly:

"We are flying through thick clouds, miles above the earth. We can't see, we don't know where we are. The pilot is someone I don't know, have barely glimpsed. Yet I trust him to lead us safely through this fog, this storm, this unknown space, and land us safely in a city I, at least, have never seen.

"If we can trust this stranger, why shouldn't we trust God who created all of this? The sky, this plane, the pilot, the ground!"

God Prepared the Table

George believes the biblical account of creation—"the most stupendous event ever recorded"—but adds his own colorful interpretation:

"It's so plausible, so logical, so in *order*—and all to prepare for the coming of man. God wanted to get everything ready, every single thing that human life would need. First of all, the air for us to breathe. The precise amount of nitrogen and oxygen surrounding the one planet in the universe where God seems to want his children to live . . . At least as far as we know right now; although scientists keep trying to find life somewhere else.

"And the water and the earth. Terra firma, the ground where God would plant the seeds, and have a place for the animals to walk—and man when he finally arrived. And the sun! Oh, how incredibly accurate and precise is that sun—93 million miles from the earth, the exact distance to keep us warm, provide the seasons, and let things grow. Any closer and everything would burn up; any farther away and we'd freeze.

"Then he got busy about food and shelter—trees, plants, bushes, grass, everything the coming animals would need—they had to get here first, in order to be ready for man. And while God was at it he made the earth beautiful for us; he'd already put stars in the sky, now he added flowers for the table. Then, just like the Bible says, he created the fish to fill the oceans, and the birds to fly in the sky and sing. Some for food, some just for our pleasure. I am absolutely convinced God was like a loving father, wanting to provide things for his children to enjoy, as well as their physical needs.

"Next came all the other creatures, animals and insects of every kind, including mosquitoes, although I can't see why— except, of course, to feed the birds." George laughed. "Maybe he compensated with the butterflies. And so many other beautiful things . . . Anyway, the point is, God put the animals here mainly to serve us. To be our companions, to work for us, or guard us, or even carry us on their backs. But whatever the animal does, every single one has exactly the same organs we do, making us one step closer to him. Even those that are here to nourish our bodies with their milk and eggs and meat. You know how I love animals, but this is a fact, and a part of God's plan. Because the whole story of creation *was* a plan, carefully executed for one reason: to prepare the world for man."

George's eyes shine as he speaks of it, his words almost sing: "I think of God not only as a father but an eager host, preparing for a special guest at the banquet table. Everything in readiness, lights, music, flowers. And oh, the food and drink— not only the main course of fish, and meat and vegetables, but even sweets—desserts of honey and nuts and fruit. God didn't have to do *that,* man could have lived without it. But God wanted to, because God is also an artist, whose greatest joy comes from his own work, and, as the Bible says, 'seeing that it was good.'

"And at last, when the table was ready, everything in perfect order, God opened the door and flung out his arms to *man* —the final, most thrilling achievement in his whole symphony of creation!"

Symbols

One Christmas, while we were still reading from the Old Testament as well as the New, we got to talking about symbols.

I said it was hard for me to understand why the ancient Jewish people worshipped God so utterly that they dedicated every act of their lives to him, even wrote his laws on their doorposts to remind them of him—when they had no hope of ever seeing him, or giving any account of themselves after death. "The prevalent feeling, until a little while before Jesus, at least, was that the soul drifted into a kind of noplace called Sheol, where it lost consciousness, ceased to exist." Gradually this began to change, and by the time of Jesus there were many people who did believe in an afterlife of some kind.

We talked about how hard it must have been—and is—to love an abstraction. But one reason Jesus came to earth was to give people a *look* at God, a physical presence, a voice, a body to love. He became a living symbol, we can love the figure of Jesus, the person.

"He was the perfect person," George said. "The kind of human being we all would like to be."

The reason Jews rejected him, we both realize, was because they misunderstood; they didn't want just to love him emotionally and symbolically, they thought the promised Messiah would be a literal king. An earthly ruler who would right all wrongs and free them from the long enslavement. For that they could worship and love him; and when that didn't happen, they were shocked.

We talked then about Christmas, the symbolism of Santa Claus. The famous "Letter to Virginia." And George said, "The author of that classic answer was right. Santa Claus *is* important too. He's the symbol of joyful love. To me, his bright red suit suggests bright red blood. The life force, vigorous, lively. And the white whiskers and fur symbolize purity. And the jolly voice and laugh remind us of the joy in giving. Santa Claus is good and kind and happy and unselfish, not looking for rewards. And the fact that he gives to children is very important. It makes us all want to *become* 'like little children,' as Jesus said."

"Santa Claus is the symbol of material giving," I broke in. "He lands on the roof and leaves presents, he stuffs the stockings. But Jesus is the *spiritual* symbol."

"Absolutely," George agreed. "That baby in the manger didn't bring anything tangible at all. *He* was the gift himself— God's gift to us. But he did bring tremendous gifts, priceless gifts—not only teaching people how to have a happy life right here on earth, but giving us the promise of *eternal life.*"

Suddenly George laughed. "Even Santa couldn't top that. And you know—Jesus and he could be friends. Maybe Santa's an angel in disguise, sent down to brighten people's hearts and help celebrate the miracle in the manger."

CHAPTER SEVENTEEN

Serpents in Paradise

Our happiness, for all its beauty, has not been unscathed; we are not immune to suffering, and we have not escaped it.

To begin at the beginning: When George and I first met, he insisted on making "a clean breast of everything." From youthful indiscretions to his passionate, total loving dedication to his wife. Some of this tore me to the roots of my soul, plunging me into such anguish as I had never known. But he felt it must be done.

He also declared that I must know all about his physical condition. He'd never smoked, and never had a drinking problem; in fact, as a former athlete, he'd been unusually healthy most of his life. "Right now I have a double hernia, but it doesn't bother me. And two years ago I lost a kidney to cancer. Everybody was shocked, thought *I* was the one who was going to die—not Carolyn!"

It had begun with blood in the urine, while they were on their usual winter vacation in Florida. His wife insisted they rush back to Pittsburgh for confirmation—and the surgery. "Carolyn was devastated, slept in the hospital, the family almost called the priest for my last rites. But I got well, and they lost their *mother*. Quite suddenly, last summer."

He had made a complete recovery from the cancer, he told me. As far as he knew, except for the hernia, he was now in perfect health. But he was going to make sure. He would have another CAT scan. "I know how much you've been through before. If there's the slightest doubt, I refuse to marry you. I would never put you through all that pain again."

A few days later he called from Pittsburgh, jubilant. "All clear, all clear! Not a shadow on those X rays. Set the date, buy your dress!"

When we had more time, he described the experience: "When I came out, one of the nurses asked me, 'Doctor, what did you think about, going through that tunnel?' I told her I was praying. 'This is the most important journey of my life. I am passing through the valley of the shadow. My destiny lies at the end, where two paths are waiting. One leads to despair and death. The other leads to heaven. Lord, bring me out safely so I can take the path to happiness with my Marjorie.' "

Two months later we were married, on a glorious Fourth of July.

The Hernias

Our only trouble at first was with the hernias. George was wearing a truss, which kept sounding the alarm at airports. And we had to fly a lot: to Canada that first week, combining our honeymoon with an already scheduled speaking date; later cross-country on book promotion tours; and finally to Greece. Going through security, the truss would shriek, and George would have to be searched. It was comical but embarrassing . . . The following year, a few months before our departure for Athens, he decided to have the operation that would fix it.

Nothing serious, but as with any surgery, we dreaded it. His daughter, Diane, and young George's wife, Liz, came to the hospital that morning to be with me. (Both beautiful, loving young women.) They kissed George goodbye when the time came to wheel him off, then stepped aside for me to walk to the elevator beside him, holding his hand, while he sang "I love you, I *love* you . . ." all the way, until the door closed.

It was a ritual journey that was to become familiar.

George made a remarkable recovery. He was home from the hospital in three days; his old vigorous, ebullient self in less than ten. In two weeks he was at his office again, seeing patients, walking the dogs, dancing, and sharing the things we both enjoy so much. Our trip to Greece was magical; Melanie and Haris lived in an apartment overlooking the Mediterranean. We walked through a fairyland of olive trees and flowers to swim in its sparkling blue waters; dined and danced in the tavernas; visited the Parthenon and other ruins; and boarded a ship for a week's cruise to the beautiful, legendary islands . . . We extended the trip to Germany: Frankfurt, Salzburg, Heidelberg, Trier, where we sailed up the Mosel River to Zell, where George's father was born. Another month of castles, cathedrals, and beer gardens, the romance of foreign travel made even more enchanting by the thrill of being in love.

All this involved a lot of climbing steps and mountains and carrying of luggage, but except for George's nightly leg cramps, physically it was flawless for both of us.

The cramps were nothing new. Like many former athletes, George had suffered with them for years. (Son George, a star basketball player, had them too.) I soon got accustomed to them. I would pop out of bed beside him to massage the muscles vigorously until the contractions stopped. Sometimes mild, lasting only a few minutes; sometimes so fierce the muscles bulged, hard as cables, impervious to my touch, and he was mad with pain. When this happened I flew back and forth to the bathroom with hot steaming towels, which finally gave him relief. Sometimes nothing helped but to get him into the tub or under a hot shower.

George always thanked me profusely, and apologized for forgetting to mention the problem before. I told him nonsense, after all it was nothing vital, and as long as he took his calcium —about all that could be done, since lack of calcium can be a contributing cause, as he knows better than I. Our fervent agreement on this basic issue was to see us through the next crisis two years later. In fact, it saved his right leg from amputation.

Circulation

George also began to have circulation problems, despite the fact that he had never smoked and was not a diabetic (two of its major causes). His feet were dry and scaly, in such terrible shape I began to massage them with vitamin A ointment. Most of the time they were also ice cold. The right leg swelled, and for months the pain, especially at night, was excruciating. Ulcers were also forming on the right foot. I had begun to treat them with warm salt water and antibiotic salves. "Dad, you really should have an arteriogram to see what's going on," George Jr. urged; but my George kept putting it off.

It was June. We had gone to our Lake Erie Paradise expecting to spend his month of vacation, and weekends the rest of the summer. Every day, despite the pain, we went down the steep cliff and along the rocky beach to swim. I would go ahead, seeking the sandiest place to go in, then wade, testing for rocks to avoid when he came in. As George kicked off his sandals, I rolled out a piece of carpeting to protect his feet from the stones.

George swam with his own magnificent vigor and joy, like a mighty animal born to the water. He often emerged way down the beach, where I met him, carrying towels and shoes, and rolled out the carpet for him to stand on again. It was glorious! We didn't want to leave.

But one morning as I knelt on the cottage deck, drying his feet and applying the salve to the ulcers, I was shocked to see that the middle toe was now dark and hot and swollen. George noticed it too, and groaned. "Gangrene," he muttered. "No doubt of it. Better pack up. I'll call George at the hospital, have him tell 'em to reserve a room." Squeezing my hand, he gazed at me a minute. "Oh, honey, I'm *so* sorry to put you through all this. If I'd only *known*—"

"Don't be silly," I said. "You couldn't have talked me out of marrying you, no matter what."

We drove all day. His son was waiting at the emergency room when we arrived, and George was admitted that night. The arteriogram, which proved to be very painful for him this time, was performed the next morning. After it was over, the surgeons entered his room looking grave.

"The arteriogram shows virtually complete blockage of the arteries that go down the entire leg from the knee. The smaller arteries of the feet are also almost completely occluded." They could try a bypass, but they didn't recommend it; they doubted if it would succeed. And even if it did, it would only postpone the inevitable. "In our opinion," they said firmly, "the leg should be amputated."

Amputated. We stared at them in disbelief.

They could begin by taking off the toe, they told us. But that too would be only a stopgap; before long he would probably lose the foot. In their best judgment the whole leg should come off just below the knee, as soon as reasonably possible. Meanwhile, the toe could be treated with medication, and we might want to get a second opinion. But if we agreed, they would like to schedule the surgery for the following week.

Dazed and stricken, we discussed it with young George. "Can't something be *done?*" I pleaded.

"Well, maybe," his son told us. "I'm not sure, but let's not be in any hurry, surgeons are always anxious to get on with the job. You *should* have another opinion—not mine, I'm too close and I'm not a vascular surgeon. Let me call Dr. Webster, one of the best men down at Pitt, see how soon he can give you an appointment."

George was to be kept overnight, for intravenous antibiotics. We prayed together before I left; and signed each other with the cross, as we always do. *Heal him, heal him!* I kept praying all the way home. *Show me how I can help. If there's anything I can do in a human way, let me help you heal him.*

God answers fast sometimes. Suddenly, lights flooding the house as I turned into our driveway, I thought of my own health book. I'd done a tremendous amount of research on every subject, including circulation. Now I remembered stuffing a few of my bulging files into a bag to bring along to Pittsburgh. Heaven knows why, or on what—the book was already published. Still, on the faint hope that I might find something useful, I decided to look.

I unlocked, let the dogs out, and ran to my study. And there on a shelf I found the folders. The only ones I had brought. All labeled *Feet, Legs, Circulation.*

Now it was my turn to stay up most of the night, reading, winnowing, gleaning, writing down every bit of advice I could find about treatment for such problems. By morning I had a scribbled list, which I typed into a possible program we might follow, and carried to the hospital for George and the doctors to consider.

To my intense relief, the doctors had no objection.

"While the situation is serious, it isn't life-threatening right now. Who knows? It might work. If not, you realize, we *will* have to amputate." . . .

Thanking God for this reprieve, we went back to the lake to begin the treatment—of footbaths, massage, and medication, but above all megadoses of vitamins and prayer—working on it the rest of the summer and through the fall. I promised George we'd have it licked by Christmas. It wasn't easy, there were setbacks, but gradually the toe returned to normal, the swelling in legs and feet subsided, the pain relented, the ulcers healed. By Thanksgiving, we were celebrating. By Christmas, dancing.

With nutrients, medicine, hard work, sheer faith, determination, and plenty of prayer we won the battle. Not only this time but twice after that over the next two years, when the ulcers returned. The third time they were so much worse George's son shook his head. "Well, Dad, I'm afraid you won't make it this time."

"Oh yes, we *will!*" I vowed. And we did.

George will always have circulation problems, but seven

years later he still had that right leg. We were not to be so fortunate with the left one.

But that story comes later.

Crisis at Christmas

The next serpent was to strike at Christmas two years later. Until then, it was the only one I was driven to write about as it happened. Before, I had been too busy trying to capture the sheer joy and wonder of life with George. Days to be savored and treasured, memories too precious to lose. The assaults of pain and worry were so sudden and unexpected they were like strangers, intruders in Paradise, they didn't belong. Acknowledge them, cope with them, but get rid of them as soon as you can. Thus they seemed to pass quickly.

Looking back, it was as if they *hadn't* really happened. Or perhaps it was just that even these painful periods still carried so much magic just because we were together, they blended into the picture. Drifting away when they were over, and actually leaving behind one reward: George's leg cramps had stopped. Maybe his body was so busy with new pain it couldn't be bothered with the old. Or maybe it was compensating. Anyway, that torment ceased altogether, the cramps simply went away and never came back.

But one morning shortly before Christmas, George left for his office early. "To study a man's X rays," he said. He was late getting home that evening; it had been snowing, the roads must be slippery, and heavy with holiday traffic. I kept vigil at the window, relieved when his car pulled in the drive.

As he got out I noticed his bowed shoulders, the look of sorrow on his face—signs that usually told me when one of his patients has died. They are his family too, some of them his oldest friends. I scurried out through the snow to comfort him. "Oh, honey, who is it?" I cried, "You've lost someone."

George shook his head and groped for his faithful black bag. Gripping my hand, he led me back into the house. "No," he said after a minute, as I brushed off his coat. "You know that man whose X rays I went in early to study? . . . Those X rays were mine."

I was too shocked and apprehensive to respond.

He'd had blood in his mucus for several days, he said; now he had found a shadow on his lungs. Canceling appointments, he spent most of the day at the hospital to confirm his own diagnosis. The former cancer had metastasized.

"Oh, *noooo!*" Never have I known such fear, such sense of loss. I felt my knees dissolving—my heart, my bones, white and sinking like the snow. Or like a body standing on a precipice in the Lake Erie fog, afraid to move, with nothing below me anymore, my beautiful marriage swept away beneath my feet.

The next few days are a blur. More tests, scans, consultations; endless talks between us, plans to be made. But the verdict was final: His previous cancer had invaded the left lung. "Cannonball lesion, they call it," George explained, "actually about the size of a golf ball." Then in his inimitable way: "Impossible, I told 'em, how come? I never play golf with my mouth open, in fact I don't even play golf!"

It would have to come out right after the holidays. Yes, we could make our usual trip to Virginia to spend Christmas with my children there, and George's son Jeff and his family in Maryland . . . Meanwhile, the confusion of final shopping and packing, while my mind wrestled with this serpent. In the case of George's leg there was something I could *do*. Wait, stop the music, let's try something else! But with cancer there was no alternative; at least not this time. Surgery had saved his life before; I must trust it now. Still I felt helpless.

My mind went back to the fierce battles I had fought against that insidious monster for Lynn. Years of treatments, orthodox and otherwise, but in the end the cancer won. With Lynn, however, there were *reasons*. George was different. His body had not been tragically damaged by radiation as a youth or by other excesses later. Both of us practiced the health rules we so fervently preached.

Why, then, *why?* But to ask why is fruitless. Now I had no weapons except faith, prayer, and a fierce and stubborn love force *that would not let him succumb.*

. . .

George is a bundle of contradictions. He whistled and sang most of the way to Manassas, but at times he would lean back, bracing himself against the wheel, and look at me with eyes that plainly said, "It's all over."

"Oh, stop playacting!" I wanted to say, but was afraid it might lead to revelations that could spoil Christmas.

Although George always presented a shining example to the world, and together we read practically everything ever written about the power of prayer and positive thinking, he has a dramatic negative streak. His son warned me about this when we first married: "Dad suffers from a chronic low-grade depression—at least when it comes to himself or his family. He sees every physical problem as hopeless, fatal, a disaster beyond repairing. It's almost comical how he'll blow things out of proportion. But when something *is* really serious, he knows it—and will soft-pedal it at first. Look out, he's a terrible actor, like a little kid trying to fool you, knowing you'll see right through him and sympathize with him."

Yet it was, incredibly, a glorious Christmas, with Melanie and Haris home with their two little boys after five years in Greece, and other children and grandchildren swarming. All of us dashing back and forth between the two houses on Lake Jackson. The lake was now frozen over as it had been six years before, when I was brooding over what to do with the rest of my life. Even the skaters were there again, playing hockey! Some of us joined them and went skimming across the ice. We laughed and danced and sang and unwrapped our presents, around a tree that seemed bigger and appeared to sparkle more brightly than ever. Friends and neighbors swarmed in. George and Haris sang duets while Haris played his guitar. Melanie and Haris taught us Greek dances, George the merriest, funniest, and nimblest of all.

We had debated telling our families; now we were glad we did. If anything, there was a heightened joy and excitement about their knowing. Instead of the worry and sympathy we feared, there was this avalanche of joyous affirmation, buoying us up. George was not pretending, nor was I. Life seemed unusually precious, our whole family so blessed by the presence of this vibrant, life-enhancing man. The sheer power of their love and the magic of Christmas would work its miracle. He *would* be all right, he was simply too dear a treasure to lose.

Swept up in the heady celebration, we put anxiety aside. Like Scarlett O'Hara, we would "think about that tomorrow."

But as New Year's Eve approached, we discussed our usual plan to go on to Jeff's vacation house at Ocean City for a few days. "The scene of the sublime," George called it, because of our courtship there. But it seemed like running away. Anxiety and dread could no longer be denied. I was almost relieved when George suddenly declared, "Let's go home and get this over with."

George did not whistle or sing on the long trip back. Instead, he drove with a fixed intensity, mostly staring straight ahead; or when his eyes roved to the farms and streams and wooded hills, many still glistening with patches of snow, it was as if seeing them for the last time. No longer pretending, or merely escaping, but honest as he had been when we first spoke of marriage—but this time frankly depressed. He expected the worst. There were certain things I should know about the house, his estate, the will. Yes, we had a prenuptial agreement, but . . .

"Stop!" I begged. "I won't have you talking like that."

On and on he went, no matter how I protested, pleading faith and prayer and the boundless resources of sheer determination and common sense. Look how we'd tackled the job of saving his leg. "I'm tough, remember? I'm strong. Lean on me, I've got a power to overcome things. I *can* move mountains!"

George seldom argues; instead he has a dignified but exasperating way of listening until you're exhausted, then negating all your arguments with logic: The cancer may have metastasized even further. Even if they got it all this time, it would probably show up again in the liver, the other kidney. "I appreciate your fervor and faith and concern, yet as a physician I know what can be happening. I've seen it too often and fought it too often with every weapon at my command. Drugs, X rays, surgery, prayer. Yet if it is determined, no matter what you or I or anyone else can do, it *will* prevail."

I was stricken, frustrated, and by the time we got home, frantic with things unsaid. Late that night, after he was asleep, I put some of them down in a letter:

You're wrong, I wrote. *You think you know me, but you haven't reckoned with me yet. You and I are special. God brought us together for a special kind of life, and he's NOT going to separate us yet. I will not release you. I will not LET you give in. You are mine, a part of me to protect and reinforce. Draw on my strength, I have plenty. Draw on my faith, I have enough for both of us.*

Rest, yes, you're going to need it. Yell to express your pain and misery if it helps. I don't mind.

But do not give up, I forbid it! You are mine and I love you. I waited for you too long, dreamed of you too long, I have you at last, the most fascinating, exciting, worthwhile human being I have ever known and I refuse to lose you. I have earned you, I deserve you.

Never mind about your family and friends and patients, who need and want you too. I am speaking with all the power of selfish love. I deserve you more than anyone else and I will not release you. I am just as jealous of your life as your first wife ever was of other women.

You are mine, do you hear? Don't you DARE leave me now!

Lung Surgery

Once again George's daughter came early to the hospital to be with us; and waited graciously so we could hold hands while they wheeled her father to the elevator, George again singing "I love you . . . I *love* you" all the way. I'll never forget the look in his eyes as I bent to kiss him goodbye.

Diane and I then went out to breakfast and began one of our daylong talks. She is a tall, slim, fair, exquisite woman, keen and astute, her cool composure protecting an intensely warm heart. She adored her dad—"He made my childhood magical," she has told me—but worshipped her mother. No day passed that the two hadn't called or seen each other. Sweetly though she accepted her father's remarriage, beautifully though she treated me, it had been very hard for her. I could never replace her mother, and didn't want to. For one thing, we both were too busy—I with my writing, she as chief microbiologist at the hospital where her father had practiced so long. But we became truly understanding friends; women who rejoice in each other's company, and can freely confide in each other . . .

Lung surgery is a far cry from correcting a double hernia. It takes hours and is very painful later; they have to cut through the ribs. It was seven o'clock that evening before we were allowed to see him briefly, still glassy-eyed and incoherent, clutching our hands and trying bravely to sing to me, not quite sure which of us was which . . . Later, as we parted in the hall, Diane and I held each other silently and wept . . .

Three days in intensive care, five more in the hospital, then home to make another remarkable recovery. With one exception. One night I heard George scream from the bathroom, "Oh, Marj, come look at *this!*" Under his arm he was cradling a swelling the size of a football. Terrified, we summoned George Jr. as usual, who raced over, and tracked down the surgeon, Dr. McCabe. If it got worse before morning, they decided, call the ambulance; otherwise be at McCabe's office by eight in the morning, in case it had to be drained.

My George was the first to start praying. "Oh, God, dear Dr. God, don't do this to me now," he groaned. "Marj has been through enough."

"You've been through enough," I corrected.

George took a pill and slept. I spent most of the night in supplication. At sunrise I could hear George whistling as he shaved. Beaming, he lifted his arm. The "football" was shrinking, not much bigger than a baseball now.

Examining him, Dr. McCabe looked puzzled. There were several medical conjectures about this sudden appearance and change, but no real explanation. Anyway, no incision was necessary. When we told him we'd been praying, he laughed and patted us on the back. "Well, you couldn't have a better partner than Dr. God. Next time you talk to him, put in a word for me."

After that, George's recovery was so fast everyone was astonished. In May, four months later, he was well enough to drive us to the University of West Virginia, at Charleston, where I was to speak to the writing students. In June we drove to Colonial Williamsburg for another speech, at the annual convention of the National Federation of Press Women. In July we flew to California to introduce my latest novel, *The Messiah,* at the Christian Booksellers Convention. In September we were off on a twenty-city coast-to-coast promotion tour.

George thrived on all this. It had introduced him to an entirely new world. His outgoing personality made him a hit at talk shows and autographing parties. I insisted that he take his afternoon nap while I was off doing more; evenings we were usually free to have a leisurely dinner, and get a good night's sleep before catching the next plane. Whatever we did, it was always an adventure, absolutely glorious after making so many of these tours alone.

"Thank goodness for that cancer operation," George sometimes remarked. "Otherwise, I'd still be in practice, trying to figure out how to get away." He had realized that after fifty-two years in medicine, although he'd sworn he never would, this was his ultimatum to retire.

Retirement

Happy as he was to be free of the obligation, submitting to retirement was traumatic for him nonetheless. And, in a curious way, for me. My heart ached as I followed George around the office trying to decide how to dispose of the things that had been such an important part of his life so long: Furniture not only below but upstairs where the family had lived when the children were small. Cabinets bursting with papers; cupboards of drugs; a vast array of medical equipment, from scales and microscopes to machines for EKGs and ultrasound. But even here there were amusing touches to ease the strain. I urged him to save the scales for weighing patients, on which he had hung his own personally hand-lettered sign:

ATTENTION! ALL YE WHO STAND UPON
THIS IS A MOOD MACHINE
IT PUTS YOU IN A **GOOD** MOOD OR A **BAD** MOOD

I also rescued several old clown masks I found in a drawer. "What in the world did you do with *these?*"

George grinned and looked a little sheepish as he explained. "Gee, those go back to the days when I was still in family practice. If I had to hurt a child—say give him a shot or maybe sew him up—I put one on to make him laugh, or think it was somebody else, and not be scared of me."

Strange wonderful George! I thought, wishing I had known him then.

I saved the masks and the scales and the signs—another one largely proclaiming: SORRY IF YOU HAVE TO WAIT. WHEN YOUR TURN COMES I WILL SPEND JUST AS MUCH TIME WITH YOU . . . It was yellow with age; George told me he had posted it his first day on the job—"When we were over on Euclid Avenue, with only a couple of rooms and a couple of patients. But I kept my word to everyone that came, and never took down that sign except to move."

Overflowing bookshelves and pictures of the family were everywhere. A handsome portrait of Carolyn graced the wall over his reception desk—beautiful and composed. Her calm sweet eyes seemed to follow us, as they had on my only two other visits before. I felt uncomfortable, like an intruder in this scene where lives had been closely intertwined and sublimely happy without me.

Sensing my mood, George took my hand as we stood looking up at her, and once more he reminded me, "Just remember, honey, if it weren't for her we wouldn't be here."

I nodded, but it failed to comfort me.

George wanted to get this parting over with too. In the end he sold the building for a song and gave most of its contents away.

His patients were stricken at losing him. There were flowers and newspaper interviews. Letters poured in, all witnessing to the great love and respect in which he was held. "You always had time for us," they wrote. "I will never forget how good you were to Mother; you made her feel like a queen."

Such tributes, together with the lively diversion of my activities, contributed to his swift healing, body and soul. Soon we were walking the dogs across the hills again, dancing and loving and swimming at Lake Erie. The reality of it passed so quickly. It seemed almost a bad dream, something that hadn't really happened. Anyway, we were home free now, or so we thought. Surely we would never have to face such a dark ordeal again.

But we were not home free. Far from it. Looking back on it two years later, George remarked almost fondly, "Compared to this, that cancer operation was a lark!"

Serpent in Spring

It was spring when the next serpent slunk back into our garden. Striking first in George's callused but swollen big toe. "Oh, darn it!" I groaned, more in anger than alarm, and rolled up my sleeves. *Ulcers* again. Well, bring on the vitamins, and healing salves, get busy on the footbaths and massage and prayers. You villain, you can't scare us now, we licked you too often before.

The toe bled profusely one time, then settled down, but the second toe seemed uneasy. Undaunted, we opened the cottage in May, expecting to spend the summer. By June, however, both toes were swollen, the foot scarlet, the second toe inflamed. I urged George to at least get X rays at the village hospital; he kept putting it off. Until one morning the second toe was black. Now we did rush to Westfield Hospital there, where they said he must be admitted for intravenous antibiotics at once.

"Not here." George was adamant. "I want to go home."

Frantically, I threw things together and closed the cottage as best I could—lights, water, food, blinds. Doing all the things you have to do when locking up a house, meanwhile with that desolate ache of wondering if you'll ever see it again. I had felt this pain every time we left; this time it was worse because I was so frightened.

George was unable to help; but insisted on driving, with his good right foot. One of the longest trips of my life. It was dusk when we finally pulled into our driveway. His son was already there, and so was Diane. Dr. Finn, a vascular surgeon, would meet us at the emergency room . . . Diane helped me find what her father would need and we packed his bag. Still in the jeans and T-shirt I'd worn all day, I hopped into her car. They took George into a curtained cubicle and began. It was nearly midnight when Diane dropped me at our door.

"Do you want me to come in?" she asked.

"No, no, I'll be all right."

The dogs were barking. I couldn't remember if they'd been fed, so I fed them again. I was glad to let them sleep on the floor beside our bed.

Thus began the long, kaleidoscopic battle.

After a weekend of "anguishing," as they put it, the team of brilliant young vascular surgeons, Dr. Finn and Dr. Krosnoff, presented their recommendation: amputation of the second toe and a bypass the length of the leg. True, we still had a choice, we could settle for just removing the toe, trusting that the wound would heal. As it might, considering our previous experience. If it didn't, however, it would be too late for the bypass that might save the leg. We too "anguished," but the gamble seemed too great. We told them to go ahead.

Such a process is a complex, arduous procedure. With patience and skill, these incredible men must turn the vein inside out and strip it of its valves before grafting it into position at the groin, then guide it down the long incision to the ankle for another graft; this done, if all goes well, it will assume the blocked artery's job of discharging blood.

George Jr. monitored the seven-hour operation, reporting from time to time as Diane and I kept vigil . . .

. . .

Daily one of the doctors or an aide would appear with an instrument called a doppler to test the blood flow; and never have
I heard a more beautiful sound than that amplified *whoosh-
whoosh-whooshing!* Signaling activity. Hooray, it must be
working!

Ten more days in the hospital, then home, with George
bedfast except for weekly trips to the doctor's; and a drive to
the emergency room one afternoon when his leg swelled
grossly. To my surprise, both surgeons walked in, still garbed in
the rumpled green gowns and little round caps in which they'd
been operating since morning. The sight of them, so young and
obviously tired but here, suddenly overwhelmed me. Awed at
the magnitude of their achievement, touched by their caring, I
rushed impulsively to embrace them, blurting, "I *love* you
guys!" I couldn't help it.

It was a long hot summer, housebound in McMurray while
our souls longed for the lake. Ghastly medical visits when the
big toe, angry again, must be knifed (debriding, they call it), "if
you don't want to go through all this again." I held George's
hand, his teeth clenched, his face white. Nights wild with pain.
His or my own? Surely my knee couldn't hurt like this . . . my
right knee did sometimes go out of whack—ever since the time I
hit it on the dock coming in too fast from water-skiing. Now I
must have sprained it jumping too long on my trampoline.

Pain, sprain, strain . . . a confusing chant. What was
happening to us? . . . Dragging myself downstairs, trying to
crawl back up carrying trays. In desperation calling my son
Mallory in Maryland. His voice saying, "I've been expecting
this, Mother, my bag's already packed." His wife, Judy, was
understanding, bless her heart, his job one he could leave.

He arrived late one night, an angel of mercy, taking over.
Carrying George to the doctor, me to an orthopedist for a cor-
tisone injection and holding me while the knee was drained.
And finally, in late August, when George rebelled at the bond-
age, Mallory packed us into the car and took us back to Lake
Erie, where we could at least feel the healing presence of sky
and water and trees. My other son, Mark, drove hundreds of

miles to help. Together they tackled the house and grounds, neglected for months—weeding, clearing, cleaning, fixing. And in November when we could stay no longer, they would both return to pack us up again, close the cottage, and bring us home.

CHAPTER EIGHTEEN

The Gauntlet

Until then the grotesquery of the past months faded, dissolved, leaving only bandages, medications, and a walker to remind us —except for George's continuing pain. We had promised to see the vascular surgeon there. "You're doing fine," Dr. Elwell told us, "the wounds are healing. The big toe is still your problem— will probably have to be cleaned out again, but only under anesthetic. Not now, wait, just call me if things go wrong."

And so we had these few precious weeks looking out on the water, even if we could no longer swim. George urged me to take the dogs and go without him, but I couldn't bear to leave him alone with that leg propped on a pillow. The only time I even went down was one rainy Sunday when Diane and her husband arrived. The two of us put on windbreakers and went slipping and sloshing down the muddy hill. She's taller than I and managed, I kept sinking in up to my ankles, she kept pulling me out, both of us laughing and grabbing at each other. Hands in our pockets, rain in our faces, we walked the beach the way she used to with her mother, she told me, and talked. She was having domestic problems; I listened, groping for answers. My own problems were too obvious to discuss . . .

George's ulcers were healing, and miraculously for several nights he was not in pain. But one night after our baths and dressing his toes, the pain that had begun as a bitter ache in the morning, and continued all day, struck savagely. We tried propping the leg with more pillows, massage, more codeine, a second sleeping pill, and after another tormented hour, he fell asleep, holding me so close I could monitor his irregular breathing.

I prayed almost all night, mystified at this terrible setback. In the morning, to my vast disappointment, the pain was still dominant. I had begged him to sleep late, but he awoke at six o'clock for his usual hour of meditation. And when I got up later, his coffee was brewing, he had picked and arranged his dear flowers, and was determined to continue our ritual of singing to me in the shower. But I could see that he was suffering; he had to take more codeine before lying down for his afternoon nap.

"If only there could be surrogates for pain-bearing," I told him, as I used to tell Lynn, "I'd gladly at least take turns."

"Never!" George declared. "I wouldn't wish this on anyone, especially you—you've had enough. I just wish I could hide it, it hurts even worse to realize how much it hurts you."

"In sickness and in health," I said. And, as usual: "You're still more fun sick than most people are *well*." And he is. At times, when the pain gets intolerable, instead of yelling he actually whistles and tries to sing.

Pain Makes You Wonder

George got up finally, at four o'clock, saying it had been too bad to sleep, but he insisted on getting ready to drive to town for the paper and our mail. When I came into the bedroom, he was sitting on the bed, pondering as he put on his shoes. He looked up, gazed at me a minute, and began this philosophic discourse on his favorite subject:

"I've been thinking about the body, this wonderful human body, God's most complex creation. The whole of it, first as a fully formed baby, then a child, a youth, a man or woman—so absolutely perfect in every way, so marvelously equipped for life, if all goes well. And then to think of the vast gauntlet of enemies it has to run to survive!

"All the diseases that can attack it, all the germs that can violate it, all the millions and billions of threats. Why, doctors can spend a lifetime trying to learn how many there *are,* let alone their symptoms and how to cope with them. All the maladies, inherited or acquired—cancer, arthritis, diabetes, appendicitis, phlebitis, atherosclerosis—syndrome after syndrome . . . it makes your head swim. The medical libraries are filled with books about them; you were with me there in the Rockefeller Institute where we saw one whole *room* just filled with information about bacteria!"

George rubbed his jaw and shook his head. "It makes you wonder, doesn't it, why God, who chose to make such a remarkable machine as the human body, surpassing every other species—what's more, to endow it with a mind *itself* able to create, to invent, to imagine, to worry and dream, able to experience human emotions, able to laugh and smile and cry . . . What I'm saying is—how strange that such a Creator also made us subject to so many perils, so much suffering.

"You and I are lucky," George said as he rose and reached for his jacket. "We've bypassed most of them, considering their illimitable numbers, we've reached this age in remarkably good condition, without a history of serious illnesses—you, at least, and me too until these last few years. My two bouts with cancer —losing a kidney, then part of a lung—and the threat of amputation because of poor circulation: those doggoned ulcers we've been coping with every couple of years. But never before have I endured so much pain.

"At least I don't remember. After surgery, yes, but that kind of pain you forget—like childbirth, women say, once it's over . . . Now I have this excruciating pain which makes me wonder about the surcease of medicines. What a mercy, what a comfort, we have to have it, I don't think I could stand this without some help. But as a physician I worry about patients who become dependent on drugs, either to block out physical pain or to block out emotional misery. Whether those drugs are cocaine, crack, alcohol—or lithium or Valium. There's really not much difference, the result is actually the same. What are we actually doing in the process? Altering or eliminating emotions along with the pain, stopping the *feelings,* terrible feelings yes, but essential ones too, good ones like love, hope, awareness. Seeking oblivion. Getting closer to the ultimate solution, which is total oblivion. Nothing more of you at all. In other words, *death."*

He paused. "I'd rather have this pain and still be alive at any cost," he declared. "Aware of you beside me, holding you, seeing you, tasting things, tasting life. Pain at least makes me realize that I'm still here, *you* are still here, *we are both alive."*

Rewards and Compensations

There are so many things George can't do for me as he used to, and this hurts him most of all. He thanks me over and over for every little thing, gets up and hobbles around trying to help— this huge handsome man who has always taken such good care of me . . . My turn now to see that the cottage is warm, feed the dogs, burn the trash, carry out the garbage. Together with the other burdens of shopping and cooking and cleaning and carrying trays; the constant bandaging and nursing—all this is sometimes almost too much. I get very tired and it's hard not to get discouraged.

Sometimes we hug each other and blindly try to comfort each other . . . I cry so easily now, the slightest thing makes me just spill over. Even the slightest misunderstanding or word that suggests impatience stabs me absurdly. This startles and hurts him too, he reaches out to touch me, hold my hand. He is in so much pain I know he can't be blamed, it's not his nature to hurt anyone, least of all me. He would never intentionally make me cry, but he has said to me, "The very fact that you do cry so easily makes you even more dear to me." . . .

But I didn't start out to write all this. I want simply to record my feelings of the past few mornings, having to do with compensations—of such simple things as carrying out the trash.

Here at the lake we have been granted the right to have our own private dump, a deep ravine in our woods a little way behind the cottage. Earlier, I had stumbled through vines and weeds and brambles to get to it, but Mark and Mallory hewed a path through it for us while they were here. Now as I carry the bags of garbage to be hurled back into the arms of nature, I can enjoy the surrounding ferns and bushes, appreciate the flowers. And I seldom come back empty-handed.

One day I reached up to pick a bouquet of fluffy white snowballs. They've faded now, so I picked a fresh one this morning, this time snowballs dyed pink as popcorn balls which the bushes are now sporting. Also great wands of goldenrod. They sprawl out in such splendor I didn't know where to put them—too big for table or even the mantel. About to throw them out, I tried them on the open counter between the living room and kitchen, where they catch the light from both sides like a golden fountain.

Since there was nowhere to recycle the papers, I burn them in the round metal container beside the garage. Some days the wind is much too high; I have to stand guard to prevent the flames from whipping too far and threatening our Paradise. Despite a lot of rain some of the leaves and sticks are brittle, I must be careful to stamp out little fires. I've learned to wait for a quieter day. By that time the accumulation has piled up; the bulging sacks must await their turn. But again as I pile them on I dare not leave—and don't want to. A lively fire is fascinating to tend, especially on a brisk blue-bright morning.

This is such a morning. And as I stood poking and stirring the fire and watching its dancing flames, its smoke coiling upward, I lifted my eyes to the majesty of the encircling trees. What a cathedral in which to worship. The whole soul is drawn heavenward, through the arches, the pillars, to the blue gems of sky sparkling through the glittering leaves. My heart cried out to God, I began to sing his praises, rejoice in my blessings, and lift my burdens to the very throne, in tongues.

What a glorious way to pray, not thinking at all, not bothering about words, just letting the Spirit speak and cry and sing out for you, as the Bible teaches. I was praying, I knew, for George's family, and mine, all the people dear to us, but above all for his healing: That the blood flow freely through his veins and arteries again, the ulcers heal, the pain stop. That his energy, and mine, would be renewed, to become the healthy happy couple we have been, able to serve him, our vitality and love an inspiration to others.

And turning back to the fire, I saw that it had died down; only its smoke was ascending now in soft gray coils. Lazily, gently leaving, drifting skyward, taking our problems with them. I felt it with a sudden sweet conviction. All this pain and worry and suffering had been burned away, this was the symbol, they were in the smoke, simply vanishing before my eyes. God must have heard, really heard, and this was his response. The few embers still glowing, the pert little remaining flames, were actually a kind of cheerful reassurance.

I know there will be more garbage to be discarded—but hopefully exchanged for flowers. More fires to be built for more trash to be burned. But God will give us strength, and for now I am encouraged. What a privilege it is to be alive, able to carry garbage and trash outdoors on a sparkling autumn day. What rewards and compensations.

The Sweetness of the Dream

Between these bouts of misery, George and I reclaimed the sweetness of the dream. Being here at all seemed unreal, like magic to be driving the country roads to the little doll villages again for groceries or to pick up our mail. Or sometimes down to the wharf for fish, or jaunts across the autumn hills to track down a colorful country restaurant we'd heard about.

Sometimes I drove, but more often George. Incredibly, he was able to drive with one foot, and he wanted to. He even hobbled out to chop wood or pick his morning offering of flowers. And every day he labored over his eloquent, tender, but also entertaining love notes, enfolded in a used greeting card, accompanied by a joke and concluding with his own little drawing of a Love Boat sailing at sunset on Lake Erie.

The trees were in their glory, the lake a silver blaze. Autumn was "A Wild Forbidden Date with That Gay Rogue October," to quote a poem George recited every year, and now more fervently than ever. (How I wish we knew who wrote it.) Grapes ripened and their winey fragrance was heady in the air . . . Then early November, as long as we dared to stay, and our own wild forbidden date was over.

My sons returned, both cars were full. I rode with Mark, whom I had seen less often; Mallory took care of George and the dogs.

CHAPTER NINETEEN

The Pain and the Promise

The toe was still sore and angry when we returned from the lake. George checked into Washington Hospital for the minor surgery of its debriding. But even that didn't help; osteomyelitis, a serious infection, attacked the bone.

Mallory had stayed on. A few weeks before Christmas he drove us into the city to seek counsel at the Falk Clinic, Presbyterian-University Hospital, where the pool of medical knowledge is world-famous. Young George had told Dr. Steed, the vascular surgeon there, the story of how we had saved his father's leg several times by our own efforts. The man congratulated us, and tried to ease our disappointment now.

"We all want to win," he said, "but we can't every time, no matter how hard we try." He unwrapped the toe, took one look, and declared it would have to come off. "The sooner, the better. I'll be glad to do it, but if you'd rather go back to Washington, nearer home, fine. The surgeons there are tops, and so is your son. We'll keep in touch—if it heals, great; if not, we've got the world's best healing facilities here." His face glowed as he described them. "We'll do everything humanly possible to save that leg."

We left reassured—just in case. But praying we'd never have to find out.

Amputation of the toe was scheduled for two days after Christmas. That settled one thing, this year we would not be going to Virginia. George had been looking forward to it; I insisting it was unthinkable—a 600-mile round trip through the snowy mountains with an injured leg. Now there was no more question . . .

Just where to spend Christmas had been an issue our first two years. I knew it would be hard for George's children so soon after their mother's death. I was diffident and confused about what to do that first year. Then, providentially, I received a call from Dr. Roy Blizzard, my friend and biblical adviser, who appears regularly on the Trinity Broadcasting Network in Santa Barbara, California, inviting us to fly out at their expense, to discuss my novel *Two from Galilee* on their Christmas show.

We were saved. This would also give us a chance to visit my daughter Mickie and her family in Mendocino.

We had a wonderful holiday and got ourselves home from the airport New Year's Eve in time to celebrate. Tired as we were from the long flight, we made coffee, sat before the fire opening presents and piles of cards, and listening for the first time to Garrison Keillor's *Prairie Home Companion* on the radio. He was so funny, the jazz and country music so enticing, we even got up and danced.

Our second Christmas the problem rose again. I still felt almost a stranger in this big Tudor house, so filled with the ghosts of Christmases past. Here, as long as the family could remember, they all were together on Christmas Eve. Their mother's preparations were legendary, beginning weeks ahead, with every possible surface decorated, and every cupboard overflowing. Even the rituals were sacred, continuing with their grandchildren.

George Jr. memorialized them in several eloquent letters to his father, which he read aloud for the whole family every season. Diane wrote me a similar letter, partly in explanation for how they felt. The house held memories almost too sweet to bear. "To us, Mother *was* Christmas in that house. Please forgive us . . ."

I felt helpless and stricken. Not that I blamed them, I really understood; it hurt, nonetheless. There was no use even getting a tree or trying to decorate, although George bought huge poinsettias for every window, and brought down a Santa Claus from the attic so big it scared me. Then he proposed a solution so obvious it's a wonder we hadn't thought of it before: We'd go back to Manassas, where he'd found me, and celebrate with whoever was there. Both daughters were still too far away, but my sons and their wives could be rounded up, and so could his son Jeff and Tanya, who still lived just around the Beltway.

Calling ahead, to see that both houses were warmed up, we departed. George, at that time with a practically new audience for his songs and jokes and tales, was in his glory. Christmas proved to be so much fun for everybody, we promised to come every year.

We had not missed a Christmas since—until now. But I had no heart for it, anyway. I was too busy and burdened to shop, except by mail. I didn't even get out to the malls, and only once to church, although Mallory insisted on taking us on a drive one night to see the beautifully trimmed and lighted houses.

Then he left to be with his wife . . . and we were alone. Vaguely humiliated, not wanting sympathy, but confident that George and Diane would figure out what to do with us. ("It's time we establish some traditions of our own," Diane had decided during that first critical year.)

They did. We were divided between them for Christmas Eve and Christmas Day. Late the next afternoon I took George to the hospital to be admitted.

The big tree in the lobby was shining, every doorway bearing wreaths or other symbols. Carols were playing softly in the background. It was very quiet. The halls, usually swarming with people, were almost deserted. It doesn't seem appropriate to be sick at such a merry season; people are taking a holiday, or trying to, even from illness.

Once again George was put in a wheelchair, his overnight bag on his lap, while I tagged along to his private room. When he was undressed and settled, they injected him to begin the twenty-four hours of intravenous antibiotics before the operation.

Amputation

The surgery took place as scheduled. They kept George ten days to continue the antibiotics. I drove back and forth to the hospital by myself and stayed most of the evening. Sometimes I went downstairs for dinner, but more often we had bedside picnics together, as we'd come to call them. The hospital always served more than he wanted. I ate what he couldn't, or took it home for the dogs. They were always ravenous by the time I got there.

The previous year, when George was in the hospital on the Fourth of July, George Jr. ordered a gourmet meal sent to the room. It was also our wedding anniversary. This beautiful gesture, served with the aplomb of a fine hotel, helped us celebrate, and eased the ache when it was time to leave . . . The hardest part of these visits was always having to tell George good night. He held my hand so tight and looked at me with such pathos, like a trapped animal, this big vibrant man I love so much.

We both dreaded the moment. And I am nervous driving at night. Luckily, the snow was mostly gone, the roads good, but once I made a wrong turn and was hopelessly lost for an hour, in a threatening neighborhood, or so I thought. It seemed wild and strange, and yet familiar . . . All cities look alike after dark, the same bright lights or desolate areas and alleys, whether in Pittsburgh or Washington, D.C. I had done this before, in another lifetime somewhere. Once I was terrified, as now, certain that a car was following me . . . I remembered praying the same prayer: "Oh, God, dear God, just get me *home!*" Then at last the joy and relief of familiar streets, and headlights flooding your own driveway . . .

From long experience with hospitals, I had worked out a strategy of getting a husband home. (George and Diane were willing to help, but not always available; and I had told Mallory not to come until I called—I would need him more later.) Make advance trips to your car with all the flowers, books, balloons, and other stuff you can push or carry, starting the night before. Check out early, and park your car near the door.

If it takes gates to get out, make sure you have the token to release them. (I once used a slug by mistake and to my horror locked in myself and four cars behind me. It took a policeman to spring us.)

A kindly attendant waits until you pull up, gets husband from wheelchair into the car, and you're off, with a glorious sense of achievement and escape.

This time, sailing through the sunlight, I realized I had made no provision for getting George into the house. The entire leg was swollen, his poor foot, lost in an enormous white bootie, must not be stepped on. He agreed that we'd have to call our neighbor Bud Parkins, who was home, thank heaven, and with the help of his son, gently lifted my precious cargo up the steps into the kitchen and then up two flights of stairs. I will always be convinced the Lord provides us all with guardian angels, and they sometimes live just across the street.

Amputation of the large toe is not a simple operation. The surgeon has to cut away the supporting bone and go very deep. It leaves a gaping hole in the foot, which is very slow to heal. We were warned it could take months. George must stay in bed with the leg propped, but could go downstairs for dinner or a change of scene when he felt up to it. This wasn't as hard as it seemed; he managed the steps on his rear end; we met him below with the walker.

He was cheerful and funny and stoic beyond belief, considering the pain. Trying to hide his frustration at being so helpless. Busy with an enormous backlog of reading, his Bible, his dictionary, his clippings and cartoons and writing his daily love notes. "Bored?" he'd protest when people asked. "I've never been bored a minute since I arrived on planet Earth!" But the pain was insatiable. Nothing helped. There were days when he was frantic. Nights were hell, neither of us slept.

At times he fell into deep depression. His greatest concern was the cost to me.

Mallory had returned to take over the burden of meals and trays and the countless jobs a good husband does—taking care of cars and yard and fixing things. Plus taking George to his weekly appointments with the doctor—which gave me a few hours to write. (Guardian angels can also be faithful, caring sons and daughters.)

But suddenly one day I reached out for a chair that wasn't there because the world was spinning . . . I could feel the rhythm of George's fingers on my wrist, then his stethoscope on my chest, hear him scream, "Call the ambulance!" . . . Male voices rumbling, big hands rolling somebody's body into a kind of sling, feel it being carried around corners, downstairs (how do they do it without dropping you?), eyes shut, don't look, don't look, this can't be happening . . . they slide you into an ambulance—like a cave, can't breathe, rubber mask pressed over your nose—"Just to give you a little oxygen," they explain —radios crackling, siren beginning that hideous wail (why scare people with such a sound of doom?).

Ridiculous, this is somebody else, they are scared, *she* is scared, ridiculous, she can't be dying. Not me, not me, absurd, *this too shall pass* . . . I had ridden in ambulances before, but never as the patient. When it's you *(if* it's you), there is a kind of silly drama about the commotion, tearing through stoplights to that siren serenade . . . the dim thunder and vibrations of wheels below . . . pulling into hospital grounds, wheels stopping at an emergency entrance where you don't belong . . . not me, not me, I'm not ready for this, it can't be happening, this too shall pass, *this too shall pass!* . . .

It was the same hospital we'd left so recently. I was there only three days, for tests and questions, and precious sleeping. Though it hurts to be stabbed for intravenous fluid, and hard to sleep on a bed that folds in the middle, with a tube projecting from your hand. How could anyone endure it night and day for weeks, as George had done? Get me out of here! . . . A mere attack of dizziness brought on by strain. (My mother had suffered such attacks, "Mom's dizzy spells," we called them, not realizing.) Take these pills, get more rest . . . The world was okay now, and so was I, let's go!

The incident increased George's frustration. He was tired of depending on people, worried about me, and discouraged about himself. The wound was not healing. After two months it remained a long, deep, bloody, and stubborn hole. The subject of total amputation could no longer be avoided. Quietly, Diane brought it up with me. "Do you think Dad could deal with the loss of his leg?"

I cringed at the thought, but told her, "Your father is the bravest man I've ever known. He'll make the best of whatever has to be."

"Why not get on with it, Dad?" Young George was more direct. "I've been discussing this with Finn and Krosnoff. They could do it just below the knee—that gives you more mobility. In a couple more months you'd be ready for a prosthesis. They're a lot better now, lighter, easier to fit. You could walk again, even take Marjorie dancing." He winked at me. "Why not get on with your life?"

His father pondered. "You're probably right. But first I'd better go back to the clinic, see what Dr. Steed says."

Mallory and I rejoiced. We'd been praying for this.

His son was less optimistic. "Sure, go ahead. Maybe there *is* something they can do. Frankly I don't think so. And again it could be only a matter of time. But talk to him first anyway."

And so, the first week of February, we pulled up before the door of the famous clinic and hospital adjacent to Pitt. As before, cars were unloading their sad cargo: people requiring wheelchairs, using canes and walkers, some on crutches. One man with a folded pant leg dangling where a limb had been. His wife was steering him gently; I couldn't watch as she went ahead to open the door.

It had been cold and windy the last time we were here, Now spring was sweet on the air. Yards were greening, crocuses popping up, and as we waited in the doctor's reception room an early robin landed on the windowsill, chirping merrily until it soared away. Then Dr. Steed strode in, as radiant and cheerful as an omen of spring himself.

He examined the cavern still raw in George's foot, and whistled softly. Took measurements. Applied the doppler. The pulsing *whoosh-whoosh-whooshing* sounded fine to me, but the doctor said not enough blood was getting through. He perched on his desk, exuding optimism as he expressed his conviction the leg might be saved if given the chance. Elaborating on what he had told us before.

Mallory and I sat mesmerized; George listened with his thoughtful smile that tells you nothing—whether he is agreeing with you or lost in some reverie of rebuttal. He roused to ask questions; the two doctors discussed risk factors and procedures, including an angioplast, and if possible another bypass.

"True, you could go ahead and have the amputation and live a nice life," Dr. Steed acknowledged. "But amputation is so *final,* you can never put a limb back on. If there's any other recourse and you don't take it, you will always wonder . . . The first time you struggle with a prosthesis, or lose your balance—you will wonder. Sure, you could lose the battle in the end, but at least if you tried you will never have that regret."

George thanked him warmly, and left samples of blood and urine, to be available when or if he returned. "It's okay if you change your mind," the doctor said, "we'll just throw them away."

Mallory rushed them to the proper desk, and went on ahead to summon the car. George was silent as we waited in the lobby. I was cautious but eager. "Well, what do you think?" I asked.

To my dismay, he shook his head. "No," he declared firmly. "It could take months, this has gone on long enough. I want to get it over with."

That night he called George to report his decision, and ask him to contact the surgeons. "I think you've made the right choice, Dad," his son assured him.

But Mallory was heartsick, and I was torn.

Reprieve

This was Friday. The amputation was scheduled for Tuesday the following week. He would be admitted to Washington Hospital sometime Sunday, as soon as a room was available.

That night George hadn't felt like coming downstairs, so

we carried his dinner up, and our own on trays to keep him company. Mallory had tried to reason with him all the way home; now, at my insistence, he kept silent. Until bedtime, when he came back to our room. "George, please—at least *try* it for a couple of weeks," he pleaded.

"No," George declared again. "I will not prolong this. This is my body and I'll decide what to do with it. I will not have any more tests, I'm sick and tired of needles in my veins and tubes in my arms; I will not have any more X rays or bypasses or all the other things they'll want to try. I've had enough, and your mother's had enough. We've got to start living again. We don't have that many more years left!"

Suddenly, I was strangely relieved. This thing had dragged on for a year, George in almost constant pain, all of us suffering. It tore me to think of submitting him to more of the misery that only proved to be so futile in the end. Later, in the kitchen, I tried to make Mallory understand. "George is right. I am not going to try to persuade him anymore, and I hope you won't either."

"But if it would save his *leg?*"

"Of course, if we knew it *would.*"

Saturday night I packed the usual things: Shaving kit, robe, pajamas, slippers . . . and suddenly froze. *He won't need both slippers anymore. Only one. Put the other one back.* Secretly, in the closet, I hugged that old familiar shoe and cried.

In bed we held each other, silent, trying to shield each other from our terrible anxiety and dread. Both of us already mourning the poor doomed leg. It was my leg too; it would take a part of my life with it. I felt almost the way I had when George told me the news of his cancer. The world was dissolving beneath me; life as I knew it with my wonderful George was being swept away, it would soon be gone.

Twice before, I had been through amputations with people I loved. One, a young man cruelly burned when his ship was bombed during the Second World War. They had brought him to the Naval Hospital in Philadelphia, where we lived then. His wife, Helen, a girlhood friend, was staying with us, to be near him. Lynn drove her to the hospital every morning, and when the worst was over, brought Harry home for weekends so they could be together. I will never forget the first time he bravely struggled up the steps.

The other, my daughter's fiancé, who had cancer. Young and scared and in a foreign land, far from home. I flew to Boston to be with them through the ordeal . . . Each time I prayed never to witness such suffering again.

Now my very soul shuddered. It was as if a cold hand had gripped me, and my own body was about to be dismembered. Yet, curiously, at the same time there was a profound sense of peace and resolution. We would adjust, as other people did. We would go on. We would learn new ways of walking and dancing and swimming and caring for each other. Anything to save his life and spare him.

The next morning while George was having his breakfast upstairs, the hospital phoned. Mallory took the call in the kitchen. They felt sure a private room would be available by four o'clock; they would call later to confirm.

Grimly, Mallory gave me the message. He paced about, stricken, almost frantic in his desire to keep this from happening. "Oh, Mother, if he would just *wait* a little longer. To have come so far and then *give up!* Won't you talk to him, try to persuade him?"

"No, honey, I won't do that, I can't."

"Then do you mind if I do? Just once more? *Please!*"

It didn't seem fair to stop him. He had given up a lot to come here, worked so hard to help us, and loved George so much. I sighed. "All right. It won't do any good, but if it's that important to you, go ahead."

Nervously, I poured fresh coffee, and opened the paper. Before long, to my astonishment, I heard feet pounding down the stairs, and Mallory raced in, face shining.

"You won't believe this, but George agreed! He's willing to do whatever you want."

"What? . . . What did you *tell* him?" I gasped.

"Well, frankly, I told him you haven't let on, but you're very upset. That it would mean a lot to you if he'd just hang on a little longer—at least *try* what they can do at the clinic."

I stared at him, aghast. Shocked at his tactic, but flooded with such relief I burst into tears . . . A reprieve! The executioner's knife had been stayed.

Wiping my eyes, I rushed back upstairs to hug George. We laughed and kissed. "It's the least I can do for you," he said humbly. "I love you so much I can't bear to think of putting you through this, if there's the slightest chance."

The phone was ringing again. The hospital had found a room—number 576. We could come in anytime before five. Still shaking, I thanked them for their trouble, and tried to explain it wouldn't be necessary, after all. There had been a change, we would have to cancel.

Now we must get busy and notify the surgeons.

George and I prayed longer than ever that night. The thing we so greatly feared had not yet come upon us. Pray God it never would.

Communion

And now, for George again the CAT scans, X rays, physical therapies, tests, intravenous medications. The first major step an angioplast—a tiny balloon inserted in a new vein at the groin. A few days later surgery to remove the infected portion of bone, and thoroughly debride the wound. George was cheerful and long-suffering, convinced he was going through it all for me. But adapting, as he always does, to new surroundings, buoyed by his insatiable curiosity and his fervor for discovery.

Presbyterian-University Hospital was a particularly rich source. It was also a teaching hospital for the medical school at Pitt. Almost every day four or five students marched into his room to observe. The first time this happened, I welcomed them excitedly, thinking it must be a quartet sent by somebody to entertain him. (People send wonderful things to hospitals these days—not just flowers and balloons—we've had a clown, a magician, and once a gorilla with a bottle of champagne.) When the youths just stood grinning until their professor, a stunning young woman, appeared, I recognized my mistake.

How young they seemed, gathering closer as George's wound was revealed and discussed. Mere kids—diffident, cheery, respectful, a little shy, but brilliant or they wouldn't be here, and having the confidence and courage to enter this tough profession. My heart went out to them. I tried to imagine George that young and bright and hopeful, setting out on his quest, but although I'd seen pictures of him with his graduating class, it didn't seem possible.

He was keeping his usual lengthy hospital journal, in which he logged everything that happened over the past twenty-four hours: The number of times he was stabbed in the night: "To test for sugar, because they *refuse* to believe I am not diabetic. I am going to have a big sign posted on the door: NO, I AM NOT DIABETIC!" . . . Colorful descriptions of everyone who entered the room, from orderlies and nurses to the priest who came every morning to offer confession and Communion.

George registers his religion as Catholic, although his parents didn't go to church. He says when they took him to be baptized, "my father didn't have any money with him, but the priest demanded payment. My dad got so mad he never entered that church again, not until they wheeled him down the aisle."

This time the priest was young and handsome. "Very tall, over six feet, blond with wavy hair and blue eyes, had a dimple in his chin. Norwegian, I'd say, still in his twenties. I feel sorry for the girls! Well, when he asked if I'd like to confess, I told him, 'I'm afraid I don't have any sins to confess, son—sorry, I mean Father. I obey the commandments, am good to my wife and family, and try to help everybody I can . . . Also, as a doctor, I am in awe of the Creator. I feel I'm worshipping God every time I examine the body, what a wonderful thing, so perfect in every detail.

" 'As for Communion, I take it all the time. Every time I eat or drink I think of the Holy Spirit in that food. Every morsel of bread or meat, every sip and swallow of milk or orange juice. The Holy Spirit is in that life-giving food that becomes a part of us. I never take anything into my mouth without thanking God and secretly blessing it.' " George briskly crossed himself. "*In the name of the Father, Son, and Holy Ghost.*"

His reenactment was delightful.

"A wonder he didn't ask you to give *him* Communion!" Mallory laughed.

"No, but he seemed to enjoy it."

George would read his journal aloud when we arrived; and if other visitors followed, read it again to them. George Jr. caught my eye as he listened one day, and later told me in the hall, "Marj, you and Mallory deserve medals for coming every day and spending so much time with Dad. There's nothing I hate worse than visiting somebody in the hospital. It's so terribly dull."

"Not for us," I told him. "Not with your father. He couldn't be dull if he tried, even in the hospital. Long-winded, sure, sometimes ridiculous and exasperating—but dull? Are you kidding? I've never had one dull minute in his presence since he came into my life."

You Can't Amputate God

But George was also pondering deeply during the long ordeal. And one day he shared his true feelings as I sat beside his bed. "Marj, I love you and Mallory for trying so hard, and everything these doctors are doing to save my leg. But I know they may have to take it off.

"And last night I lay there in despair. I felt just as you do— who wouldn't? How horrible, to have any part of your body amputated. Especially a leg. But then I thought—God, who made us, doesn't have any legs. With the human being that he has made, legs are invaluable. With the Holy Spirit, there are no arms and legs. And the thought came to me: Why should I be so distraught? When the Holy Spirit that produced me has no legs, no feet, no arms. God has nothing that the human being has, yet he has everything. And he is right in *you*.

" 'Don't worry about your feet,' I told myself. God doesn't have feet, but he gets things done. He doesn't have any hands, but he has thoughts—the spirit, the power, even though you can't see it. He doesn't have any vocal cords, but you can hear him, he speaks to you in other ways . . . If I lose this leg, I've got another one—God gave me an extra, just as he gave us an extra arm, an extra ear, and an extra eye. All these wonderful things he created in pairs, to work together, and to keep on working if one of them goes wrong.

"If they have to take my leg I'm going to rejoice in the leg I still have. Thank God for it. I know from my experience as a doctor, life doesn't depend on that leg, the spirit doesn't depend on that leg. I still have life and power, and God is a part of me. *You can't amputate God.*"

George paused, his voice serious, but smiling. "And one more thing, because we'll both have to face it sometime, honey: If you fear death, remember you are a part of God. When *you* go, God goes with you. There is no way you could cease to exist. You can never be apart from him, *you can't amputate God.*"

Déjà Vu

Actually, Mallory and I enjoyed the drives into the city. Through Mount Lebanon, down Route 19 to Banksville Road, through the Fort Pitt tunnel, and across the bridge—into the sudden magical light and wonder of buildings soaring around us, almost leaping and shouting in their vitality. But sometimes the haunting déjà vu returned. As if I had traveled these same miles before . . . As if life may be a circle, winding back on itself, repeating the same experiences. Or does our past run beside us in parallels? Like railroad tracks we cannot cross, though we hear a ghost whistle ahead, ghost wheels bearing down, not sure where the danger is coming from, but afraid to look over lest we crash.

Once I said, "Well, honey, this brings back memories. We've been through a lot together."

"We sure have." My son nodded and patted my hand. "But this time it's different. You're happy again, Mother."

To our left, on Forbes Avenue, a historic church was being torn down. Whole at first, when we passed it, but day after day, we saw the silent hammer swinging, battering it into oblivion.

Walls and windows and Gothic arches, victims of that immutable swinging. Then only a skeleton remained, except for the beautiful entrance, still proud and serene. And finally it too staggered, sank to its knees defeated, the last to crumble. Together we mourned its going. We would have stopped the battering if we could. We felt helpless—as we were beginning to feel about George.

Lively and promising as all the things going on at the hospital were, nothing seemed to be happening. The gaping wound, dressed carefully three times a day, was getting no worse, but neither did it seem to be getting better . . . Give it time, give it time; another bypass might help. But George vetoed that emphatically. "Why not hyperbaric oxygen?" A doubtful solution, we were told, and very expensive. "Not enough proof of success . . . "So what do we do?" "Give it time." "How much?" "A couple more months, at least." "More?" "Possibly." "Not *here?*" "Well, you could go home, continue the intravenous antibiotics—arrangements could be made." "I'm tired of this, let me go home!" "All right, next week." "No, *now!*"

The doctor sighed and mopped his brow. He is a beautiful guy, very fair, with curly hair and the face of an angel. And he'd tried so hard, I wanted to comfort him. "Okay, if you insist, and you're probably right. But please don't rush into anything; if it's still stubborn after two months, I give up, I have done all I can. But I want you to know I'm still hoping to save your leg."

And so, after two weeks, with George's foot still in the big white bootie, and bracing himself with the walker, we brought my darling home. Instructions had been carefully given. Visiting nurses had been ordered to supervise, bringing the sterile gauze and gloves and everything else needed for the dressings.

Once more we plumped up the pillows, arranged the flowers which people kept sending, carried his trays, listened to his brave bright jokes and songs and stories . . . and waited.

But oh, how good it was to have him back again. I flew to my typewriter for a couple of hours each morning. A tremendous excitement and sense of achievement possessed me. Somehow, it *had* all been worthwhile. It was only a matter of time.

In such a mood I urged Mallory to drive home for a while

to be with his wife. We would be fine, I could manage. I promised to call him if anything went wrong.

I really thought I could.

But my own strength was beginning to wane. However strong the spirit, the body has its limits. And when the body begs for rest even the spirit is threatened. I began to question, I had unworthy thoughts . . . I could not forget George's dream about Carolyn: How she appeared to him all in white, holding my book—and told him she had hidden it where he would find it . . . because he would *need* me . . . *Was I actually no more than the fulfillment of that dream? Another woman's choice to take care of the man she loved after she was gone?* No, no, don't think about it, unworthy of me, unworthy!

I was just so *tired*.

This is what I wrote in my journal not long after Mallory left:

Fatigue

Fatigue is an enemy too. Ah, but fatigue is an enemy and a sickness too.

I feel limp, drained, scared. I feel sometimes as if I'm skidding toward a precipice and I must resist, fight back, struggle not to pitch over . . . but I am so tired, so tired . . .

I am a fortunate woman, even so. My heart is with the beloved who calls to me, to whom I carry trays, whose wounds I dress, and with whom I still make love and laugh and sing and pray. This man I love so much, so kind and funny and desirable. So sympathetic and grateful, thanking me as fervently as if this were something special. Not merely a duty or a kindness, but almost an honor. As if I am doing something brave and noble. Which I'm not. I am just a wife doing what any decent woman does when her man is suffering . . . Even as I did for my husband before him, who suffered almost constantly, for some reason or other, so many years.

George is different, though. He is a doctor, and certainly no friend of suffering; he is the rescuer, the restorer, the enemy of pain. That he himself should suffer so much now in these years when he belongs to me is ironic. *Unfair, unfair!* my soul cries out.

But no, these thoughts are not worthy of me. I am alive! I survived that other long sentence of suffering. And I am grateful to be the one chosen to be beside this beautiful man when it is his turn to suffer now . . . Now, after our few years of enchantment, the pain. Pain for both of us. But he's worth the price. And even this time of suffering has its own enchantment. There is a magic about George that makes even this vigil far better than not having him at all . . .

The fatigue is my only enemy—the exhaustion. It doesn't mean that *I* am protesting, it is my body protesting. I cry from sheer exhaustion, I droop from sheer exhaustion. I feel drained, squeezed by some monstrous force that is trying to trick me, grab me, skid me toward a precipice and pitch me over it if I don't hang on!

Oh, but I've been through all this before . . . long before George. Over and over, so many times. I was scared then too, exhausted, afraid of crashing. But I never let go. And I will not now.

With the help of God and my own fierce love, *I will hang on.*

The Price of Paradise

Five days later it happened. I awoke that Sunday morning to hear George groaning, "Oh, God, dear God, not *this!*" His leg had swollen overnight to almost twice its size. He could scarcely roll up his pajama leg. "A blood clot, it's got to be, I was afraid of this. A thrombosis is always a danger when you lie in bed so long." He'd been trying to exercise in bed: stretching, bending, aerobics, going through the motions of swimming, but unable to step on the foot. Now there was no choice but to call son George again.

He came at once, although he had a plane to catch. He was speaking at a medical convention. "Dad, you've got to go to the hospital right away. This could be serious, it could go to the lung and kill you." He turned to assure me, "Diane or one of us will help you get him there."

"No—no, I'll be all right, I can do it."

I thought I could. I kept praying I could. I detest any show of weakness. I didn't want to bother them; Liz was expecting a baby, everybody was so busy. I didn't want to fail . . . But I was trembling, and uncertain. What if I got dizzy again and caused an accident? Pocketing my pride, I called Diane, who said, "Of course. What time?"

She came early, followed by another car carrying her daughters Pam and Robane, and the curly-haired toddler, Jessica, George's first great-grandchild. They all swarmed in, bubbling with youth and love for "Grandpap," and tried to help. Sending us off with almost a feeling of some joyous celebration.

I was grateful to have Diane taking over; she is so splendidly efficient and direct, helping her father in and out of the car; promptly finding a wheelchair and pushing him swiftly along the halls, while I followed.

The staff had been alerted; a bed was waiting, although there'd been no time as yet to find a private room. Diane briskly whisked the curtains that separated the beds, then introduced herself to the other occupant. When George was settled, his nurses busy, she suggested we go downstairs for coffee.

Looking around as we walked to the elevator, I remarked, "This feels like home."

"No *wonder!*" she snapped. "You two have been in *hell* since your marriage."

Her tone was so vehement I was startled. "We've been in Paradise too," I insisted. "Everything has its price. Especially Paradise . . . But your father is worth it."

Dr. Krosnoff is a tower of strength; a composed and quiet man who works almost without expression, His eyes rove as he speaks, and what little he says is in low tones, sometimes hard to understand. But as he bent over George, there was no mistaking his pronouncement: "Got him here just in time. Any later and it would've been 'Goodbye, Charley, you're on a ship that ain't comin' back.' "

It was so sudden and surprising, coming from him, it struck us funny. We all laughed, and the strain was relieved.

The tubes from George's arms now were filled with fluids to dissolve the clot, as well as to guard against infection . . . Ten more days in captivity, ten more nights having to say goodbye. Then Mallory was with us again, and the pain of parting a little easier . . .

Spring

And now spring, when "beauty just hurls itself into the world," as George once phrased it. Easter is almost here, and George is getting stronger, able to walk to the window with only his cane, to look out on trees draped in their delicate green chiffon of leaves, or pink and white with apple and cherry blossoms. The hills are paved with the impudent gold of dandelions; the violets along the stream where we will surely walk the dogs again are bonneted in blue. Daffodils bloom in the garden, and scarlet and yellow tulips. He sees a world bouncing and sparkling with life after the long winter sleep.

Birds are singing their merry anthems of resurrection. Before long you'll be back at the lake! they seem to be promising. Another month or two, certainly before the summer is far gone. The wound is smaller, just a little, but definitely smaller; the leg no longer swollen, but as slim and trim as its partner. (That leg you almost lost.)

Before long you'll be walking along the beach, maybe even running and swimming . . . My seven-year-old grandson Alexis had a vision, he told his mother. "I saw George running beside the water. It was a beautiful day, the sun was shining, I saw him, Mother!" Melanie had called to tell me about it. And I saw it too, through that little boy's eyes, and believed.

My husband is getting well. We will return to Paradise, for as long as the Lord allows. We found each other late, but we packed more experiences into our nearly nine years together than we might have had in a lifetime. In those years I had written three books, and with George made three promotion trips. We had gone to Canada, Bermuda, Germany, and Greece; and traveled to countless American cities for writers conferences, book conventions, and speaking dates . . . The first five years of our marriage George had continued to practice medicine. His retirement, sad as its cause, gave us even more time to enjoy each other, wherever we were, especially those lovely summers at Lake Erie.

How was all this possible? I've been asked, and sometimes ask myself. But I have a theory of time: time telescopes, it expands and contracts, revealing new worlds without seeming to affect the old ones. It allows you to do the things you were meant to do—*must* do, while also making room for the normal demands of life. And even the interruptions of sickness and suffering.

Indeed we had spent our time in hell. George's daughter, Diane, was right. We had been in hell over and over, regularly these last few years, like a sentence to be served. In her intense love and compassion, she had protested, and rightly, for to her the hell seemed paramount. In our minds, however, it was the Paradise that prevailed. The painful detours hadn't lasted very long, at least in retrospect, and when you really love each other, heaven is never far away, no matter where you are.

George and I will never cease to marvel over the miracle that brought us together. Every day we thank God for it. In sickness or in health, no two people could have been happier. That this happiness came late only makes it more precious.

We feel, as the groom was told at the wedding in Cana: *"You have saved the best wine for the last!"*

EPILOGUE

We finally lost our long battle to save George's left leg. This time, although using the same therapy of God and vitamins which had saved his right one several years before, we failed. After six trips to the hospital and three postponements, the pain was too great; in September we brought him home from our beautiful place on Lake Erie, and the leg was amputated just below the knee.

His spirit was phenomenal. He even came back from surgery singing and waving his stump. But the ensuing journey was very rough. As I wrote in our Christmas letter that year, "George is making a noble effort to use his prosthesis; but learning to walk all over again isn't easy, especially for a guy who's a wonderful dancer, and was once a champion athlete for Pitt."

Again Mallory arranged to be with us throughout the ordeal. I don't think I could have made it without him; or the loving support of Diane and George Jr., who not only looked after his dad's medical care but produced a grandson, Eric, eager to be on his feet.

"My George says it's a race to see who learns to walk

first," I wrote. "So life goes on. We have resolved to treat this experience as an adventure instead of a tragedy—or are trying to. Grateful for just being alive and *together*. We have so much to be thankful for."

Gradually George improved. By spring he had adjusted to his prosthesis so well he sometimes forgot to use his cane. We were so encouraged. He even promised to dance with me at his 55th medical school class reunion in Baltimore in May; and maybe have a fling in New York before coming back to Virginia for Mother's Day with my children. But as the time approached, he began to feel so miserable we realized we'd better cancel everything except the Virginia trip and a few days at his son Jeff's summer home in Ocean City.

We came back to face what added up to a triple blow. His lung cancer had returned, which would mean months of radiation; and there was severe pain in his remaining leg. Strange wonderful George. Sometimes, driving to the clinic for his treatments, the pain got so bad he would *sing*. Even so, at last in August, Diane and her husband got us safely to our Lake Erie Paradise, where we hoped to enjoy the brilliant autumn months. But after a couple of weeks, for the third summer in a row, we were forced to return to the hospital at home, where, exactly a year from his first amputation, the other leg was taken.

Once more Diane and her brother George were with us, which helped so much. And my George was so brave it almost broke my heart. Just before they took him away, he kissed my fingers and dabbed at a tear darting down my cheek. "Oh, honey, I'm *so* sorry. But please don't cry. We still are richly blessed. I still have eyes to see you. I still have arms to hold you. I still have ears to hear you—"

"And you still have a beautiful voice to sing to me," I managed to remind him.

"You bet!" George exclaimed, and burst into song. The one he always sang as they wheeled him down the hall: "I love you, *I love you,* that's all that *I* can say . . ."

Earlier, facing the inevitable, we had cheered each other with the old rally: "We did it *before* and we can do it *again!*" We even speculated that having learned so much from the first experience, the second might be easier. Somehow it didn't occur to us that with *no* leg to stand on, it would be twice as hard. Nothing could possibly prepare us for what lay ahead. But George was so brave, his faith unscathed, his humor intact, an inspiration to everyone else.

One day, when I walked into his room, I was frightened to find a doctor and nurses swarming around his bed. They had taken him down for physical therapy, one of the nurses explained. He had collapsed—the parallel bars had been too much for him. After they left, I sat down to hear George's version of what happened: "It was those darn parallel bars," he said weakly, but grinning. "Never saw so many bars—a bar here, a bar there, on both sides of the street. By the time I stopped for a shot at each bar, no wonder I fell down!"

When he finally came home, it was to a hospital bed and all the equipment in the living room. Here he resumed his precious rituals: love songs morning and evening, reading to me twice a day, and fervently writing his ardent love notes to be read at bedtime. Although he could no longer pick or buy flowers for his breakfast bouquets, he would present me with a rose or a couple of tulips from the beautiful flowers others had sent us . . . He was still very funny. Once I caught him signing his thank-you notes "Two stump George."

"Now I have a matched set," he said of those curious members that lay on the bed before him. All that was left of those magnificent legs—so docile, looking like sleeping hounds, I thought, although I never told him—mute creatures vaguely smiling, mindless and impotent, unaware of the anguish they represented. But they were also uniquely precious—I was so grateful that Dr. Krosnoff had saved even this much of him for us. I felt a great tenderness for them, and kissed and caressed them, perhaps to comfort them—and George, and myself.

In his inimitable way, George pretended to enjoy his stumps. Often wagging them up and down like puppets and giving them voices to entertain visitors. Especially children. "Do you like this little boy?" he'd ask, as the stumps nodded joyfully. Privately, he confided, "One nice thing about stumps —they're always positive, they can't shake their heads."

But he was profoundly aware of the enormity of his loss.

One day I saw him gazing sadly down at those scraps of him-self, and heard him say, "Well, now the Lord has *really* brought me to my knees."

I slept on the couch beside him, where I could at least hold his hand. My own soul felt his growing despair, and he was very tired . . . Three days after Christmas he went into a com-plete relapse and was rushed to the hospital.

He died January 12, semi-comatose, still striving to write me one more love note.

His eyes, now closed, had been blue—so blue. Never have I seen such blue eyes in a man. He always wore blue for the office. His services were held in Canonsburg, the suburb where he had practiced so long. He was dressed all in blue as his patients remember him, still so handsome, with his stethoscope and battered old doctor's bag beside him, and a copy of the book that had brought us together, *I've Got to Talk to Some-body, God.*

The night before our final goodbye, his family asked me to participate in a brief eulogy. I didn't think I could do it; but later I lay awake remembering how proudly he'd always called me a pro. Pros don't cry in public. He had gone with me on so many promotion tours and speaking trips, I could do no less for him. And there were special things about my George that only I could tell them . . .

His grandson George III, a captain in the Air Force, told "Grandpap" stories. How the grandchildren all adored him be-cause he was so much *fun*. "Grandpap was always reciting po-etry. Some of it hilarious, like our favorite, 'Piddlin' Rex.' " . . . George Jr. gave a beautiful summary of his father's life, focusing on love. "Dad was loved so much because he exuded love. Everywhere he went people felt it. He loved every living thing, he wouldn't kill even a fly if he could help it . . . And Dad was very lucky during his lifetime to have the love of two women who made him happy: My mother. And Marjorie."

A tribute I will always cherish.

I said that I fell in love with George (as many women did) because he was so handsome and delightful. But not until I married him did I realize the brilliance of his mind: his wisdom, his imagination, his eloquence. His originality. His vivid descriptions and figures of speech. "What a mate for a writer! Never before had I let anyone but editors read my manuscripts. But with George I could hardly wait. He had wonderful judgment, and he was a fountain of ideas. Some of the best ideas in my last four books, written since our marriage, came from him."

I told them how close he was to God. How he woke up early every morning and spent an hour just meditating and scribbling in his alphabetic journal of blessings. I held up one of those "A–Z books," as he called them, and read a few selections from the many listed under *L:* "*Lungs* that let us breathe 25,000 times a day . . . *Light bulbs,* invented by Thomas A. Edison—how wonderful, turning night into day . . . *Lawyers,* what a help, especially my son Jeff . . . *Life,* the miracle of being a part of God's plan . . . *Laughter,* to brighten the journey, and help heal the body. 'Better than a good medicine,' the Bible says . . . *Love,* God's greatest gift. Without love, life wouldn't be worth the struggle. But with love, how rewarding, what a joy! God is love and with love we have God." . . .

George and I had this joyful reward for ten years, six months, and twelve days (he always counted them). The last decade of both our lives. For me, this final decade has been the happiest, most romantic, inspiring, and beautiful of all.

The wedding feast is over. And the best wine *was* saved for the last.